PEROT

AN UNAUTHORIZED BIOGRAPHY

PEROT

AN UNAUTHORIZED BIOGRAPHY

BY
TODD MASON

BUSINESS ONE IRWIN
HOMEWOOD, IL 60430

Jacket photo by: Jim Knowles

This publication is designed to provide accurate and
authoritative information in regard to the subject matter
covered. It is sold with the understanding that the
publisher is not engaged in rendering legal, accounting, or
other professional service. If legal advice or other expert
assistance is required, the services of a competent
professional person should be sought.

*From a Declaration of Principles jointly adopted by a Committee
of the American Bar Association and a Committee of Publishers.*

Sponsoring editor: Jeffrey A. Krames
Project editor: Jane Lightell
Production manager: Ann Cassady
Compositor: Carlisle Communications, Ltd.
Typeface: 11/13 Century Schoolbook
Printer: The Book Press, Inc.

Library of Congress Cataloging-in-Publication Data

Mason, Todd.
    Perot / Todd Mason.
      p.   cm.
    ISBN 1-55623-236-5
    1. Perot, H. Ross, 1930–   . 2. Businessmen—United States–
–Biography. I. Title.
HC102.5.P42M37 1990
338.7'61004'092—dc20
[B]   89–71424
                                          CIP

Printed in the United States of America
  5 6 7 8 9 0 BP 7 6 5 4 3 2

To Meg
"For what could be more
glorious than to be united
with a being incapable of
an ignoble thought?"

CONTENTS

PREFACE

This was an impressive mouthful of foot, even for me. I had called a close friend of Ross Perot to ask for an interview. His secretary wanted to know what Perot thought about my book. It was a fair question and one I should have anticipated, but my mind balked. How could I describe his reaction? My answer made this a very different book than the one I began.

Perot was unequivocal in our first conversations. He did not want a book written, period. He was not done with his accomplishments, he explained, so a biography would be premature. What's more, he thought he should own the rights to his life since he was the one who lived it. He understood that he didn't. No, he didn't want to collaborate on a book of his opinions and philosophy either. He didn't have time.

He was brief and to the point a month later when I called him to tell him I had signed a contract to write the biography anyway. I wanted him to be the first to know. You won't get access, he snapped and brusquely concluded the conversation. He had regained his composure when he called back perhaps five minutes later. Make sure I had an editor I respected and a publisher that was serious about the project, he counseled. Call him back when I knew what I wanted. It was nothing I said. He still didn't want the book written, but he didn't want it written without him either.

That's how the game is played between the press and public figures. Perot seldom loses at it. I'd made a modest request of him the day before I stammered through this conversation with his friend's secretary. I had approached for interviews two people whom Perot had instructed not to talk to reporters. I asked him to lift the restrictions, and he agreed.

Which meant what? The secretary began helping me. Was it authorized? No, it is an unauthorized biography. Well then, did he approve? No, again. Well, I ventured finally, I guess I could say he blessed the book. Perot called back in a matter of hours. It was as if someone had thrown open a window to the Arctic. He had not blessed anything. He had not seen so much as an outline. The media was carving him up like a piece of meat. He was done helping me. I was crushed.

I decided after a few days that I was also free. I had nothing more to lose. I approached the chore as a historian would. I pored over the newspaper and magazine articles written about his life and deeds over the past 20 years. Perot dismisses these thousands of stories as myths, but I found patterns. He repeated his stories, his country witticisms, again and again. I searched out accounts in his words in radio and television interviews. I found Congressional hearings reports, transcripts and tape recordings of press conferences, and court transcripts and depositions. I collected 20 of his speeches. Then I began conducting interviews in Dallas, Austin, Houston, Texarkana, Washington, and Detroit. I finished with hundreds of hours of tapes.

These are not the people who know him best—as a friend, husband, father, and brother. The book suffers as a result. By most accounts, he and his wife, Margot, have raised five well-adjusted, industrious children under difficult circumstances. His friends could tell me countless stories of his generosity and compassion. I found a number of people he has helped. Since they are acquaintances, colleagues, and even strangers, their testimony is more compelling.

Instead, I wrote a business biography. There, I had unique access. Perot's old company—and new enemy—Electronic Data Systems Corporation (EDS) opened its archives and its doors to me. I approached Perot's former colleagues directly. EDS would tell them that the decision to cooperate was theirs. The vast majority did. Most of them were trying to understand, as I was, how Perot could attack a company he once thought of as a member of his family.

EDS's help became controversial, as you will see. EDS's lawyers showed me material that is still confidential under the terms of an agreement among the parties of *EDS* v. *Ross Perot,* a civil lawsuit in Fairfax, Virginia. Arguing that EDS had acted in bad faith, Perot's attorneys got EDS's case thrown out. I was profoundly disturbed to become a part of the story. I don't believe I lost my objectivity. The EDS attorneys showed me both sides of the disputes and left me to reach my own conclusions. It's the reader's job to decide.

I saw things differently when I finally sat down with Perot in mid-summer in fact-checking exercises. (I was not to quote him directly for this book). They didn't go well. You will learn that Perot is utterly, absolutely convinced of his rightness. I had assembled evidence that he had been wrong on several occasions, but Perot simply won't travel that road. It is an affront to him that I would give any credibility to his enemies. Perot requires people to accept him on faith. I had lost mine in the course of my research.

I have not lost my admiration and respect for him. He says what he thinks and accepts the consequences. He is willing to risk everything for what he believes. I hope you will not seize on his failings and miss the context. I've done my best to be fair and honest, but it's not easy to keep the middle ground in a profile of a strong personality.

I set basic rules for myself. You will not find unnamed sources in this book or mysterious documents. I have not re-created dialogue, or indulged in mind reading or 25-cent psychoanalysis. You will know precisely what I think as the story unfolds, but I won't ask you to accept opinions on faith. It was my aim to give you enough of my reasoning and evidence so that you can decide for yourself. I accept your verdict. The opinion in this book, for better or worse, is my own.

I can't possibly thank the hundreds of people who helped me. But let me at least recognize the people who put up with me for days on end at EDS, the *Dallas Morning News,* the *Dallas Times Herald* and Dallas's exceptional J. Erik Jonsson Central Library. Thanks also to my bosses at *Business Week,* Steve Shepard and Keith Felcyn, for giving me time off, and to my friend and colleague Kevin Kelly who inherited the Augean stables in my absence. My editor, Jeffrey A. Krames, was a source of boundless enthusiasm and help when I needed both. Thanks also to Dallas attorney Tom Leatherbury, for his comfort, and Philip Nalbone, for his sharp eye. And I offer special thanks to Meg, Lowell, and Katy, who smiled indulgently as I swung from the heights to the depths and back, and went right on with the work in the Mason household that really matters.

TODD MASON

INTRODUCTION

OF OYSTERS, PEARLS, AND GRAINS OF SAND

The halls of justice in Fairfax County, Virginia, are surprisingly warm. There are no cold marble floors, hard benches, or foreboding darkness here. On one side of the corridor are floor-to-ceiling windows. The opposite wall is paneled in blonde wood. It is late afternoon on October 19, 1988. The fifth floor corridor is empty except for a mother and daughter, both blonde and well dressed. The pair is lost in tears and hushed conversation. This is the third richest county in America, but money can't stem the tide of human failings. It only raises the stakes.

Suddenly the doors to Courtroom 5H swing open, and a noisy procession fills the hall. A short, slight man is the center of attention. He is physically unremarkable except for his erect posture and expensive clothes. A dozen reporters crowd around him with notepads and tape recorders. Ross Perot makes a virtue of being ordinary, but onlookers must first recognize his celebrity status to appreciate how easily the billionaire founder of Electronic Data Systems Corporation (EDS) banters with the men and women of the press. The mother and daughter turn back to their own problems.

EDS is now suing its founder in a lawsuit that has all the drama and bitterness of a custody case. Four years earlier, General Motors Corporation acquired EDS and enlisted Perot to help combat the threat of import cars. But Perot and the GM bureaucracy clashed so violently that GM paid the charismatic leader $700 million to go away. Perot didn't. Instead, he started Perot Systems Corporation on the first day his agreement with GM permitted and began hiring executives away from EDS. EDS asked the Virginia courts to stop him.

Perot's comments at this impromptu press conference alternate between the futility of EDS's case and his disappointment in old colleagues. EDS is making Perot Systems a household name, he crows. "By the time this is over we're going to be better known than Coca-Cola." The reporters scribble furiously. Furthermore, Perot insists, EDS is driving employees into his arms. The company is accomplishing this by physically searching employees who prepare a bid proposal being challenged by Perot Systems and thereby demonstrating that it does not trust them.

EDS's public relations manager, William Wright, watches Perot's performance from a distance of 10 feet. "Go tell him that [search] policy was instituted in 1980," Wright whispers to a reporter.[1] The writer approaches Perot.

"What son of a bitch told you that?" Perot shouts.[2]

The hall is silent. The mother and daughter are staring at him. His folksy manner is gone. His ears are deep red. His face is contorted into a scowl and has the unblinking intensity of an eagle. His voice, reedy and colored by a Texas twang a moment earlier, now pierces the corridor.

"Get that son of a bitch over here!"

Wright walks over. Perot doesn't acknowledge him at first, but Wright persists. EDS first began frisking employees the last time EDS bid for and won the disputed contract, Wright explains. Perot was then chairman of the company, and EDS's current chairman, Lester M. Alberthal, Jr., headed up all of EDS's health insurance business. Perot backpedals. "That was Alberthal," he snaps. "I would have fired him on the spot if I had known that."[3]

Alberthal is standing only a few yards away. Round-faced and fair, Alberthal is not a demonstrative man. His face is a study in neutrality as he explains why EDS had to defend itself. Most EDS employees didn't want Perot to sell EDS to GM in 1984, he says. They felt abandoned when Perot sold out and left in 1986 and betrayed when he hired away eight EDS executives to start Perot Systems.

It's not Alberthal's nature to volunteer details. He had tested his executives' loyalty in the anxious days when he knew Perot Systems was coming. When the eight came in to resign, Alberthal had written them off. Men who were once friends now walk past each other in these halls without acknowledgment. "All these personal relationships have been torn apart by one man's decision to jump the gun and start a new company," Alberthal says.[4]

Who is Henry Ross Perot? We have always been fascinated by men of great wealth as witness in the newsreel indulgences of John D. Rockefeller and H. L. Hunt croaking little tunes and passing out dimes and pecans. Forbes estimates his wealth at $3 billion and ranks him the fourth richest American. Perot's hold on us is stronger; it is the stuff of myth; it leads us to make more of him than he is. Although Perot encourages our myth making, it frustrates him at times. "No," he once corrected NBC reporter Maria Shriver, "I'm not a living legend. I'm just a myth."

In our rush to judgment in the late 1960s, we dismissed the crewcut U.S. Naval Academy graduate as a right-wing nut. Similarly, although EDS was one of the shrewdest startups ever, and Perot was a billionaire at age 38, but we saw only a computer services company that acted like the Marine Corps and dressed like the FBI.

Liberal commentators still haven't forgiven him for his politics. While it's true he televised "Town Hall Meetings" in 1969 to give voice to the so-called silent majority and tacit support to President Richard M. Nixon, it's not Perot's nature to follow anyone blindly. He had plenty of critics in the Nixon administration when he attempted to deliver Christmas gifts, food, and medicine to American prisoners of war in 1969.

Two decades later, an openly antiestablishment Perot would strain his welcome at the Reagan White House. He was convinced that the Defense Department was covering up the continued captivity of Americans in Southeast Asia. He undertook his own investigation in 1986, as well as another private mission to Hanoi in early 1987. The Reagan administration was dismayed by his meddling.

By then, we saw Perot in a new light. We applauded him as the man who sent a commando team to Iran in 1978 to rescue two executives from prison. This exploit was the subject of Ken Follett's *On Wings of Eagles* and of a two-part television miniseries. The tens of thousands of us who had been absorbed, spun off, reassigned, demoted, and fired by impersonal corporations over the past 20 years admired his loyalty to his employees and his sense of personal commitment. After Iranian revolutionaries took 52 Americans hostage, plunging the United States into 15 months of anguish, a Dallas country-music deejay penned this song:

> Where are you when we need you Ross Perot?
> When it came to a showdown in oilrich Iran,
> We wound up with our pants down without a hope or a plan.
> Where are you now when we need you, Ross Perot?*

Perot achieved the same pinnacle of popularity when GM bought him out to silence his criticism of GM Chairman Roger B. Smith. Pickets walked the sidewalks in front of GM carrying signs that read "Keep Talking Ross." Again Perot stood out as a concerned, committed defender of average Americans. GM factories were dark and cold, and thousands of laborers were out of work. But Smith, seemingly oblivious, still wheeled his complimentary Cadillac into his heated parking garage and rode the elevator to his aerie. We were tired of the indignities rained on us daily by the Japanese, Taiwanese, and Koreans. Perot told us that ordinary Americans weren't to blame. We were being betrayed by our leaders.

Perot's defense of the GM working man requires a footnote. Perot has no use for unions himself. He closed an EDS business unit in Concord, California because it had dared to

---

*Copyright© 1979 by Glad Music.

organize in the early 1970s. United Auto Workers (UAW) members once pressed him for his thoughts on unions. Retired UAW vice president Donald Ephlin reports, smiling, "His answer was, 'If I worked on an assembly line and was treated as you are, I would get together with my fellow workers for collective action.' That's a pretty good description of a union. That's as close as he could come."[5]

Antigovernment patriot, antiunion populist, antimanagement capitalist, loyal boss who sold out twice to GM, billionaire defender of the underdog, perhaps no contemporary American has been written about more and explained less than Ross Perot. Writers have tried out dozens of labels on him that all fall short of solving the paradox.

Ron Rosebaum, writing for *Esquire,* reached back to the Middle Ages:

> We long for the kinds of social relationships that ensure that someone will save us in our hour of need. There's a word for a social system that offers such solace to its vassals: *feudalism.* And it is to a future of corporate feudalism that Perot's gesture points us—a future already taking shape in Japan, where employees sing anthems to their corporations and look to them for the patriotism, loyalty, security, and sense of family that nation-states and nuclear families no longer provide.[6]

Rosebaum misread the future, but he was dead right in his description of the EDS organization. Perot ruled EDS as its charismatic leader. He even owned EDS employees in a sense. They couldn't quit without losing the stock awards that Perot dangled just in front of them. Nor could they join a competitor without breaching the noncompete agreements Perot required them to sign. The Virginia lawsuit centered on those restrictions. Perot had carved out one safe haven for EDS employees in his final deal with GM—his new company. Perot Systems Corporation alone could hire EDS employees without triggering their noncompete agreements. EDS claimed that Perot tricked GM into a bad deal.

Charismatic organizations have their virtues. Followers have simple choices and clear paths to success. All a young warrior needs is a grasp of the group's beliefs, the strength of his convictions, and the courage to act on them. His reward is knighthood. At EDS, men in their 20s found themselves running business units with thousands of employees and tens of millions of dollars in revenues. They believed in themselves and in Perot. They tackled any task he gave them and often triumphed simply because they refused to quit.

That was the can-do spirit that Roger Smith hoped to infuse in GM. Smith had been frustrated in his attempt to revitalize GM by the company's vast bureaucracy. He wanted GM's functionaries to see holy warriors in action. Smith turned over 7,800 GM employees and all of GM's computer operations to Perot.

Smith made the same mistake as Rosebaum in identifying Perot as the model savior of embattled corporate America. Charismatics leaders and bureaucrats don't mix. At EDS, Perot used his company's superior grasp of computer technology to blow holes in the status quo. All that remained was picking the brave, ferocious fellow to lead the charge through the breach. The inevitable by-products, swagger and spoils, don't go down well among the ranks of the vanquished. The GM and EDS "alliance" touched off a stupendous clash of corporate cultures.

As the gulf widened, a gun-shy GM stopped Perot from distributing at a banquet a slim book called *Leadership Secrets of Attila the Hun*. But the damage was done. Smith, in effect, had ushered a small band of Huns inside the castle walls and put them in charge of morale. Perot was right about GM's ineffectual leadership.

Perot was wrong about EDS. History proved that EDS could compromise with GM without risking collapse. The dire consequence he waved almost daily under the nose of Roger Smith. Perot—a man who demands as much loyalty as he gives, and perhaps more—reacted badly to the news that EDS could live without him. Consider Paul Chiapparone, one of the men he freed from prison in Iran. Perot wanted Chiapparone to join his new company. Chiapparone declined. The following year, Perot declined an invitation to Chiapparone's dinner honoring the men who delivered him from Gasr Prison.

Perot also misunderstood the challenge at GM. The rules of warfare are different inside the castle walls, where the focus is not maximizing gains, but minimizing losses. Feats of individual bravery are less important than cooperation. Every response must be measured against the resources remaining. When the rift between Smith and Perot was out in the open, Perot snorted that GM's philosophy was "ready, aim, aim, aim. At EDS it's ready, fire, fire, fire." Perot's approach is more appealing, but it is no way to defend the city.

EDS executives at GM began checking their swagger immediately, but Perot would not bend on the subject of spoils. Says EDS Senior Vice President Gary J. Fernandes:

> We created as certain as I am sitting here, the seeds of Ross's departure [from GM]. Hiring thousands of people that GM had no say in and creating a cost bubble of the dimensions we did was bound to cause a dramatic counteraction. . . . [Also] we put forward an extensive round of stock options to people we would never have thought of before. . . . Their compensation people pointed out to us that we had some trainees on the list.[7]

To adapt Perot's metaphor, a strategy of fire, fire, fire is as distorted in its own way as aim, aim, aim. In the first stages of my research, I toyed with a Robin Hood metaphor to explain the public's delight at Perot bashing GM in the media to restore the poor. The analogy melted away in the thousands of pages of legal documents generated by the 1986 stock buyback. They showed Smith bending over backwards to make the best of a bad fit, and Perot refusing to budge. After reading them, it seemed to me that the press attacks had less to do with Sherwood Forest than with the World War III that Perot promised if Smith did not hew to the letter of the agreement. It's a tribute to Perot's power of persuasion and GM's reticence that the story has remained as one-sided as it has.

Perot's media gifts are the first key to understanding Perot. Writer Helen Dudar scored a near miss with this nifty turn of phrase, "The instant friendliness, the pearly smile, the firm handshake, the almost mesmeric gift of speech, the profound belief in himself and his product, the blurring of distinctions between the two—it is pristine Americana, Willy Loman come of computer age with, at last, the right territory."[8]

Her mistake: not recognizing that Perot's product is Perot—no blurred distinction here—and his territory is not computers but the media. Modern public figures rarely exercise the degree of control that Perot has maintained over his story. Perot is easily the most articulate, forthright, and accessible folk hero most reporters will ever encounter. Outsiders themselves, reporters are particularly susceptible to Robin Hood imagery.

Perot trades access for control. He wielded his No. 2 pencil on three drafts of *On Wings of Eagles*. His contract with Morrow and Co. allowed him to kill the book if he was willing to repay Follett's $1 million advance. Perot also reviewed the NBC miniseries script and vetoed the casting of Robert Preston as rescue commander Colonel Arthur Simons. Unlike the book, the miniseries embellished the story of the rescue. Perot shrugged: Television had visual and dramatic reasons to tweak history. Perot said his interest was protecting his men and himself from caricature.

Norman Pearlstine, now managing editor of *The Wall Street Journal,* was among the first to recognize Perot's hunger for publicity. Based in Dallas in the 1960s, Pearlstine wrote that EDS executives were pushing him to write a profile on Perot and that the entrepreneur's supposedly anonymous gifts were being touted by press agents. Pearlstine drew a parallel between Henry Ford's peace ship, an antiwar gesture on the eve of World War I, and Perot's Christmas flights. They were both attempts by businessmen to seek a broader stage.

Pearlstine was on the right track. Perot, like Ford, is driven by a personal vision of the world. Apparent contradictions or not, Perot's view of it has barely changed since he became an Eagle Scout in 1943 at the age of 13. In Perot's world, ordinary folks are basically good and capable of heroics. His credo is the Scout's Oath. He has never apologized for being square. "Have you read the Scout's Oath?" he snapped to one reporter. "If anyone wants to label me that, fine."[9]

Perot held on to his vision of an ideal world even after reality intruded. When he crossed swords with his skipper in the navy, he discovered that captains of ships are almost always right in the navy's eyes. The setback soured him on the navy and startled his classmates at Annapolis, who considered the young midshipman a sure bet for admiral. He quit IBM in 1962 after a similar clash with the company's local managers. Later, he competed fiercely against IBM, preying on his former colleagues for both employees and customers.

Thomas J. Watson, Sr., the father of IBM, also helps us understand Perot. Both men defined their companies in terms of their values and assembled a following as fanatically devoted to them as any Japanese corporation today. Watson, 60 years ago, and Perot, 30 years ago, were perfecting the techniques of symbolism, shared value systems, and empowerment. Those are buzzwords today, as consultants and scholars lament the drought of leadership in business. There's no surprise in the current fascination with leadership. We applauded managers, the caretakers of the status quo, while American corporations were ascendant. We pray for leaders, the agents of change, now that domination is slipping out of our hands.

We can study Perot's techniques and improve our leadership quotient, but charismatic leadership is also a trick of the genes. Perot is a unique specimen. He does not have what Texans call "book smarts," but his intuitive grasp of situations is uncanny. He dazzled a Washington cocktail group with his impromptu analysis of the Carter administration's failed Iran rescue, Perot compared the mission to that of Hannibal. Once he started over the Alps with his elephants, he was committed because there was no place wide enough to turn his procession around. In contrast, Perot pointed out, the helicopter mission could be scrubbed at any time, and a half-dozen officials were standing by to give the order.

Perot's ability to state the problem, to articulate our vague dreads, leaves us gasping and willing to follow his lead. Perot is one of the most effective, broad-spectrum critics afield. Despite his popularity on the dinner circuit, he speaks for free and as often as his schedule allows. Perot wowwed journalists with his speech at the National Press Club on November 17, 1988:

Right after we elected a president, we started . . . saturation bombing about the economy on the front pages . . . and all over television. I have only one question. Why didn't we do that all through the campaign?. . . I have a message for all of you men and women in the press. I think you were the dwarfs and wimps in the last campaign. . . .

I like to talk to ordinary people and they come up and say 'Ross, how come all of the money is in Japanese banks?' And I say it's this simple . . . 'They make the best products in the world.' I remember back during the depression as a child, if you . . . got an orange for Christmas, you knew your parents loved you. If they gave you a Japanese toy, you weren't sure. . . .

This is from the horse barn, not from Harvard Business School. Junk bonds by definition are junk. I didn't name them. The guys who created them named them. They are going to be worn like animals around the necks of the companies that have sold them. . . . [Junk bonds] have nothing to do with restructuring. They have nothing to do with anything except making fees.

Perot is also unique in his absolute, bedrock conviction. Once he has settled on a course of action, his cause becomes a holy mission. The only two possible outcomes are complete victory or utter defeat. "Think about that," says Fernandes. "How many people have the certainty that they are right, and in addition to being right, righteous?"[10]

Our approval or disapproval hinges on whether we are in front of him weathering his relentless attack or behind him enjoying his gains. He is not always right. Perot's headstrong ways led his loyal troops at EDS into other disasters besides the GM affair. Stockbrokers quit in droves after Perot took over the failing duPont Glore Forgan stock brokerage in 1971 and tried to remake it in the mold of paramilitary EDS. Perot put it in Chapter 11 bankruptcy protection three years later.

EDS succeeded because Perot traveled to Camp Pendleton and Fort Bragg to recruit men who shared his vision of America. They shrugged off most Perotisms: stock awards instead of pensions, for example, or summary dismissal for extramarital affairs. Even EDS evolved. His knights couldn't live on spoils when EDS stopped winning in the late 1970s. By 1979, Perot was stepping back from day-to-day control of

EDS, and his company was developing a management counterpoint to his leadership.

Fascination with power is another trait of leaders. People who specialize in the means develop a remarkable, sometimes alarming, ambivalence about the end at question. Watson, for example, admired Mussolini's successful mobilization of Italy in the 1930s, much to the consternation of his friends. Similarly, anti-Communist Perot can savor Mikhail Gorbachev's challenges in implementing glasnost. Of Gorbachev, Perot says:

> He is providing really very crisp and strong leadership. You can say that he is leading them in the wrong way, whatever your opinion is, but, by golly, he is out there trying to reshape Russia. . . . Once you let the Russian people start criticizing their government and criticizing their officials, once you release all that pent-up energy from all these years when they just had to take whatever was dumped on them. . . . Once you release all that energy, somehow you have to control the steam. Now if he can control the steam, he can generate all of the electricity in the world.[11]

One senses that he would buy the first Aeroflot seat to Moscow if he could somehow shoulder some of Gorbachev's burden.

Hundreds of petitioners do seek out Perot. Philanthropic promoters experience three stages in their dealings with Perot. First, of course, is joy that he not only signed the check but also shows personal interest. Shock follows. Perot is not merely interested; he is obsessed. The last stage is a roller coaster ride of exhilaration, dread, despair, and elation. GM's Smith stamped out brush fires all over GM as Perot bulled his way into labor relations, advertising, customer service, and more. Perot is not a patient person.

Perot has won hundreds of awards for his single-minded campaigns for the public good. Among them are the prestigious Raoul Wallenburg Award for humanitarianism, the Jefferson Award for public service, and the Churchill Award for exceptional achievement. Perot captured his own essence perfectly in his Churchill acceptance speech. "As a young man I wanted to be a pearl," he said. He gave up that dream. He wasn't an oyster either. "Unfortunately my lot in life is to be the grain of sand that irritates the oyster," he concluded.[12] The oysters in the audience, including Roger Smith, could only smile wanly.

Winston Churchill, a Perot idol, was a loose cannon himself. He was returned to power in 1939 only after the threat of waging World War II without him overshadowed the dangers of handing him the helm. He was retired again in 1946. Charismatic leaders, people who have THE answer, don't do well with ambiguous questions.

Perot's public service campaigns aren't the sterling successes they are made out to be. Texas legislators tried to tell him that imposing draconian sentences on drug dealers wouldn't drive the criminal element from Texas as Perot predicted. Instead, mandatory sentences would fill up the state's prisons. The legislators were right. Texas prisons began releasing convicts early, and Jamaican gangs moved into Dallas to take over entire inner-city neighborhoods.

The gangs, operating 15 miles from Perot's 22-acre compound, came from a different world than he. Perot demonstrated how little he knew about it in 1988, when he suggested to a newspaper editorial board that the police cordon off minority neighborhoods and proceed door to door. Fences were the wrong symbols to hold up to people who felt excluded from the Dallas mainstream. Perot drew angry charges of racism, even though Dallas inner-city schools were among the first of his charitable projects 20 years ago.

Not even critics can slow Perot. His campaigns for educational reform turned around public education in Texas. His drug campaign, emphasizing public education in addition to tougher laws, had beneficial results as well. In a two-hour meeting with First Lady Nancy Reagan, Perot sowed the seeds of her "Just Say No" campaign. The education efforts are helping to save middle-class children from drugs.

In any event, Perot gets an A-plus for effort. He keeps a brutal schedule of meetings, public hearings, and speeches during his campaigns, spending millions of his own dollars on them. He is willing to jeopardize his own safety. His travels in Southeast Asia and visits to Chiapparone and Bill Gaylord in Gasr Prison show that Perot's courage is beyond question. "Threats are kind of like going to the barbershop on Saturday," he says. "You take a ticket and stand in line."[13]

Perot remembers his roots in working-class America. Among the dozens of Perotisms that express EDS values is this one: "A man is never more on trial than in a moment of excessive good fortune." To remind himself of his responsibilities as a corporate chief, he walked the length of Braniff International Airways' terminal in Dallas on the morning after the airline filed for Chapter 11 bankruptcy protection. Braniff workers had come to work even though they had no jobs. He saw men and women in tears, he says, and came away shaken and humbled.

He credits his success to luck. Success, he tells us shrugging, is just like Halley's comet. It comes around every so often. "I was working jobs like boys did just to make a little money: breaking horses, roofing barns, stringing barbed wire," he says. "If you had stopped me and said, 'Son, what do you want to do when you grow up?' I'm sure I would have said I want to get enough education so I can work indoors. I know that much."[14] If he were only an "aw-shucks" billionaire, we would admire him as the anti-Trump.

The reader must realize by now, however, that Perot sought out the world stage, and saw activism as his responsibility. As he wrote in the *Nation's Business* in 1970:

> The key to our future is for millions of private citizens like you and me to start once again to act like proud part owners of our country. We will not always agree and that is not important. We will be involved in doing everything we can to see that the things we feel need to be done are done.

Perot caught scent of his destiny early in his life. Perot disputes this assertion because it ruins his "just-folks" image, but it is true. The first piece of evidence is housed in a glass case in the Perot Scout Center in Texarkana. On display is every promotion card he earned in his 16-month, meteoric quest of Eagle rank. Next to it is a duplicate set he obtained in his late teens when, apparently, he believed the originals to be lost. The case also houses canteen, campaign hat, sash laden with merit badges, and his *Handbook for Boys*.

Granted, many of us have such collections, thanks to our mothers. But Perot was a 23-year-old on his own in 1953, sailing around the world on the destroyer USS Sigourney. He collected coins from every port of call, Hong Kong, Ceylon, Suez, Europe. The coins are on display in his office. Among the other exhibits are memorabilia from Annapolis, the Walther PPK wielded by Iran rescue commander Colonel Arthur Simons, a picture signed by all 1,400 POWs, and a flag emblem from an infantryman's flak vest. The inventory would fill pages. Perot has been curator of his own museum for 40 years.

The best evidence of his sense of destiny stands on the corner of 29th and Olive in Texarkana. Perot's father built the trim little brick bungalow in the 1920s when 29th Street was the edge of town. It's still an attractive house in a well-kept, middle-class neighborhood. Perot grew up in the house, and his father lived out his days there until his death in 1955. His mother finally sold it and moved to Dallas in the 1960s. The new owner painted the bricks white.

These bricks were the principal item of business when Perot repurchased the house shortly after he became a billionaire in 1968. Mason contractors told Perot that no amount of sand blasting would restore the original look. Undaunted, Perot had the walls taken down brick by brick and rebuilt with the unpainted inside of the same bricks facing out! Perot has a caretaker living over the garage. The house stands empty but spotless. The grass and bushes are always perfectly trimmed. It's a national shrine with no identification, the place where it all began.

CHAPTER ONE

A BOY SCOUT FROM TEXARKANA

Ross Perot was not voted the most likely to succeed in Texarkana High School's class of 1947. That honor went to a man who is running a nursing home in nearby Atlanta, Texas. Nor did Perot chart ambitious goals for himself. In a list of the class members' nicknames, pet peeves, hopes and aspirations, Perot's entry is blank. He wasn't a scholar either. He carried a respectable B average, but he trailed at least a dozen classmates. "Ross was not the kind of guy you noticed much," says Donald Rochelle, a classmate who is now a Houston heart surgeon. "He never got into trouble, but he never did anything outstanding. . . . He was a quiet fellow. He didn't seem terribly brilliant, not terribly full of personality."[1]

That sort of youth could have been a disappointment to the national reporters who began calling on Perot in 1968. They asked what everyone wants to know about Perot: How was he exceptional? Where did he learn the secret of success? He answered that he was lucky, and he was partly right. Going public in a raging bull stock market in 1968 spelled the difference for Perot between being rich and super rich. He could have left his explanation there. Writers would have dashed off a few lines about his humble origins, which aren't unusual among successful entrepreneurs.

15

Instead, Perot turned his ordinary youth into a virtue. His was a triumph of the system. In America, pluck and vision can still win out over class and privilege. "The secret of America is common people achieving uncommon things," quoth Perot. He told stories that celebrated the essential goodness of small-town America, sometimes with a splash of wry humor. In any of his stories, listeners can close their eyes and imagine the scene as a Norman Rockwell painting. Thus, it is no accident that three Rockwell originals hang in his Dallas office. Perot confesses, "Rockwell painted what I strived to be."[2] Perot was exceptional, of course, but he had few opportunities to shine in Texarkana. His childhood was very ordinary indeed.

Perot is descended from French traders on his father's side. His great-grandfather drifted into Texas from Louisiana well before the Civil War and opened up a general store in Boston, Texas, some 20 miles west of Texarkana. Perot's grandfather, Gabriel Elias Perot, followed his father in the merchant trade. He also became a cotton buyer, a wholesaler who paid cash to planters for their 450-pound bales and undertook the risk of shipping and reselling them to textile mills or exporters. Gabriel Ross Perot, his father, followed his forebears in the cotton trade. Around the end of World War I, the older Ross Perot moved his business to the big city of Texarkana.

The *Texarkana Gazette* in 1947 hinted at the elder Perot's appetite for business. As a young cotton buyer new to Texarkana, Perot's father arranged credit at a local bank to buy 50 bales. Soon he was financing 50 bales a day. Perot, Sr., lined up a planter who was willing to sponsor him at the bank. The planter had to deliver a wagon wheel first. Perot's father threw the muddy wheel in the back of his brand-new Dodge, delivered it, and raced back to town. At a community dance, the prosperous young businessman met Lulu May Ray, a secretary for a lumber company. Lulu Ray, two years Perot's senior, was born April 15, 1897, in a small town immediately south of Texarkana. They were married February 25, 1923.[3]

Though comfortably middle class, the Perots were not counted in the Texarkana elite. The county Historical Museum has collected volumes about the city's first families. But the museum had to ask Lulu Perot to contribute information on her family after her son became famous. Its Perot collection consists largely of what she submitted: a typewritten family history and a handful of press clippings, most of them about her son.

Even if the Perots had felt slighted, they would not have shown it. Aspiring to exclusive society was considered a character weakness in populist east Texas. Ross Perot, Sr., once pulled a practical joke on an acquaintance who had moved to Texarkana from a nearby small town. Meeting a visitor from his friend's former town, Perot clucked in consternation that their mutual acquaintance had developed an inexplicable taste for golf and spent his days piloting a cart around the Texarkana Country Club. It was a fib, Perot told the reporter. "He hates golf," Perot chortled. Golf and other "high-hat" pastimes were considered cardinal sins.

In this way, Perot is very much a product of small town east Texas. Texans are different from you and me. They have been since the first wagon creaked to a stop in the early 1800s and discharged its load of Scotch-Irishmen. Texas was the last stop on the bitter odyssey of this pioneer stock. In the 1600s they were uprooted from their native Scotland and transplanted to Ireland to serve their British masters as a Protestant buffer to the Catholic natives. By the end of that century they were emigrating by the boatload to the United States.

They found no better luck in Georgia, Alabama, or Mississippi. Losing their homesteads to the plantation builders and their banker allies, they splashed "GTT" (gone to Texas) on their cabin doors and drifted west. Occasionally they vented their frustrations first. It was a point of polite society in east Texas well into this century not to ask a neighbor from whence he hailed. To do so forced the poor man to choose impoliteness by ignoring you, dishonesty by lying, or foolhardiness by naming the state that sought his extradition.

It's not hard to imagine why Perot's neighbors turned surly in the company of politicians, bankers, and the landed gentry. The Scotch-Irish heritage explains many of Perot's other traits that seem to be contradictions, like antiestablishment patriot, antiunion populist, or dogmatic individualist. The people who settled Bowie County moved there to be left alone. They wanted the right to work hard and to enjoy the fruits of that labor. In east Texas, a man answers readily to his God and to his conscience, and occasionally to his neighbor. Authorities need just the right question.

Debt was another sin. Perot's father was forced to borrow in 1925 to build the family's $4,000 brick bungalow at 2901 Olive Street. He paid off his mortgage in a year or two. One of the Perots' distant neighbors was the late U.S. Representative Wright Patman, the populist former chairman of the House Banking Committee and scourge of money-center bankers. The elder Perot paid cash for a 1929 Dodge sedan. The huge hearse-like vehicle remained the family car until 1947.

The Perots' one extravagance was their children. They spent $15 per month in the waning years of the Depression to send Perot and his sister, Bette, to an experimental grammar school. Patty Hill School was named after a Columbia University advocate of kindergarten education. The school was opened in a modest white frame house in 1921 by one of Professor Hill's students, Mary C. Patterson. The most vivid memories of the school centered on the daily Bible verses and Mrs. Patterson's ruler. The students had to answer roll call with a memorized verse. The ruler dispensed discipline. The child who drew his knuckles away was swatted until he didn't.[4]

The curriculum stressed artistic expression and frequent student performances. The attic was outfitted as an auditorium. Several times each year, Patty Hill put on full-blown stage productions at public school facilities. Perot usually turned up in the chorus and sometimes toting his accordion. (By most accounts, accordion lessons were wasted on Ross Perot.) He never starred, but then this was a fast crowd for grammar school. Classmates included Fullbright scholar and CBS correspondent Fred Graham and Hayes McClerkin, a speaker of the Arkansas House and unsuccessful candidate for governor. Temple-Inland CEO, Arthur C. Temple, Jr., was a Patty Hill student in the 1920s.

Perot was called Ray in those days. At birth, he was named Henry Ray Perot after his uncle. When Perot moved to the public schools in the fifth grade, his parents changed his name to Henry Ross. The Perots' first child, Gabriel Ross Perot, Jr., died of spinal meningitis on June 24, 1927. Perot's older sister, Bette, explains, "The doctors told her she couldn't have any more children without risk, so of course she went out and had two."[5] His parents wanted a namesake for Perot's father, who was also called Ross. It's hard to say how much this very deliberate passing of the torch registered on the boy. As an adult, Perot doesn't think it did.

The elder Perot set a high mark. He conducted business at 110 North Lelia Street in a faded red frame building only a step or two superior to a shack. The sign above the door announced "G. R. Perot Cotton Buyer; Sell it. You can't eat it." His seasonal business allowed him plenty of time with his children. Father and son were fanciers of the Tennessee walking horse. The Perot family kept them in a vacant lot across from his home. Perot's contemporaries recall seeing him and sister Bette astride the tall horses with their father idling behind them in his huge Dodge.

Lulu Perot also helped out with Cub Scout and Brownie troops. She hung in her son's room a Norman Rockwell calendar showing a Boy Scout at prayer. Apparently, she was aiming her son at heaven if not the stars. Solid families are a common thread in the lives of strong leaders. Loving, secure homes provide a bedrock for the conviction leaders must have.

None of this registered on Perot's contemporaries. His home life looked perfectly ordinary to them. His folks spent their evenings at home with their children, in the parlor or out on the front porch in the summer. Perot's friends describe his mother as sweet and friendly. They remember his father as the archetypal Southern gentleman, courtly, dignified, and quiet, a portly man in a cotton suit and a wide-brimmed planter's hat.

Perot's circle of close friends in high school was a clean-cut crew. Says high school classmate Ed Overholser, now a retired advertising executive, "Our idea of doing something really tacky was finding a sign that said 'Men Working' and putting it on the lawn of the football queen, Joyce Green. Man, that was really ribald."[6] Perot became estranged from many of his contemporaries when they discovered beer. Perot promised his father he wouldn't smoke or drink. In fact, the serious youth made his best impression on the parents of his classmates. Friendly, thoughtful, and a bit cocky, Perot invariably left them smiling. As late as 1980, he knocked on the elder Olverholsers' door in Texarkana and sat down for a visit and a slice of apple pie.

In his own age group, Perot was given to long, thoughtful silences. Perhaps he was measuring himself, as if he were trying on various suits of glory. He dumbfounded classmate Howard Waldrop during a scout meeting. "Ross had thought up a way . . . to be a member of the board of directors of General Motors," Waldrop recalls. "For a 12- or 13-year-old in retrospect it's quite amazing. His idea probably couldn't have been successful. . . . His idea was to get proxies from hundreds of thousands of minority stockholders. Ross probably won't remember it."[7] Perot doesn't.

Unfortunately for the diminutive Perot, the only real glory available to boys in Texarkana was on the football field. The two Texarkana high schools met in a fierce rivalry every Thanksgiving. Classmate Bill Wright, a starting tailback for Texas High School, was the athlete in Perot's clique. He too caught a glimpse of Perot's competitiveness. Perot challenged Wright to a tennis match, an unfamiliar sport to Wright. The loser was to buy the winner all he could eat down at the drug store. Says Wright, now an accounting professor at Abilene Christian College, "I wrote him [after Perot became famous] saying he had conned me out of my last 87 cents. He sent me a check for 87 cents."[8]

Little did Wright know that Perot had been playing tennis almost every Saturday on a private tennis court. Classmate Jim Morriss, now executive director of the Texas rural electric cooperatives, was Perot's regular opponent. "Ross always beat me," Morriss says. "He did it with the unorthodox but effective style of being able to slice it so the ball bounced away from you. He had one of the silliest, most raucous laughs. I can hear him today. When he'd get the English on the ball and get one past me, he would laugh like he was in second gear. . . . It used to make me furious."[9]

His classmates noted one other portent of greatness. Perot joined Boy Scout Troop 18 shortly after his 12th birthday in June 1942. By October of the following year, 16 months later, he made Eagle Scout rank. His determination is obvious in the Perot Scout Center display of his memorabilia. Perot literally thumbed a groove in the pages of his scouting *Handbook for Boys*. Scouting was one of Perot's first charities after he became rich.

By most accounts, Perot's scoutmaster, Sam Schuman, influenced young Perot. Schuman's family fled Russian conscription in Lithuania. Schuman joined the scouts in Texarkana over the protests of his mother who remained suspicious of any uniform. He volunteered as an assistant in 1927 and stayed active for 40 years. Schuman's patriotism was heightened by his immigrant experience.

Scout meetings in those days were held on the top floor of a downtown office building. After the meeting, Troop 18 would walk 10 blocks to Bowie Park to play "wolf over the river," or "capture the flag." Afterward, Schuman would gather them for what he called the "scoutmaster's five minutes." Most of the scouts, Overholser and Rochelle included, didn't listen. Rochelle had a second opportunity to hear Schuman's thoughts on duty and country many years later as a troop assistant. This time, Rochelle listened raptly. "I thought to myself, 'Damn, someone should be recording this.' "[10]

Rochelle saw an unexpectedly forceful Perot during a hazing at scout camp. Perot commanded the group in charge of Rochelle's hazing. The final ordeal was a rubber hose filled with flour. Blown into the open mouth of the victim, the flour instantly dried up the throat and created the sensation of choking. Perot bustled about and barked orders. Rochelle was surprised at how tough he was.

The stories Perot tells of his youth emphasize his enterprise. Again, his objective is to make a virtue of being ordinary. He is eager to show why Harvard Business School is not a required stop on the road to success. He presents instead a homespun Texarkana school of common sense.

His father's dealings with the same planters year after year, for example, illustrate that business was about relationships rather than transactions. He describes how, as an eight-year-old, he used his head to break horses for $1 each. After multiple concussions and a broken nose, Perot says he learned to tie up the horse's front leg with rags. Horses have an innate fear of broken legs. A three-legged horse is a petrified animal. Selling garden seeds and Christmas cards door-to-door, he says, taught him the pitfalls of seasonal enterprises. He learned to bargain watching his father trade horses. Perot's point is well taken. A country horse trader can teach a computer salesman a thing or two about psychology.

Such stories take on an air of myth. Reporter Bryan Woolley quotes Perot at length describing a paper route he established in Texarkana's black ghetto. He talked the newspaper into giving him a bigger cut of the subscription money because the circulation managers thought he was wasting his time, but his route turned out to be a bonanza:

> I was making $25 to $30 a week. The newspaper thought that was too much so they tried to change my rate to what the other carriers were getting. I appealed directly to the Publisher, Mr. C. E. Palmer. "Sir," I said. "I made a deal and these guys are reneging." Mr. Palmer started laughing. He laughed and he laughed. He said "Well, son, I'm going to assume you're telling the truth and we're going to honor our commitment." Since then, whenever I've got a problem, I always go to the top.[11]

The story continues in Ken Follett's *On Wings of Eagles,* a book over which Perot had editorial approval:

> The *Texarkana Gazette* cost twenty-five cents a week in those days, and on Sundays, when he collected the money, he would wind up with forty or fifty dollars in quarters in his pocket. And every Sunday, somewhere along the route, some poor man who had spent his week's wages in a bar the previous night would try to take the money from little Ross. This was why no other boy would deliver papers in that district. But Ross was never scared. He was on a horse; the attempts were never very determined; and he was lucky.

It is not possible today to verify or disprove those stories; the principals are dead, and the adults who were peripherally involved didn't take note of children. For their part, Perot's contemporaries are skeptical and point out discrepancies. For example, Rochelle's older brother, J. B., now an internist in Texarkana, delivered the *Texarkana Gazette* in the black ghetto several years before Perot did. He had taken over the route from another boy. (Delivery, of course, may have lapsed.)

Nor were paper routes particularly hard to get. Boy power was much in demand during the war years. Perot himself had three paper routes. D. W. "Sonny" Atchley says he turned over Route 36 of the afternoon *Daily News* to Perot in the early 1940s. Perot used a bicycle, Atchley insists. He still has a mental image of Perot on his bicycle with a snare drum strapped to the luggage rack over the rear wheel. Atchley, now a retired executive in Louisiana, bought Perot's drum for $14. He also married Perot's junior college sweetheart, Jane Maxwell. In Atchley's opinion, his tales of newspaper routes by horseback "are bullshit. It's harmless. It makes good copy."[12] Perot says Atchley and Rochelle are wrong.

Perot uses his days in Texarkana to point out the essential goodness of people. He says, "I threw newspapers for whore houses. I knew all the women. I threw papers to flop houses, to some of the poorest people in the world. They tried to hold me up every Sunday. . . . They weren't bad people. They were desperate. I learned that no matter how poor people are, they're good people and those are things you can't learn at the Harvard Business School."[13]

In his homilies, his family was poor as well. He recalls his family's visit to the 1936 state fair in Dallas. "My most vivid memory of the fair was the cars. Times were so harsh I didn't think I would ever have a car. I was asked to turn on the lights at the state fair in 1986. I couldn't resist thinking. 'In 1936, I didn't think I could own a car. In 1986 I wound up the largest shareholder in General Motors. That's the kind of thing that can happen in America.' "[14]

All of us romanticize our pasts. Even his Texarkana friends, who fled as quickly as they could 40 years ago, now remember Texarkana in Norman Rockwell images. The facts tell a different story about life in Texarkana. A lynch mob carried out its deed there during World War II. The red light district along Fourth Street was not populated only by kind-hearted whores and good men reduced by circumstances. Gazette reporter Sally Reese learned to stay late at the newspaper on Saturday nights to cover the inevitable crimes. An Army general declared Texarkana off limits to his troops during a maneuver in the area shortly before World War II.

In 1946, a grisly string of unsolved murders focused national attention on the city. During that spring, the "Phantom" murdered four people and wounded two others. One of the victims, Betty Jo Booker, was the girlfriend of Perot's classmate, Jim Morriss. The initial murders occurred at secluded lovers' lanes. They cast a pall over dating for Perot's remaining years in Texarkana. Near the end, the authorities prohibited newspaper deliveries before daylight, as much to protect the carriers from a panicked citizenry as from the Phantom. A man of a different temperament could have used the *Police Gazette* instead of Norman Rockwell to describe Texarkana. Perot chose the romantic view.

Perot blossomed at Texarkana Junior College in 1947. The college was run by the local school board and shared the same city block as Texarkana High School. The college was growing again thanks to Perot's class and a wave of returning veterans. Perot displayed initiative his freshman year by restarting "The Bulldog" yearbook, which had not been published since 1931. Perot assumed correctly that the college had regained its momentum.

Perot was becoming an unstoppable natural force. When Dorothy Rumsey Bakie took over as editor of the sophomore yearbook, she recruited allies to keep Perot from running the show. "He was very domineering," says Bakie, now a Cincinnati housewife. He was also a loyal friend. "He is the sort of person you just love. Other times you could kill him."[15]

Perot was elected president of the student council in his second year. In that role, he locked horns regularly with the dean of students, Lucille Couch. There was no swagger in his assertiveness. His friends considered his take-charge nature to be compulsive rather than obnoxious. Jim Morriss recalls that he was ebullient one Friday, bragging that he had "airtight" argument for the Texas junior college debate finals. He came to school on Monday crestfallen. Morriss asked him twice what was troubling him and then concluded, "they found a hole in your argument didn't they?"[16]

The junior college also gave Perot his first taste of public policy. The college was running out of room. Perot and a group of students urged the college board to relocate the campus. They argued that the college couldn't grow without more land, and that the college would be more attractive if its students weren't forced to share the campus with mere high school students. Jim Alexander, freshman class president Ross Perot, and Preston Dowd made an appeal to the board on April 27, 1948.

As Perot tells the story, his appointment to the Naval Academy was another lesson in luck and pluck.

In the account he approved for *On Wings of Eagles*, his appointment was a casual bit of unfinished business as Senator W. Lee O'Daniel was packing his boxes to leave in Washington in 1949. An aide reminded the Texas Democrat that he had not made a selection for Annapolis. The book continues:

> "Does anyone want it?" the senator said.
> "Well, we've got this boy from Texarkana who's been trying for years. . ."
> "Give it to him," said the senator.
> The way Perot heard the story his name was never actually mentioned during the conversation. Applicants had to be sponsored by senator or a congressman and of course the Perot family did not have the right contacts. . . . (H)e just kept writing to senators begging for sponsorship. He succeeded—as he would many times during later life—because he was too dumb to know it was impossible.

Actually it was not yet difficult to get appointments to Annapolis out in America's heartland, where the pounding of the surf was faint. Economics was the academy's main appeal. Don Rochelle had applied also, and when he and Perot talked about it as junior college freshmen, they most liked the fact that the academy paid its students rather than the reverse. When Rochelle's appointment came through, he declined, having decided to become a doctor. Perot had second thoughts also. He was going to be a lawyer. Bakie recalls him confiding one day that his goal was to become a Supreme Court Justice.

He was enjoying himself right where he was. He was dating college freshman Jane Maxwell, a pretty, strong-willed brunette from the Arkansas side. His parents had joined the Texarkana Country Club. Although no one remembers them indulging in anything as high-hat as golf, Perot's classmate Hayes McClerkin says, "They did it as much for Bette and Ross. . . . We [teens] hung out at the swimming pool."[17]

The idyll was ended by his academy appointment. "He wasn't very happy about it," says Jane Maxwell Atchley. "He said his daddy wanted him to [go]. He wasn't very enthused about it originally at all."[18] Perot says Mrs. Atchley is mistaken. She says Midshipman Perot visited her once while he was home on leave. The meeting was brief and definitive. His Texarkana days were over.

CHAPTER TWO

LEAD OR
STAND ASIDE

Yearbook editor Dorothy Rumsey Bakie learned a lesson for free that cost General Motors Chairman Roger Smith $700 million and much of his public standing: As a subordinate, Ross Perot is a mixed blessing. A transformation comes over Perot once the objective is clear. His considerable people skills fly out the window. Scowling, barking orders, and striding briskly, Perot elbows aside anyone who dawdles in his path. This behavior is particularly disconcerting when the idler happens to be the person in charge.

Perot gets what he wants. The National Register of Historic Places originally insisted on authenticity in the renovation of the Saenger Theater in Texarkana. But Perot could not be swayed. He's putting up $800,000, and it's to be renamed the Perot Theater after his parents. He won't have 1920s-style safety glass, "those damned chicken-wire windows," even if they are authentic. (The windows are modern safety glass.)

Bureaucrats have an instinctive, bad reaction to people like Perot, and the feelings usually are mutual. Yet twice in Perot's life, for a total of 13 years, he was able to work and to prosper inside a bureaucracy. He became class president at the U.S. Naval Academy and a star salesman in the Dallas branch office of IBM.

He also quit both organizations with some measure of disgust. As he tells the stories, he felt stifled under the Navy's lock-step promotion scheme and ran out of opportunity at IBM. There's more to it than that, however. Perot has great difficulty concealing his contempt for people who thwart him. The spark touching off these confrontations usually is not personal, but rather, the result of some unfortunate person stepping between Perot and his objective. However, the clashes get very personal once they start. Perot lives his life like the bumper-sticker slogan, "Lead, follow, or get the hell out of the way."

The Perots of the world are valuable, if prickly, resources. Perot did well in the navy and in IBM under savvy leaders who recognized him as a natural force and turned him loose. Those leaders often paid for it. You can't make pearls without irritating oysters. Still, it was inevitable that only a world of his own making could live up to his ideals. Ordinary mortals are unnerved by people who actually subscribe to the philosophy, "Death to expediency."

The navy suited Perot perfectly at the start. Not even Rockwell could have painted a happier backdrop for him than the Naval Academy in 1949. Political connections didn't matter as much in those days. The class of 1953 had its share of "navy juniors," as the sons of admirals were called, but it had many more of Perot's common folk. Classmate Billy Gene Starnes, an academy standout and later an EDS executive, was born on a tenant farm near Memphis, Tennessee. An office worker at his high school had pled his case with his Congressman and then collected $5 each from her friends to buy Starnes a train ticket, his first.

Arlis J. Simmons, one of Perot's buddies in the First Company, First Battalion, quit high school in Georgia before he realized how important an education was. He returned for his degree and excelled. He came to Annapolis because no other college was within his financial means. Harold L. Shrewsbury, another First Battalion midshipman, was working nights to put himself through the University of Oklahoma. With the navy picking up his tuition and paying him $7 per month besides, Shrewsbury figured he could concentrate on his education.

Perot, Starnes, Simmons, and Shrewsbury weren't disadvantaged by their lack of pedigree. The new middies shed most of their class privileges and prejudices when they exchanged their civvies for navy uniforms. If anything, it was the navy juniors who labored under a handicap because they were not as overawed and eager. A meritocracy emerged during "plebe summer," a boot camp of sorts. These were the plebes who were the fleetest, strongest, smartest, and the most poised. One of them was Perot.

Poise was essential once the upperclassmen returned in the fall. Of all the slang phrases the plebes learned, the most dread was an order by an upperclassman "to come around" after hours for hazing. The ordeal had two objectives: It washed out the midshipmen who were weak of will and thus unfit to lead, and it made the plebes allies in adversity.

In cases where navy conduct did not protect them from superiors or each other, the midshipmen supplied their own unspoken rules. As Shrewsbury put it, "These rascals would steal my girlfriends. We would box together. We had to live in this constant competition. Amazingly enough, it turned out. . . . We all figured it was a fair fight and that the best man would win."[1] In the unspoken code, a midshipman who spent every extra hour with the books was a "slash," someone who would cut his buddies' throats to improve his class standing. A generation later, ex-servicemen would describe a similar style of foxhole camaraderie at EDS.

Many of the midshipmen had two years of college behind them, but the academy was faster paced and far more regimented. The midshipmen marched to classes. Plebes marched everywhere. Even in Bancroft Hall, the academy dorm, plebes marched to the exact center of a hall intersection and executed military turns. Every hour of the day was scheduled. Middies had an hour of study for each hour of class. The necessary work habits and the ramrod posture usually stuck for a lifetime.

Perot struggled with the curriculum. The academy education is equivalent to a bachelor's degree in electrical engineering. Perot's long hours of study were aimed too much at survival to earn him a reputation as a slash. He finished almost exactly in the middle of the pack, ranking 454th of 925 in his class.

Perot was no standout in athletics either. Physical education instructors introduced the middies to dozens of sports, from fencing to crew, hoping for a happy intersection of interest and proficiency. Perot never found his sport. He was often paired in PE classes with the First Company's James Chesley, a wiry marine who won his appointment from the enlisted ranks. Perot's boxing and wrestling encounters with Chesley, who made the varsity wrestling squad, were one-sided to describe them charitably. Perot never sulked or complained.

If books and sports had been the sum of the Naval Academy, as they were in Texarkana, Perot's four years there would have been equally unremarkable. His classmates in Annapolis describe him in much the same terms as his Texarkana peers do, with one crucial difference.

Perot now had exceptional poise. Arlis Simmons remembers making mental note of Perot during plebe summer. The plebe units squared off in a series of competitions as September drew near. One of the events was a debate, and the standout was Perot. "He did a superb job," says Simmons. "The whole class knew who he was. That's really how he got started."[2] Most plebes were trying to perfect the art of invisibility. Instead, Perot showed the knack of the timely and salient public remark. Chesley took to calling him "Senator Perot."

Still, Perot was very private. Perot passed up drinking and hell-raising, which explained part, but not all, of the distance. He still wasn't telling anyone his pet peeves, hopes, and aspirations. Moreover, his poker face was nearly perfect. There weren't many of his stony silences that told his friends at Texarkana Junior College he was disappointed in himself. He had fewer occasions to be disappointed. Already disciplined, he flourished in the academy's regimentation. The principal mission of the U.S. Naval Academy was to develop leaders of men. At long last, Ross Perot was a natural.

The academy gave Perot plenty of opportunities to shine. Midshipmen run their own affairs at the academy, supervised by regular navy and Marine Corps officers. The top student officer wears six stripes. Company commanders wear three. Promotions aren't a matter of chance. Three times each year, every middie is evaluated by his company classmates, the members of the next higher class, and the regular officers who commanded him. These aptitude ratings were averaged with class academic standings to determine rank.

It was no surprise that top scholar Trost wore six stripes, or that Billy Starnes, who stood in the top 10 percent academically and starred in football and soccer, wore four. For Perot to wear four stripes despite his average grades made him an oddity at the academy on the order of the National Basketball Association's Spud Webb, the slam-dunking five-foot-seven guard for the Atlanta Hawks.

Perot conformed, but that's not how he won respect. The navy drummed into the middies the need for absolute authority and unquestioning obedience. A slim book called *Message to Garcia* illustrated the ideal. (Naturally, Perot has a copy of it in his office collection.) It tells how a naval lieutenant named Rowan delivered a letter from President McKinley to a Cuban insurgent at the turn of the century. Rowan sailed to the island, plunged into the jungle and came out the other side three weeks later. Author Elbert Hubbard editorialized somewhat breathlessly:

> Rowan took the letter and did not ask, "where is he at?" by the eternal. There is a man whose form should be cast in deathless bronze and the statue placed in every college of the land. It is not book learning young men need nor instruction about this and that, but a stiffening of the vertebrae which will cause them to be loyal to a trust, to act promptly, concentrate their energies to do the thing—"carry a message to Garcia."
>
> . . . . My heart goes out to the man who does his work when the "boss" is away as well as when he is at home. And the man, who, when he is given a letter for Garcia, quietly takes the

missive, without asking any idiotic questions, and with no lurk-
ing intention of chucking it into the nearest sewer, or of doing
aught else but deliver it, never gets laid off nor has to go on
strike for higher wages. Civilization is one long anxious search
for just such an individual.

In the real navy, quite often it was the task that was
idiotic. Sailors waited anxiously for someone who could finesse
the situation. Perot was that Rowan. While the student commanders were extensions of the academy staff and faculty,
each class also had elected officers who represented the students as a body. Perot was elected president of his senior class;
Trost was vice president. Forming a student tribunal at Annapolis was Perot's major accomplishment. Like its counterpart at West Point, the tribunal sat as a student court on cases
of alleged misconduct.

Few humans can match Perot's single-minded devotion to
the task at hand. Admiral Bob Inman became a Perot "project"
in 1984. Perot was dismayed that Inman would quit as deputy
director of the Central Intelligence Agency to head an important computer research consortium. Perot wanted Inman to
stay in government. Failing that, his second choice was to
recruit Inman to EDS, or more precisely, to fill the admiral's
pockets so he could get back to government. Perot tagged along
with Inman in an effort to persuade him during an auto trip
between Washington and Annapolis where Inman was speaking. He ignored Inman's declaration that he was through with
government.

Recalls Inman, "From 17th and Pennsylvania to Annapolis, Ross put me through his own special blend of ringer. 'Why
the hell are you doing this? It's never going to work. Can't
you get out of it? Take this [EDS] job and get back into government.' " The one-sided debate still raging, Inman went into
the hotel ballroom to deliver his speech. Perot sat in the lobby
reading a book.

Inman continues, "We get in the car and . . . the whole
way back it was, 'How are you going to make this work? How
will you recruit? How will you do this?' . . . You would never
know the other conversation took place at all. . . . His last

statement was 'would you be willing to live in Texas again? Well, you're going to.' He became, behind the scenes, the driving force to bring the consortium to Texas. He has the most marvelous ability to bring all of his energies to bear on a single issue and not be deflected."[3]

The class of 1953 recognized that it had a master in its ranks. First Company Midshipman Mark Royston remembers the middies returning from Dwight D. Eisenhower's inaugural parade in 1953 and complaining that still another West Point "kay-det" had won the nation's highest office. "We were asking when we were going to have a Naval Academy graduate as president?" Royston recalls. "We decided at that time that Ross was going to be the one."[4] His classmates assumed that he was a sure bet to become an admiral.

His peers were wrong. Perot left Norman Rockwell behind when he joined the regular navy. The academy expected midshipmen to test student government against the ideals they were being taught. Against a backdrop of black and white, Perot is a creative, resourceful, and even diplomatic leader. The captain of a ship at sea, however, is an absolute ruler. Junior officers seldom win, particularly those who say "death to expediency" and mean it.

Perot got a plum assignment on the destroyer USS Sigourney. Ensigns on small ships are given responsibility faster than they would earn it on larger ships. The Sigourney sailed around the world, calling on ports from Ceylon to France. Perot loved it. By 1955, he was chief engineer, a fast tracker by navy terms.

Perot's problems began when the command of the Sigourney changed hands. Neither Perot nor the navy will talk specifics, but the young lieutenant clashed with his new captain. Perot was reassigned, but the incidents followed him— an unfavorable fitness report, perhaps, or formal complaints by Perot, the captain, or both. The story has several variations.

Sam Byrd, an academy classmate, and boyhood friend Hayes McClerkin, by then a navy officer himself, ran into Perot in Norfolk as the drama was unfolding. Perot ultimately sat down with the chief of naval personnel. The brass was sympathetic and perhaps a bit amused that the young officer took his responsibilities so seriously. The chief told Perot that the incident would not affect his career. He told him he couldn't help him either. Perot was transferred to gunnery control aboard the aircraft carrier USS Leyte. In show business terms, his reassignment was a move from a major supporting role to the fifth row of the chorus.

Perot made his mental break with the navy in Norfolk. From Perot's narrow focus on the mission, the navy was maddeningly obtuse and unresponsive. Years later, he would snort derisively in his speeches, "If we did not have such a thing as an airplane today we would probably create an agency the size of NASA to build one. It's a good thing the Wright brothers didn't know any better when they made the machine fly."[5] Inventor Thomas Edison was an example of the triumph of the individual. "Everytime you land in an airplane at night and you look down at all those lights, think of a guy whose teacher thought he was dumb. Thank goodness we didn't have a National Science Foundation anywhere. They never would have given him a grant."[6]

Perot made up his mind to resign from the navy. He told Byrd that he was going to join a small high technology company in Dallas called Texas Instruments Incorporated. He urged Byrd to buy TI stock. Byrd bought a washing machine instead.

He told McClerkin that his fiancé, Margot Birmingham, wanted him to leave the navy when his tour of duty ended in 1957. They had met on a blind date during Perot's academy years. She was a student at nearby Goucher College and a native of Greenberg, Pennsylvania. They were married in her hometown in 1956.

His navy career did get back on track. In two years, he rose from the gunnery decks to the bridge as assistant navigator, a job that put him in charge of the ship. There he met a naval reserve officer who was an executive for IBM. The executive urged Perot to apply for a job at his company. Perot passed IBM's aptitude tests on the east coast. Henry Wendler, manager of the sales branch office in Dallas, invited him to drop by the office for an interview. The Perots, then married a year, threw everything they owned in the trunk of a 1952 Plymouth and drove west.

IBM was, in the words of Yogi Berra, déjà vu all over again. Perot loved the company, admired Wendler, and worked effectively under him until he was reassigned to Washington in 1961. Perot lasted less than six months under Wendler's replacement. His IBM years were pivotal nonetheless. IBM served first as the model for EDS, and then as the start-up's mortal enemy. IBM's founder, Thomas John Watson, Sr., is perhaps the closest historic parallel to Perot.

Back in 1957, IBM was an elitist crew, if not quite a cult. Its messianic leader had died one year before Perot joined, but his liturgy lived on. Today, we would describe its culture as Japanese-like, at the price of standing history on its ear. IBM was populated by wild-eyed zealots in the 1930s, well before the Japanese discovered fanatical corporate loyalty and commitment.

Sixty years ago, Watson was chairing all-day sales revivals in circus tents pitched on the company lawn in Endicott, New York. Company songs celebrated Watsonian victories, and the speeches drew on IBM tribal mythology for their power. While IBM had no specific dress code, the revival-goers— sweating in dark suits and long-sleeved white shirts—followed an unwritten one so closely they appeared to be wearing uniforms. A generation later, EDS would look suspiciously similar, and Dallas radio stations would air songs extolling Perot deeds.

Watson's successor, his son Thomas J. Watson, Jr., gradually expunged most of the rah-rah elements of IBM culture. They seem corny from the vantage of history. But they worked marvelously. The U.S. Justice Department sued IBM in the 1930s and again in the 1950s alleging antitrust violations. Government lawyers argued that IBM used predatory product strategies and pricing to dominate the U.S. punchcard tabulating business. Thomas Watson, Jr., signed a consent order in 1956 settling the second case, but neither he nor IBM employees were contrite. Although shrewd product stategies brought customers into the IBM fold and kept them there, in the end IBM delivered unrivaled service. Fanatical devotion to the customer explained IBM's domination of the market.

The philosophy IBM practiced so well was, "Do business with us, Mr. Customer, and we won't let you fail." IBM salesmen, drawing on IBM's engineers, often became surrogate data processing managers for their customer-companies. They designed computer systems, installed them, helped the customer find qualified managers and staff, then trained them, and stayed on call night and day to help them fix malfunctions.

It's hard to imagine how primitive the technology was then. The IBM 1401 computer, a commercial workhorse of the early 1960s and the progenitor of the modern IBM mainframe computer, was the size of a refrigerator. Nonetheless, it could hold perhaps four pages of this book in its memory at one time. Today, a seven-pound laptop computer could hold the entire book.

Software, the computer code that harnesses the machines to useful tasks, was equally crude—when it existed at all. Data processing managers were the 1950s' corporate equivalent of witch doctors. They represented mighty gods of efficiency and held the organization's destiny in their hands. Regardless of this inherent power, they were looked on with dread and suspicion. The attentive IBM men offered management an extra degree of comfort.

Sales trainee Perot showed his mettle from the start. As an apprentice technician, Perot stepped into the breach at a difficult installation at a trucking firm. At one critical point, Perot moved a cot into the computer room. He was feeding data into the machine, a task that took days. When the card reader stopped clicking, Perot would wake up and feed it another stack. "Right away you think this guy is not run of the mill," says Dean Campbell, a retired IBM salesman and Perot's one-time partner.[7]

Perot finished at the top of his sales training class, the last step to becoming a full-fledged salesman. Wendler, a cagey manager more interested in results than protocol, gave Perot the toughest accounts in the Dallas office. Since Perot stood to make the most money at these accounts, he didn't argue. IBM's commission scheme obliged young Turks.

To make sure salesmen sprang out of bed to help customers on the coldest of nights, IBM made them financially responsible for their territory. If a customer returned leased equipment to IBM, the monthly income was subtracted from the salesman's quota and ultimately from his paycheck. Since selling and installing computers represented such a lengthy process, IBM split the commission, half on the sale, half on installation. If the seller moved on before installation—as often happened—his replacement got a crack at the installation half of the commission, so long as he agreed to repay the sales half if the deal fell through. In practice, the sales plan created a certain number of accounts in each branch office that no one but the brave dared handle.

Wendler's problem account was Southwestern Life Insurance Company. A middle manager at Southwestern had signed an agreement for an IBM 7070, the largest commercial machine IBM made. Southwestern didn't really need that much computer power. Worse, from Wendler's point of view, Southwestern's curmudgeonly chairman, the late James Ralph Wood, didn't like salesmen in general or IBM in particular. Wendler paired Perot with Campbell. The team was collectively responsible for some 20 insurance company accounts, but they divided them up from the start. Perot would work full-time on the problem accounts, Southwestern and Blue Cross, and Campbell would take the rest.

Truth be told, Ross Perot was not a born salesman. He had all the skills but was too intense. At the start, he dug a deeper hole for IBM. The Southwestern manager who had ordered the computer was accustomed to coffee and small talk. After a visit or two with a relentless Perot, he complained. Wendler took the young salesman aside and urged him to lighten up. Tom Spain, who was district manager in Dallas, remembers Perot as plain-spoken. "He wasn't sensitive to political ramifications," Spain says, "although he was by no means a bull in a china shop."[8]

Perot learned to harness his compulsive energy. "He would literally isolate himself and study," Spain says. "When he came

out of isolation he knew as much about the company or individual as anybody."⁹ Perot would practice his pitch on his
sales managers, anticipating questions. Poised, articulate,
knowledgeable, Perot seldom failed to impress.

But his style was still closer to horse trader than silver-
tongued salesman. Perot wasn't there to seduce anyone. Rather,
he would lay out the business case for owning a mainframe
computer. Perot's country wit cut straight to the heart of the
issue. When Perot would tell his negotiating partner, "You're
making me feel like a hunk of sausage, slicing me up a piece
at a time," the latter might laugh at the earnest fellow across
the table with the nasal twang and the country images, but
he also would get the point.

Perot enlisted IBM's president then, Gilbert E. Jones to
solve his first problem—getting in to see Wood. When the IBM
delegation walked in, Wood was snapping pencils in two and
throwing the remnants against the wall. I hope you're not
going to waste my time, Wood said, in the way of pleasantries.
I could be quail hunting. Perot spoke up in the embarrassed
silence. He had done his homework. He made a succinct and
compelling case for harnessing a computer to Southwestern's
problems. The meeting settled nothing, but Perot had his foot
in the door. Wood asked his subordinates if the young guy had
a life insurance background.

Still, Perot couldn't move Wood. Southwestern Life didn't
need a computer as large as the 7070. Perot proposed an off-
beat solution. What if Southwestern sold unused time on its
new 7070 to another company? One day, Perot stopped his partner, Campbell, and told him he was about to close the deal. How?
A government agency in Dallas called the Agricultural Com-
modity Price Stabilization Service flew to New Orleans several
times each week to use a rented 7070. Perot's plan was to secure
a contract with the government agency to buy time from Southwestern Life instead and use that contract to make an irresistible offer to Ralph Wood. Campbell wondered how selling
the U.S. government time on a nonexistent computer was any
easier than selling anything to Ralph Wood. Not long after,
Perot reported that he had closed the deal with Wood.

Perot's math won Wood over, and that was not all. Most IBM computers were leased in those days. The antitrust settlement obliged IBM to begin selling its equipment, because the government considered leasing practices to be anticompetitive. At first, Wood wasn't interested in buying the 7070. Well, Perot said, how would you like to rent a machine for 10 percent less than IBM charges, with the same support, saving some $3,000 per month? Now Wood was interested.

Perot declared to Wood that he had been looking forward to early retirement from IBM. If Perot bought the computer and leased it to Wood—even at a 10 percent discount—he could make handsome profits because his overhead was so much lower than IBM's. Service conscious IBM would take care of his machine in any event.

Where would you get $1.3 million? Wood shot back.

Mr. Wood, Perot replied, your word is good in this town. Based on our contract I could go to any bank and borrow the money. I don't think you like the idea of paying your competitors 6 percent interest, so I'm going to let you buy it instead.

Hearing this story, Campbell was agog. What would Perot have done if Wood had accepted his dare? Perot would have followed through, he answered. A computer leasing industry sprang up to exploit IBM exactly as Perot was proposing. Until IBM learned to deal with this new industry, computer leasing was a hot concept on Wall Street. Still, Perot was probably bluffing Wood. Financial manipulation offends his populist sensibilities.

Perot's role as an unpaid broker of Southwestern's second and third shifts put him into a gray area with his employer. Granted, it was a quaint notion that customers could switch off something as expensive as a 7070 mainframe after eight hours and go home. But on the face of it, a company that bought Southwestern's second shift to satisfy its computing needs no longer was looking to buy a computer of its own. Former IBM manager Gayle Tinsley says "It wasn't widespread, but it was done."[10] Defenders used a potato chip rationale. A company that started out leasing two hours of computer time soon needed six, and then eight, and so on.

The Campbell-Perot partnership couldn't stand prosperity. Perot began complaining to Campbell once or twice a week that it wasn't fair for Campbell to claim half of the $24,000 commission when Perot had done all the work. Campbell pointed out that Perot had never visited the 18 accounts he was managing, but the pair had been splitting those commissions. (The Southwestern payoff, of course, was far larger.) Campbell also argued that he would have been on the hook to repay the earlier Southwestern commission had Perot failed. Unable to agree, Campbell and Perot turned the question over to their managers. Campbell was aghast when IBM agreed with Perot and cut him out of the commission. "I nearly dropped dead there," Campbell says. "I said, 'I'm splitting this team right now. I know what it is costing me this time. God knows what it will cost me next time.' "[11] Perot declined comment.

Perot remained an unpopular loner in the branch office. His work habits set him apart. He skipped the morning coffee sessions in the office and the evening happy hours. He spent the time instead with his customers. His heavyweight commission income didn't help matters. Wendler was forced to defend himself and his ace troubleshooter. "Ross was doing so good, and selling so much business they thought I had given him all the juicy accounts," he says.[12]

When Wendler was transferred to Washington, Perot became just another salesman. If you walk into any bar where salesmen congregate, you will hear the same two-part gripe, The home-office idiots cut my territory and they raised my quota. Perot was no longer exempt. To top it off, IBM changed its commission scheme to prevent top salesmen from earning more than their bosses.

Under the new plan, IBM set quotas for each salesman depending on how his sales prospects actually looked. If the salesman met his quota, he received his full allocation from the bonus pool. IBM reps howled in protest; IBM was playing God with their salaries. That wasn't precisely true. If a salesman sold twice his quota, he doubled his bonus. Home runs were still possible—only now IBM was moving the fence backward for the heavy hitters.

In effect, IBM already had decided what it wanted Perot to earn in 1962. The company knew he was closing a sale of the most expensive computer IBM made, an IBM 7090. Perot had been courting the Dallas city leaders who wanted to start an advanced engineering school. The Graduate Research Center of the Southwest at that point had little more than an impressive list of supporters and a fancy name. Perot wanted to sell them a computer.

The sale was the final straw for Perot. He delivered the Graduate Research Center sale and others in January of that year to meet his 1962 quota. (Meeting annual quotas in January was not an unheard-of phenomenon at IBM. Thomas Watson, Jr., holds the record; he made his quota one year on January 1.) Perot was not obliged to hang up his spurs. He could have doubled his income that year had he been able to double his quota. That was the rub. His sales manager, James Campbell (no relation to ex-partner Dean Campbell) asks, "Where was he going to go to sell another 7090? That sales plan was totally flawed. There was no motivation to go out and sell a smaller computer."[13]

When Perot asked his new branch manager to consider him for a promotion, the man sent him out to a Los Angeles office to look over an opening for sales manager. Returning, Perot declined. Years later he guessed that he would have become a frustrated, middle-management problem for IBM had he stayed.

Perot found his epiphany in the barbershop one Saturday as he thumbed through the December 1961 *Reader's Digest.* (Yes, he has a copy of the magazine in his office.) He says he was transfixed by one of those bottom-of-the-page quotes, " 'The mass of men lead lives of quiet desperation.'— Henry David Thoreau."

Writers have spent decades trying to reconcile the contemplative Thoreau and the firebrand Perot. Perot should have been reading the memoirs of another results-oriented leader, Sir Winston Churchill. The young cabinet minister was sacked during World War I after the British navy came to grief executing Churchill's strategy in the Straits of Dardanelles. As the British army suffered further humiliation at Gallipoli, Churchill could only watch from the sidelines. "Like a sea-beast fished from the depths, or a diver too suddenly hoisted, my veins threatened to burst from the fall in pressure," Churchill wrote. "At a moment when every fibre of my being was inflamed to action, I was forced to remain a spectator. . . ."

Perot resolved to be his own boss. Why not sell data processing services rather than computers? IBM was delivering on its promise—buy our computers and we won't let you fail—largely because of the heroics of IBM employees. Why not skip the hardware and sell the people? Perot was zeroing in on the comfort factor: Buying hardware doesn't guarantee success, only the opportunity to try. Pay me for the results instead.

Technically, this was not the birth of the computer services industry. Other companies, IBM included, had been selling payroll, billing, and other basic data processing services for years. These service bureaus picked up raw data every evening, processed it overnight at their own facilities, and delivered the results before business hours the next morning. For the first five years of its life, EDS operated much the same way.

Perot's wrinkle was applying the same no-sweat approach to more exotic problems. Computers could calculate insurance premiums faster and more accurately than clerks, for example; but installing one was the organizational equivalent of open-heart surgery. The computer savant needed to know both the insurance business, in order to understand its problems, and computer technology, to provide answers. Finally he needed the skills to manage the slippery transition from manual systems to automation. EDS would specialize in those three skills.

Typically cautious, Perot eased into private enterprise. When he quit IBM, he joined Blue Cross-Blue Shield of Texas, Inc., a health insurance provider, as a consulting data processing manager. He also incorporated Electronic Data Systems Corporation on June 27, 1962, his 32nd birthday. He had an office and a secretary waiting for him in the Blue Cross building in downtown Dallas. But first, he and Margot flew to Hawaii for a two-week vacation. Until he sold EDS to GM 22 years later, he would not report to anyone on a direct-line basis.

CHAPTER THREE

A TEXTBOOK START-UP

One of the enduring fictions about EDS is that it was a wing-and-a-prayer start-up. Yes, the company was capitalized with $1,000, but that happened to be the minimum requirement of Texas corporation law. (Perot has the check under glass in his office.) That was by no means the sum of the Perots' resources. IBM was paying him a full annual salary in 1962 and Blue Cross was contributing a second regular paycheck. Margot, a school teacher, brought home a third. Perot says, "We had never cashed her checks. We really lived very modestly. I had never bought a new car. We didn't own a washing machine, and we had saved our money. . . ."[1]

EDS never required outside capital, not even at its public stock offering in 1968. Perot's financing of his start-up was one of the two strokes of genius in EDS. The company was profitable from the start. Perot only had to part with stock to entice engineers to join the company. (Recruiting was the other brilliant stroke.) When the company went public six years later, Perot owned 81 percent of EDS stock.

Perot had few expenses. He paid $100 per month to rent his office at Blue Cross. He had one full-time employee, his secretary, Betty Smith. The only other expense of note was his telephone bill. He worked mornings for Blue Cross. Then he began telephoning the 110 corporate owners of IBM 7070s and offering them the off-hour shifts at Southwestern. His 79th call, to Collins Radio Company in Cedar Rapids, Iowa, was a home run.

Collins needed more computer time for a major software development project. In October of 1962, Collins began flying boxloads of computer tapes and platoons of programmers to Dallas on Friday evenings to take over the Southwestern computer room until Sunday night. Perot found moonlighting operators to help the Collins engineers. When Collins was through, Perot four months an entrepreneur had $100,000 in the bank.

On February 13, 1963, Perot sold the EDS concept for the first time. Potato chip giant, Frito-Lay, had been struggling for two years to develop a sales route accounting system, so it was quite susceptible to Perot's results-oriented sales pitch. That isn't to say that computer services was a snap to sell. Perot was still asking Frito-Lay to trust him in the most basic sense of the word. Frito-Lay was agreeing to hand over the most intimate details of its business every evening to be carted away, processed, and returned. Thomas J. Marquez, EDS employee no. 3 and the account manager at Frito, jokes, "Without references we had to say good things about each other."[2]

The first step in any EDS account was a full-scale feasibility study. The study had a foregone conclusion—hire EDS—but it had the effect of putting cash in the company's pocket at the start. It also allowed EDS to size up the task very carefully before quoting the customer a price. EDS was seldom surprised.

Even when EDS began hiring more full-time employees, Perot did not have much in the way of expenses. The account teams went to work at the customer's offices, the only practical place for them to be. The processing was done at night on rented computers; Perot didn't actually own a computer until 1965. When the staff needed to meet, they convened at Perot's office at Blue Cross.

The risk was hiring people before their jobs existed; if the contract fell through, their salaries would be a dead loss. Perot explained the situation carefully to his prospective employees. He assured them that he had a year's salary for them in the bank; thus, they had 12 months of job security. By 1964, EDS had spread the risk over enough contracts to remove most of it. Jack Hight, a former IBM lobbyist in Washington and early EDS employee, recalls, "EDS was 15 or so people in 1964, maybe four accounts and $500,000 in annual revenues. By the same token, with five-year contracts. . . [its future work under contract] might be $10 million in the bank."[3]

What remained was to recruit people who could deliver on Perot's promise. The first target of opportunity was IBM. Marquez was a sales trainee in the IBM branch office in Dallas when Perot recruited him. To staff the Frito-Lay project, Perot hired away Jim Cole, the senior technical man in the IBM Dallas branch, and IBM engineers Thomas Downtain, Cecil L. Gunn, and others. As 1963 wore on, Perot struck again, hiring his cousin, IBM sales trainee Milledge A. Hart III, and insurance software specialist Bob Potter. Each man represented perhaps $10,000 in training costs to IBM. As EDS's needs grew, Perot raided IBM offices as distant as Atlanta. Its top-gun programmers came from an IBM unit in Houston under contract to the National Aeronautic and Space Administration (NASA).

Perot's former IBM colleagues reacted badly. Quitting IBM just wasn't done in the early 1960s. To leave implied it was not the best company in the world, so IBM employees chose to believe it was the quitters who were imperfect. It was hard to hang on to that rationalization while Perot was pulling out ace engineer after ace engineer. Perot's sales manager, James Campbell, had relocated to California for IBM. "I was glad I was gone," he says. "He really did pick over the office. He was able to identify the very best."[4]

Perot already was a controversial figure in the IBM Dallas branch. The Graduate Research Center sale fell through after Perot collected his 1962 wages and quit. Ultimately, the Center bought a much smaller computer from IBM, a 1401, and Perot's managers wound up subtracting most of Perot's commissions from their own sales-incentive totals.

The IBM branch managers seethed when EDS began stealing customers. Frito-Lay had an IBM computer on order when Perot convinced them that hardware wasn't the answer. Frito-Lay's first act after signing on with EDS was to cancel its IBM order. Perot had gone into the business of unselling computers for his former colleagues at IBM . "Every sale we made," engineer Cecil Gunn remembers, "in essence knocked IBM out of a sale. We became very bitter competitors in the early days."[5]

The Dallas branch struck back in the fall of 1963. EDS was making a sale to an insurance company called Mercantile Security Life Insurance Company, and planning to use a brand-new piece of IBM software called 62-CFO. In those days, IBM gave away its software free. Often there was no other way to sell computers except to throw in software that didn't exist anywhere else.

One day, an IBM salesman turned up in the office of Mercantile Security data processing manager, David W. Soelter, to drop some broad hints. "It definitely was implied that because we weren't buying the hardware of choice, the 1401, the software wasn't going to be available to us," says Soelter.[6] Perot wrote a letter of complaint to IBM headquarters, which ordered the Dallas office to turn over the program to EDS. It wasn't a hard decision to make. IBM could not afford, seven years after its consent order, to be seen beating up on a 10-man firm. "One reason we could compete effectively with IBM is because we knew them so well," Gunn says. "They were like a dinosaur. You could jab them in one place and they wouldn't feel it for a long time."[7]

Perot was positively gleeful about the indignities he inflicted on IBM. The joy was still evident 25 years later in Court Room 5H in Virginia. Perot had taken the stand to defend his right to hire EDS employees at will. The opposing attorneys tried to paint that right as extraordinary. When he started EDS, they asked, was he able to pluck employees at will from a rival? Perot's eyes sparkled and his lips curled into a wicked grin. "Yes," he shot back.

That brings us to the second genius stroke in EDS. How was Perot able to rob a company as rich and prestigious as IBM? The answer, in a word, is bureaucracy. He wanted people who were capable of walking into Frito-Lay or Mercantile Security and taking charge. He knew from his own experience that self-starting employees would always be frustrated by the bureaucracy.

Once he found the right person, the rest was simple. He could offer them a company virtually free of politics and procedure. In practice, EDS was a confederation of independent businessmen. Perot handed them the world's most concise procedural manual: "Do what makes sense." His budgetary policy was equally brief: "Spend the money like it was your own." And it was their money; the stock awards made them part owners of EDS.

Perot honored his own commandments. The first was to avoid forcing headquarters "wisdom" on the men in the field who were actually dealing with the problems. "He'd call you if he saw something he didn't think you were doing right," says Joe Wright, a retired EDS systems engineer. He only required a thoughtful answer. "He gave you in some cases too much leeway," Wright continues. "You didn't get enough help."[8]

EDS often tackled development jobs with a fifth or even a tenth of the staff other companies would assign to it. EDS also did away with the usual development project hierarchy. Systems analysts design computer programs. Programmers then write the lines of code that execute it. EDS's systems engineers do both tasks and consider this positive since it afforded them more control over their projects. (They were less thrilled to change hats a third time and become their own keypunch operators.) Perot made sure that nothing stood between his people and the sheer joy of harnessing the computer to their will.

Obviously, this management style wouldn't work if EDS systems engineers did not prize the joy of accomplishment. People who loved to win, results-oriented employees in today's management-speak, didn't need supervision. They worked as hard as necessary. "Whatever it takes" became EDS shorthand for working a 14-hour day and crawling back to a hotel room that had been home for five months.

The difficulty of finding such people forced EDS to create its first formal department. EDS recruiters were hardly bureaucrats, however; they were sharks. They would call a computer shop and ask hazily for "John." They were able to rack up five or six names before they got their request straightened out with the helpful employee on the line. They then arranged an interview with the programmer who sounded like the best prospect. They asked him who had a hotter hand than he with a deck of punch cards. Newly hired engineers brought along more names and perhaps even the company phone book. Until 1965, Perot refused to print an EDS directory lest some company repay the favor.

Coming up with a hot prospect was only half the battle. The interviewing process was so intricate that job candidates complained, You guys screen everyone like you're hiring vice presidents. The stock reply was: we are. The first application form ran to 20 pages and asked such pregnant questions as, What do you consider the biggest accomplishment of your life? Perot insisted on sitting down with the candidate's wife to gauge how strenuously she would object to the EDS workweek and, of course, to win her support. Everyone in the company sized up the hopeful prospect. "The 18th guy was hired in a room with 17 guys sitting around asking him questions," Gunn says.[9]

As the process was streamlined, full-time recruiters took over responsibility for the initial screening and the home visits. The application form shrunk to a more manageable size, but it still asked about the applicant's finest moment. Interviews were conducted by a team comprised of the prospective manager, an old hand, and a relatively new employee. The interviewers answered three questions about the prospect: Would they hire the person? Would they work with him? Would they work for him?

When Perot exhausted the recruiting possibilities at IBM, he turned his attentions to other Dallas companies. The Bell

Helicopter plant in Fort Worth yielded several EDS engineers, including the third president in the company's history, Morton H. Meyerson. Perot reached into his own past to satisfy EDS's insatiable appetite for talent. Tom Walter, who served with Perot on the Sigourney, signed on ultimately to became EDS's chief financial officer. Bill Starnes, Perot's classmate at the Academy, represented a bold experiment. He had absolutely no computer background when EDS sent him out on his first job.

Starnes's fast start inspired the second formal corporate department at EDS—a training staff led by David Behne. An IBM engineer, Behne had resisted Perot's entreaties until IBM made him a programming manager at NASA in Houston. Frustrated, Behne not only jumped to EDS but brought along the men who became EDS's top programmers, Frank Besadesky and Hal Ragsdale. Behne and former IBM engineer Downtain tackled the job of teaching computer technology to novices.

The two of them debriefed Starnes on his experiences. Starnes told them that his real struggle was trying to figure out what his customer, Mercantile Security Life, did for a living. Behne fashioned Phase One of the Systems Engineer Development program as an answer. EDS first assigned recruits to the customer's offices to learn what happened there and why, and to perform data entry and other menial tasks. Once they understood the industry, they came back to classrooms in Dallas to learn computing. Quiet, unassuming Behne didn't look or act like a pillar of EDS. Yet he was the elder at EDS who introduced newcomers to corporate life and customs. His counsel to the most promising new hires, and his recommendations of them to Perot, gave him considerable stature and influence at EDS.

The EDS recruiting pitch borrowed a page from the U.S. Marine Corps—The Few, the Proud—but the company did not yet have its shores of Tripoli or halls of Montezuma. The company went straight to work building a winning tradition and a corporate culture Texans would describe as "stronger than garlic."

One bit of EDS lore was born in an alley outside Southwestern Life. By 1965, EDS had purchased one of the first of the new IBM 360s and installed it there. Because it was not large enough, EDS rented night shifts in computer rooms all over Dallas and Fort Worth. Like gypsies, EDS operators gathered at dusk to pick up the programs and the raw data they were crunching that night. Tapes tucked away in the trunks of their cars, they fanned out across the area.

The systems engineers had the worst of this dispersal. When the operators telephoned them at night to tell them their programs had gone awry, the first fact the bleary-eyed engineer had to ascertain was exactly where the operator was. They learned to carry their listings and program tapes in their cars so they wouldn't have to go back to their offices first. They joked that they knew every dark alley and night watchman in Dallas.

Perot called an all-hands meeting when Anne Ellis applied for a system engineer's job in the mid 1960s. She was eminently qualified by temperament and training. She had already broken the gender barrier in two other computer shops. But could EDS in good conscience send her out in the middle of the night? And if so, should a male engineer accompany her? The gentlemen of EDS decided to offer Ellis a job but no escort. Some of them still wonder how the strong-willed Ellis would have responded if they had made such an offer.

Conditions improved for operators after EDS moved into its first offices on Mockingbird Lane in 1967. EDS still couldn't buy and install computers fast enough, but at least the operations people were working day shifts and didn't have to lug tapes and forms around Dallas.

The systems engineers suffered still. Innocents in the 1960s could have strolled into any bar in the world where systems developers gathered and heard this complaint over and over, The damned operations guys won't give me the system long enough to check out my new program. EDS was no different. The systems engineers still went to work at midnight and remained on good speaking terms with Dallas night watchmen.

Naturally Anne Ellis has the best war story. A night watchman at Great National Life Insurance was the bane of

EDS engineers. He had a habit of slipping away at night to sleep, and he slept so soundly that the bell at the employee entrance couldn't rouse him. One night, Ellis was locked inside when the watchman did his disappearing act. Checking doors, she finally found one she could open from the inside. She let herself out onto a patio surrounded by a 10-foot fence. She slid her attache case under the gate and scaled the fence.

Perot during this period was performing his own brand of heroics. EDS engineers can't articulate how Perot worked his motivational magic. He wasn't a billionaire in those days or a hero; no one knew of him outside the Dallas business community. Moreover, the early engineers were peers, usually older, and always more skilled. His influence over them was unmistakable. Ellis puts her puzzlement in words, "He is one of the most unique people I have ever known, the type fellow who could almost get you to jump off a cliff, and I am not that gullible."[10]

Perot's technique was no secret at all. He asked Ellis, Wright, and the rest to tackle jobs that stretched their skills to the breaking point. And he sent them out so confidently and relied on them so explicitly that they could not help but believe in themselves.

Most people picture leadership as Teddy Roosevelt leading his Rough Riders up San Juan Hill. Leading by example is important—don't ask anyone to do something you wouldn't do yourself—but it isn't the noblest form of the art. Perot took his place instinctively in his fighter's corner, wringing his towel, biting his lip, and waiting for the round to end. He gave his small stable of fighters a shot at the title. When they won, he turned the spotlight over to them.

They all feel a sense of obligation to him. Gunn is retired now in South Padre Island, at the southern tip of Texas. He says, "If Ross asked me to drive to Alaska but he couldn't tell me why until I got there, I would be in my car an hour later. Not only that, my wife would be packing my suitcases before I hung up the phone."[11]

Perot courted his workers' spouses. The annual black-tie dinner was largely for their benefit, as were the picnics at the Perot's lake cottage just outside of Dallas. Perot also used direct, personal appeals. In early 1963, Perot disappeared uncharacteristically one afternoon. He reappeared in late afternoon but shrugged off questions about where he had been. His men found out that night at home: He had visited each of their wives to thank them for their patience and to present them with a 100 shares of EDS stock, worth $400,000 25 years later.

He seemed to have a sixth sense that told him when a wife was nearing the end of her rope. He took the Gunns to dinner at the Cattlemen's Club in Dallas one night to present Mrs. Gunn with stock in her name. "He said, 'I hope it sends your kids to college,' " Gunn remembers. "My wife said it was a nice gesture. She thought it was just a piece of paper. It did send our kids to college, and my son is a doctor."[12]

EDS managers still make it a point to remember anniversaries with flowers and children's birthdays with gifts. Perot also pulled out the stops during crises. When Jay Coburn's son was born with a congenital heart defect in a New York City hospital, Perot rounded up his neighbor, a heart surgeon, to take command of the emergency from Dallas. The infant underwent corrective surgery and lived. Perot found a top ophthalmologist for Meyerson's wife, Marlene, when she accidently splashed drain cleaner in her eye.

As exemplary as life was at EDS, it was not without its drawbacks. A sure way to get fired was to discuss salaries with other employees. Wives could get their husbands fired. Perot was determined to avoid the backbiting and petty jealousies directed at him and Margot at IBM. Several years later, when Wright took on the job of computerizing the EDS payroll, he discovered there were wide divergences in salary that could not be explained by ability. The systems engineers EDS hired in Dallas were relative bargains. EDS had to pay dearly to hire professionals away from generous employers in Rochester, New York or Minneapolis.

Perot was frugal to the extreme. He left concrete proof of his stinginess when EDS moved out of the Mockingbird Lane offices in the mid-1970s. He had been unwilling to pay for false floors in the EDS computer room. Instead, he drilled through the concrete floor, snaked the connecting cables through the false ceiling of the floor below, and brought it up through another hole. The floor was riddled like swiss cheese by the time EDS moved out.

Perot fretted over personnel costs, the largest variable under his control in the early days. Perot made loans to newly hired employees to cover their moving expenses, and forgave the loans if the employee was still with EDS a year later. Relocated employees in those days received no financial adjustment at all. Even in the early 1960s, moving from Dallas to New York, Washington, or Chicago was a financial shock.

Perot sometimes seemed to be purposely vague about expense policies. He told Downtain to find his own health insurance policy, since EDS was not big enough at that point to qualify for a group plan. Only after Downtain had shopped carefully did Perot tell him that EDS was picking up the tab. Travelers had no guidelines to measure their expenses on the road. "Spend the money like it was your own" was far more effective. Engineers stayed two and three to a hotel room and ate sandwiches on their beds so they could turn in modest expense reports. Dallas lunches weren't reimbursed at all. Lunch and business didn't mix, in Perot's opinion. EDS staff members couldn't drink at lunch no matter who paid.

EDS failed on more substantive issues. Twenty-five years later, Perot would aim scathing criticisms at GM for dividing itself into labor and management; but he made the same mistake in the early days of EDS. Operators were second-class citizens to be excluded from banquets and other corporate functions. Since the engineers had to leave after-hour phone numbers, there was no way to finesse the slight. Worse, operators weren't cut into the stock option program or encouraged to become engineers themselves. The class system was a vestige of Perot's moonlighting operations staff and perhaps also of the military. Once production became as tricky as system development, he realized his error and made amends.

Nor did EDS give its first employees the freedom to fail. Perot called Downtain back from Washington to Dallas after one of his previous accounts fell into difficulties. Perot, accusing him of believing his own press clips, rode him mercilessly until he got the problem fixed. Downtain's brief assignment in Washington was a costly one; EDS didn't pick up the moving expenses in either direction. Employees had other reminders that Perot played hardball as a businessman. He sued insurance software specialist Potter after he left EDS and tried to sell the 62-CFO package himself—the same software that IBM handed over without a struggle. Perot won a three-year injunction against Potter.

For their part, EDS engineers had trouble right from the start remembering that the customer is always right. Ross Perot, the part-time data processing manager of Texas Blue Cross, discovered this himself. EDS employee Charles Folsom commanded a team there in 1965 developing a Medicare processing system. One day Customer Perot asked Folsom to make his engineers start work at 8 A.M. when the Blues computer staff arrived. Perot said it didn't look right to have them straggling in at 10 or 11. Folsom planted his feet, "Some of these people work all night. I'm not going to tell them. . . . You want them to come in at 8, you tell them."[13]

Folsom won the confrontation. He had to be forgiven because he produced. Time after time, EDS would rest its defense on the argument, "The job's done isn't it?" There's a certain amount of irony in the fact that Perot would bridle at an elitist strain in EDS, but there it was.

And despite Perot's gestures, families bore the brunt of EDS zeal. The company was something of a family-life neutron bomb. Most of the marriages and homes were standing afterward—EDS didn't hire men with faint-hearted wives—but Dad was nowhere to be found. Perot's own family turned out well despite his brutal hours. His family had first claim on the rest of his time. Perot had the right attitude. He startled the counselors at his daughter's summer camp several years ago when he stuck out his hand and announced, Hi, I'm Nancy Perot's father.

He often lost track of what he was asking his employees to do. Gunn was living in New York in the late 1960s. He picked up a new assignment in Chicago and shuttled back and forth between there and Dallas. Finally, a colleague prodded

Perot, You know Gunn hasn't been home to New York for three months.

Folsom saw his failings one evening during a rare dinner at home with his family. His youngest son had been born after Folsom joined EDS and he barely knew his father. During dinner, the youngster asked his mother to ask "him" to pass something. Folsom was stricken. "I decided right there I brought those kids into the world. Whether I was good father or not, I had to start making the effort to be one."[14]

Perot tried to oblige. He offered to reassign Folsom to a job that would keep him in the EDS computer center. Folsom wasn't interested. Folsom recalls, "He says to me, 'well, here you are leaving and the goose is about to lay the golden egg.'"

Folsom was not to leave with any golden eggs. For the stock Folsom purchased, Perot reimbursed his money plus six percent annual interest. But Perot valued the stock he had given to Folsom as worth $0. Folsom laughs about it today, "I don't know how you take a gift back."[15]

EDS stock awards, golden handcuffs in effect, were designed to buy Perot time to deliver on his experiment. It was an experiment; EDS was built on sand like every other high-technology company. It drew its worth initially from the exorbitant price of computers. Using the second and third shifts of other companies' computers was beneficial to everyone except IBM. Even when EDS bought its own computers to keep up with demand, it installed them in huge, cost-effective information factories that wrung out their last useful seconds. Even back in 1962, however, Perot knew that ever cheaper and more powerful computers were depreciating EDS. He also knew that his customers eventually would become proficient and no longer would need EDS.

The evidence of his fallibility mocked Perot daily. Commercial customers were willing to pay EDS handsome profits to develop new computer systems. Once EDS had the systems installed and shaken out, however, the customers began dropping subtle hints like, "Gee, how come you charge so much when you make it look so easy?" When the contracts came up for renegotiation, the customers' own data processing managers became unofficial competitors of EDS. They usually won if the task had been reduced to turning on the lights in the morning and cranking out the work. The in-house bidders didn't have to mark up their costs to yield a 40 percent gross profit. In the late 1960s, EDS lost the business of Frito-Lay, PepsiCo, Continental Emsco, Keebler, and others. Unless it solved its retention problem, EDS would be stuck on a treadmill.

It must be said that Perot was not thrilled at his first glimpse of EDS's future in 1967. A Dallas insurance conglomerate called Diversa Inc. wanted Perot take on not only its life insurance processing, but the operation of its computer center as well. There was a catch; EDS had to offer jobs to Diversa's 30 computer-room employees. This was an unpopular notion inside EDS where employees saw themselves as the Few, the Proud. Perot compromised. EDS would employ Diversa employees for a 90-day trial. He would offer jobs to some or all of them. As it turned out, Diversa employees weren't thrilled either. "Half of them ran out to the bar," says Jerry Dugger, one of the two Diversa workers who cast his fate with EDS and the only one who survived.[16]

As unpleasant as the experience was for both sides, it generated two pluses for EDS. EDS had invented the brand-new business of facilities management. The facilities management contractor steps in at a foundering computer center, takes responsibility for the existing staff and equipment, and endeavors to make it work. The concept was not a functional evolution. EDS still was selling results by a different means. But it represented a major leap in tactics. EDS was inside the tent in a facilities management deal. Controlling the staff and the facilities, the company was in a much better position to pick up additional development assignments. Best of all, a facilities management contract left no one inside to oppose EDS when the contract came up for renewal.

A desperate customer was a given in facilities management. The beleaguered insurance industry remained the best target of opportunity. In the late 1960s, EDS divided itself into two divisions, one to pursue health insurance business and the second, life insurance customers.

Southwestern Life, Perot's long-time ally, dashed the hopes of the latter division in the early 1970s. Perot had convinced Southwestern to help him create a data processing standard for the life insurance industry. President William H. Seay declined to renew the contract, however. "I felt that to leave that data processing function [outside the company] was almost transferring destiny of company to someone else," Seay explains. "Ross must have called on me five times. He hated to lose that facilities management contract."[17]

The health insurance group's successes made the loss of Southwestern more tolerable. When the government began Medicare in 1965, it badly underestimated the health care demands of Social Security pensioners. The private health insurance companies hired to process Medicare claims were staggering under the flood of those claims. It was also clear that doctors and hospitals were looking upon Medicare as a 365-day-a-year version of Christmas. The Social Security Administration was being stoned for both sins. Half of Congress was up in arms because their elderly constituents were being hounded by bill collectors for claims Medicare had yet to pay. The other half was outraged about the cost of Medicare and the mounting evidence of fraud.

There was one success story in the Medicare debacle. The government's contractor in Texas, Blue Cross and Blue Shield of Texas, Inc., was churning out checks on time, thanks to the programming talents of one Chuck Folsom. The controls that Folsom built into the EDS Medicare processing system also looked promising. His system initially rejected so many claims for unwarranted or uncovered procedures or inflated prices that Texas Blue Cross had to relax standards temporarily to get the claims paid.

Here was a mess that would last for years—EDS could march across the country from one state's Blue Cross plan to the next. Perot had found himself in the right place at the right time. But readers know it wasn't mere luck. Perot had built a seaworthy corporate vessel and assembled a talented, determined crew. Then he had staked out a promising stretch of the ocean of commerce and waited for the wave that would carry him to glory. And this was it.

There were parts of this future, however, that Perot still found distasteful. The Social Security Administration would fight to control Perot's profits. Perot would resist the meddling bureaucrats so vigorously that Congress and the press would question his integrity. He finally had the raw material for sustained growth, but he was smiling through clenched teeth.

CHAPTER FOUR

BLACK AND WHITE, BLACK AND BLUE

Perot's four-year fight with the Social Security Administration shows him in all his infuriating, paradoxical glory. One minute, he is a reasonable, conservative businessman. The next minute, he is a holy warrior willing to risk everything rather than compromise his sense of right and wrong.

The government wanted to audit EDS's books. Perot refused on principle. EDS was giving the government a fair price and doing an honest job. It wasn't entitled to more, Perot insisted. Social Security managers finally began vetoing new contracts between EDS and state Medicare contractors. Medicare account manager Mort Meyerson, then 30 years old, found a solution that kept both EDS and Perot's ironclad principles intact. Meyerson would be called upon repeatedly over the next 15 years to perform this miracle. He was one of a small handful of people who could step in to save Perot from himself.

EDS employees learned to appreciate the ornery streak in their boss. Yes, he was unconventional and uncompromising, but he was right more often than not. Even when he led them through nine yards of hell, the trips ended uncannily well, as if Perot were somehow charmed. Consider, for example, EDS's first major contract in Iran, in 1975. The deal with the Iranian Navy introduced the Texans to the quaint Middle Eastern practice of baksheesh, or bribery. His salesmen were in favor of paying it, but they could not convince Perot to go along. "He would get right up to saying yes," says Gunn. "Finally Ross said, 'I don't think it is right and I just won't do it.' "[1] Just months later, the U.S. Justice Department began indicting American companies for bribery in Iran.

Perot's constancy is no small part of his magic as a leader. EDS trusted him to do the right thing, and his example inspired them. International business executive Malcolm Gudis led a Spanish cabinet minister into Perot's office in 1986 with considerable trepidation. On a normal day, Perot would be charming, gracious, and devastatingly effective. But the United States had launched an air strike against Libyan strongman, Moammar Khaddafi, the day before, and the Spanish government had refused permission to fly over Spain. Gudis checked Perot's ears for the telltale red. He heaved a mental sigh of relief when the visit started off warmly. Then Perot excused himself to take a phone call. Recalls Gudis, "Ross was doing something for the wives of the downed pilots. I don't know what it was. [When Perot came back] he tore that guy up one side and down the other."[2] Gudis made the sale anyway.

Perot's example, inspires us also. We don't have to trade our ethics for success. Perot makes that point in his speeches to college audiences. "Don't compromise," he counsels. "You can live with yourself that way. You say, 'Gee Perot, I want to make some money.' You can still make more than you can spend. You can make more than the cute guy. Do the right thing. Stand on principle. Take the licking that goes with it."[3]

Perot risked financial and legal ruin to rescue EDS executives Paul Chiapparone and Bill Gaylord from prison in Iran. The Shah's government had jailed the men in late 1978 to force EDS to return to work on an Iranian Social Security computer system. When EDS declined, Iran set bail for the men at $12.75 million, the exact sum of its payments to EDS. Iran wanted its money back. The government fell before EDS could post the bail. So Perot sent a rescue team to Iran to spirit the men out of the country, turning Perot into a genuine folk hero.

Perot would be the first to say that his transformation to hero is a trick of luck and timing. When Perot defied Ho Chi Minh and the U.S. government in 1970, we saw him as an extremist. In 1980 we saw Perot as a purposeful, effective leader—even though his defiance of Iran and the U.S. government was equally extreme. His rescue team had dozens of opportunities to be captured or shot while fleeing Tehran by truck to Turkey. He exposed himself to damage claims, prison, or both. As he accepted an award from the Texas Broadcasters' Association in 1980, Perot admonished his admirers, "If the rescue hadn't worked, I would have been portrayed as an idiot for having tried it, irresponsible for having gotten some of our people killed and you sure as hell wouldn't be giving me an award for it."[4]

Perot had no inkling, when he took his family skiing in Vail over Christmas, of the danger confronting Chiapparone and Gaylord. Most of his 150 employees had left Iran in early December, partly because the Iranians hadn't paid EDS for months, and partly because of the escalating revolution. EDS knew that the Iranians were looking for the two top EDS executives, but the company thought the U.S. State Department would help. Chiapparone and Gaylord turned over their passports to the U.S. embassy and left for an appointment at the Iranian Justice Ministry on December 28, 1978. They didn't return. To the Iranians, the jailing was a business decision. Even after the rescue, the Iranians told EDS it could return them with no questions asked—intimating that EDS also could go back to work on the computer system. Chiapparone and Gaylord were, in effect, human performance bonds.

Learning of the situation the next day, Perot returned immediately to Dallas to take charge. Within days, he had a three-pronged plan of attack. Keane Taylor, a banking project manager in Iran, would press the Iranians to release the two men. Perot would tap his connections in Washington, including Henry Kissinger, to apply political pressure to the Iranians.

Finally, Perot asked Col. Arthur "Bull" Simons to train a team of EDS executives as a rescue team. The latter effort was dubbed Project HOTFOOT, or Help Our Two Friends Out Of Tehran. The eight executive/commandos were called the "Sunshine Boys."

Of course, Taylor told the Iranians that EDS would not go back to work on the contract. The company could not put 150 people at risk to win the release of two. Eventually the Iranians asked Taylor and Dallas attorney John Howell to post the $12.75 million. The partially installed computer system was worthless without the Americans. EDS could have the two men; Iran would recover its investment.

Officially, Chief Prosecutor Dadgar was looking for corruption. "No charges were ever brought," Taylor says. "[The Iranians] were looking for middleman payments they thought must be some there somewhere. . . . We gave them every file we had. . . . They must have had hundreds of people looking through those files. . . . They never were able to prove anything. . . . They lost interest in that after awhile."[5] The Iranians had picked the wrong company to investigate for baksheesh. Much to Perot's disgust, the U.S. State Department did not accept EDS's innocence and stayed on the sidelines. Nor was Kissinger successful. It was up to Perot to buy them out or break them out. Simons was already training the eight executives-turned-commandos in suburban Dallas.

Perot adored the hulking, lantern-jawed Simons, who began his Army career in World War II as a member of the elite Army Rangers. Perot met him in the early 1970s after he led a raid on the Son Tay prison camp on the outskirts of Hanoi. Simons was a natural leader; EDS executives describe an almost palpable aura of authority around him. Perot was captivated and awed. He brought Simons to Dallas in the early 1970s to give seminars at EDS on the art of leadership. When Simons died of a heart attack shortly after the Iran rescue, Perot drove his aides crazy providing Simons with a funeral of clipboard-and-stopwatch precision.

The Sunshine Boys regrouped in Tehran 12 days after Simons took command. The team learned that its intelligence was wrong; Simons had drilled them to storm a minimum-security prison. They found much tougher defenses. Then Chiapparone and Gaylord were moved to a maximum-security prison with thick stone walls and machine gun towers. A commando attack was impossible.

Taylor and Howell also were frustrated in their attempts to pay the $12.75 million. Bankers and bureaucrats were afraid to make decisions with the Ayatollah Khoumeini in the wings. Howell and Taylor finally arranged a money transfer that satisfied nervous officers of the Bank of Omron. "We went to the final meeting where the bank officials were going to accept the letter of credit," Taylor says. "People came in and said 'There's a curfew. It starts immediately.' Five minutes later, John and I were sitting there staring at each other. Everybody else was gone."[6]

Simons formulated a new plan. The mobs in the streets were blowing up government buildings by then. Simons would go out every day to walk among them and to study them. He instructed three Iranian nationals, EDS employees, to agitate the crowds for an attack on the prison. Perot himself traveled to Tehran to prepare Chiapparone and Gaylord for the ordeal. He entered the country on a private jet ferrying videotapes for the National Broadcasting Company. He simply strolled into the airport with tapes under his arm, dropped them off, and disappeared into the city. Signing his own name at the prison some days later, Perot told the two men that it was up to them to make their way to the Hyatt Crown Regency Hotel. Simons' instincts were right; the prison was stormed.

The press wrote skeptically of Perot's subsequent claim, that Simons engineered "the largest jailbreak in history." Perot admitted that the plan barely qualified as one because of its uncertainties, but he wasn't questioning Simons. As he explained in a 1981 speech, improvising dialog to make his point:

> Imagine trying to sell this one in the war room of the Pentagon.
> "[We'll] go to a morning meeting of the revolutionaries and urge the folks to storm Gasr Prison."
> "Wait a minute. Can you trust the Iranians?"
> "Well, I dunno."
> "Are you sure there will be a morning meeting?"

"Probably."

"Well, when they have these morning meetings, do they do what they decide to do?"

"Rarely."

It was a very iffy deal. How did [Simons] know it would work? He was inside the mobs on the ground. He had the skin feel of being there.[7]

The news that the prison had been stormed came in a phone call to the EDS command post in the Hyatt. One of the company's Iranian employees reported that Chiapparone and Gaylord were free, but alone somewhere on the streets. The Iranian, called "Rashid" in Follett's book to protect his identity, raced to the hotel.

Taylor met him at the elevator. "He had ammo clips hanging out of his pockets. He just reeked of smoke from the fires. I shouted, 'Where's the gun? Where's the gun?' " The hotel staff wouldn't let him enter with it so he handed it to a man going out the door, keeping the ammunition. "You could tell his mental state," Taylor says.[8]

EDS kept an open line between Dallas and the Tehran Hyatt rather than risk placing emergency calls. That morning, Senior Vice President William K. Gayden was talking to Senior Vice President Thomas Walter in Dallas. An EDS tape recorder caught this exchange:

GAYDEN:

We got the guys! We got the guys!

WALTER:

How about that.

GAYDEN:

Fantastic.

WALTER:

They are there? Bill? Hey, come back on.

GAYDEN:

We got the guys; they just walked in the door.

WALTER:

Hey Bill? Hey Bill?
You there? How 'bout that. Bill? Bill? The guys are physically in the room?

CHIAPPARONE:

How are you?

WALTER:

How are you, buddy?

CHIAPPARONE:

I'm all right. What's going on?

WALTER:

We were wondering where you guys were.

CHIAPPARONE:

So was I for the last three hours.

WALTER:

How did you get to the hotel, Paul?

CHIAPPARONE:

Fortunately Keane left me a lot of money one day. I walked for about 2 ½ hours dodging bullets. Got a couple rides.

Simons took over for the last leg of the escape, the trickiest part. The U.S. embassy refused to return the two men's passports without notifying the Iranian government. Perot grew even more bitter after the state department in Washington leaked the news of the rescue while the escapees were still in Iran traveling overland to Turkey. Since the revolution began in Tehran and moved out in concentric waves, they were traveling into the fighting. The EDS team was stopped and repeatedly interrogated by village militias. A pass forged by Rashid and "validated" by an Iranian library stamp saved the team at one inquisition. Taylor's EDS identification card saved them at another. Another team was waiting in Turkey with a helicopter and a light plane on standby. The team made its way by bus and plane to Istanbul, where it met Perot in triumph.

Safely home, Perot sued Iran from Dallas to collect back payments on the Social Security contract. Says Perot, laughing, "Dadgar came into this country while we were in district court and pled the case for the Iranians. . . . I have to admit a number of us thought of some practical jokes we wanted to play on Dadgar because he was so jumpy."[9] EDS won a $16 million judgment.

Perot's victory was doubly sweet. He had his men back and his money, too. When President Jimmy Carter released Iran from American claims in late 1980 in exchange for the release of the embassy hostages, the EDS judgment stood because the executive branch could not reverse the judiciary. EDS alone left Iran unscathed. Perot's triumph over American and Iranian bureaucrats was complete.

Perot cast the rescue as a contrast between plucky individuals and callous bureaucrats. His POW adventures had soured him on the state department a decade earlier. This time he practically spat out: "Nobody gave a damn. These were two Americans hung out to dry, and nobody cared." In contrast, Perot says, "Col. Simons was in complete charge. There was no committee thinking on this mission. That's why it succeeded."[10]

By 1979, America was fed up with committee-think and impressed by decisive individuals. A newspaper editor in Dallas, moonlighting as a country and western songwriter, captured Perot's appeal:

> Bull Simons lies a-sleepin'
> McArthur's dead and gone
> George Patton is fighting somewhere
> but it is in the great beyond
> Appeasement is an art form
> and Rembrandt's at the helm,
> There are no real life heroes
> throughout this wretched land
> Where are you now when we need you, Ross Perot?*

---

*Copyright © 1979 by Glad Music.

The government failed us in Vietnam, and again in the Watergate scandal. Business failed us in the marketplace against foreign competitors. Another holy warrior, Khoumeini, had humiliated President Jimmy Carter by holding 52 Americans hostage for 444 days. We were tired of compromises. We wanted action.

Perot was no different than he was 10 years earlier. The decade of the 1970s was the wrong one for him. The streets were full of kindred, antiestablishment souls at the time, but he had the wrong politics for them. Government and business, meanwhile, recognized that he was a dangerous man when he began poking around the status quo. They viewed him as an unpredictable extremist. Roger Smith could have saved himself a world of grief if he had passed up Follett's *On Wings of Eagles* and read transcripts from 1971 and 1972 of the House Committee on Government Operations—Perot's showdown with the Social Security Administration:

The dispute began in late 1967 when federal auditors recognized how well positioned Perot was to capitalize on the Medicare snafu. He was in *two* right places at the right time. Not only was Perot president of EDS, he was also half-time data processing manager at Blue Cross-Blue Shield of Texas, Inc., the Medicare contractor in Texas. The feds discovered this fact while reviewing the bills for Chuck Folsom's Medicare work at Blue Cross. Like good auditors everywhere, they were suspicious of Perot's presence on both sides of the negotiating table. Worse, the potential for conflict was escalating as EDS and Blue Cross forged more ties.

In late 1967, Perot and his part-time boss, Blue Cross President Tom Beauchamps, were getting ready to take over the Texas Medicaid health insurance program. This time, Beauchamps would hire EDS for the processing work as well as the development of the system. Beauchamps says there was nothing sinister about it. "We needed help in a big way," he says. "[Hiring EDS] was the only way out that we found that was practical."[11]

Social Security stepped in to straighten out Beauchamps. The auditors told Beauchamps in November that they wanted

competitive bidding for the data processing contract. Beauchamps protested. How could anyone bid against EDS without
first developing software? Oh no, the auditors replied. EDS
developed its software using federal funds, and therefore the
government owned it. EDS was to make it available to any
bidder. The auditors weren't sure they had convinced Beauchamps. "While it appears that Mr. Beauchamps agrees completely with us," one auditor's memo concluded, "I am somewhat
reluctant to believe the problem will be resolved without further discussions."[12]

To make sure that Beauchamps complied, Medicare director Thomas Tierney wrote a letter to him November 22
setting out the government's requirements for competitive bids.
The letter dropped this subtle threat: "We further pro-
pose . . . that we negotiate . . . for the amount which Social Security will pay you for the services performed under the
arrangement with EDS . . . through December 31, 1967."[13]
Translation: Blue Cross would have to plead for reimbursement of the fees it had already paid to EDS, and the Texans
could expect more of the same unless they knuckled under.

Unknown to Tierney, the new EDS contract was already
a done deal. EDS had a team hard at work on a Medicaid
processing system under the direction of Meyerson. His troops,
decked out in bright red jumpsuits, worked to the point of
exhaustion every day before slumping onto their cots in a
nearby dayroom. This continued for six weeks, including
Thanksgiving Day. Perot resigned his position at Blue Cross
on December 1, 1967, and executed a facilities management
contract on EDS's behalf on January 5, 1968.

Social Security administrators were furious when they
learned of the contract. A House subcommittee on government
operations found no evidence of wrongdoing after it examined
EDS's relationship with Texas Blue Cross in hearings in late
1971 and mid-1972. But Congressmen didn't approve of Perot's
or Beauchamps's conduct. Yes, Perot resigned before the deal
was executed, an SSA official testified. "How close is close?"
he groused.[14]

Beauchamps was within his rights to enter the contract.
He didn't need the federal government's blessing for subcon-

tracts that cover primarily nongovernment work. When Beauchamps notified the SSA in February that he had signed a
contract with EDS anyway, 53 percent of it covered Blue Cross
work rather than government work. That was a thin defense.
By the time SSA auditors got their first look at the EDS contract in June, Beauchamps admitted that EDS's workload had
already swung to a majority of Medicare business. An SSA
official complained to the House subcommittee, "We were disappointed that a contractor would commit us to a $5 million
contract without at least consulting us, regardless of what the
percentages were."[15] The contract was highly unusual besides.
EDS was being paid not on the basis of its costs, the standard
government practice, but rather by a flat rate of $1.06 per
claim processed.

Explaining why Perot thumbed his nose at the government is a complex task. The press and Congress found it easier
to seize on his obvious financial interests. He had a sizable
lead over his competition in Medicare processing. The last
thing in world he wanted was to hand his software to the
government. Nor did he want the government to base his pay
on his costs. EDS typically offered to take over the customer's
computer operation at its current budget. EDS counted on its
efficiencies and economies of scale to drive down its costs substantially—and push up its profit margin. A year after its
Medicare work began, EDS had heady pretax margins of 40
percent.

The government asked to see EDS books. Perot declined
on principle. In his opinion, EDS was offering the government
an attractive price. How much of it he kept for himself was
not the government's business. IBM had 70 percent gross margins, he complained. Did the government ask to see IBM's
books? Where would America end up if the government punished creative people by confiscating their work and rewarded
efficient people by cutting their prices?

Perot was suspicious of the bureaucrats. Of all the Medicare contractors, Texas Blue Cross was coping best, thanks
to EDS. He thought the Social Security Administration wanted
to shut him out of the market so that the state contractors
would fail. Then the government could step in and take over.

Each of these motives was as real to him as the dollars and cents argument. Says EDS general counsel Richard Shlakman: "Ross does things for multiple reasons, each one of which is critical to his decision. . . . He is equal parts, not any one thing."[16]

Beauchamps was the man on the spot. The government followed through on its implied threat to cut off reimbursement. The administration eventually relented and paid Beauchamps 55 cents per claim, or roughly half of what Beauchamps was paying Perot for the work. The government made him sweat for almost two years before making Blue Cross whole.

Perot didn't make Beauchamps's life any easier, either. Perot danced right up the edge of agreeing to show the government his books and then changed his mind. Two disappointed auditors turned up at EDS one day thinking that Perot had finally relented. "Practically what we did the entire day was listen to sales pitches by Ross and his staff as to what a wonderful job he could do if he could take over the entire Medicare computer program," one auditor wrote in a memo.[17]

Brief flirtations with compromise are another pattern in Perot's behavior. He tries a tentative step or two toward a shortcut, but he cannot bring himself to ignore his internal moral compass. EDS was going public when he was trying to sell facilities management to Southwestern Life. Southwestern President, Dawson Sterling, asked Perot for 2,500 shares at the opening price of $16.50. Perot arranged for him to buy 1,000 shares. Sterling then asked Perot to sell him 1,500 shares of unissued EDS stock. Perot agreed, provided Sterling had the blessing of his board of directors. He found out that Sterling didn't, after the Southwestern president left the company abruptly. Bill Seay replaced him and completed the EDS contract. Sterling sued Perot for breach of contract. Perot could have settled and avoided the embarrassment of a trial. Instead, he told his side to a jury in 1970 and prevailed.

Finally, the government delivered an ultimatum to Perot in a meeting in Baltimore. Administration would not approve another contract between EDS and Blue Cross contractors until Perot agreed to audits. EDS had been landing one Medicare contract after another. The ultimatum would stop EDS in its tracks.

Meyerson persuaded Perot to back down by reminding Perot of his suspicions that the government wanted to grab the business. If the bureaucrats want the business and ask for the books, Meyerson asked, what better way to frustrate them than to give them the books? Perot took a tiny step toward compliance. He gave the government the books of EDS Federal, the subsidiary handling Medicare work.

The Social Security managers celebrated their victory, but the party fizzled fast. EDS Federal had no profits! The subsidiary was paying the parent, EDS, more money for computer time and manpower than it was collecting from the government. EDS was a public company by then, and James Naughton, the House subcommittee's staff attorney, noted that EDS reported a 42.3 percent gross profit in 1968. "It occurred to me," says Naughton, "that if they were making that kind of money, quite possibly, the taxpayers were paying it and ought to get a better deal."[18] Not surprisingly, the Social Security Administration asked to see the books of the parent, EDS.

EDS's defense was the same chapter, new verse. Perot argued that EDS was getting the Medicare job done while charging the government less than competitors. How was it the federal government's business to know what profits EDS made? In this case, the customer had a powerful argument. The customer was the federal government, the fiduciary of the American people.

Perot was not swayed, just as he was unimpressed with GM's arguments 15 years later that parent corporations should be able to see the books of their subsidiaries. Perot was free as an individual to resist the illegitimate demands of authority, even to respond in bad faith. Consider Perot's crafty evasion of the International Brotherhood of Teamsters in the late 1960s. The Teamsters had told EDS that the union moved everything at PepsiCo, even computers. Perot instructed Gunn to ask the union for a $1 million surety bond. While the Teamster business agents were off scratching their heads, Gunn rented a truck on a Saturday and presented the union with an accomplished fact. EDS could pull stunts like these because the company performed.

The Social Security Administration was coming around grudgingly by the time Naughton's subcommittee put EDS on the examining table in late 1971. By then, the administrators had watched eight "transitions," as EDS euphemistically described its takeovers under facilities management contracts. Medicare Director Tierney and his subordinates had realized that technology was only part of EDS's magic. EDS was turning around the Blue Cross shops by its tried-and-true formula of all-out attack, week after grueling week.

Tierney told Naughton's congressmen: "EDS has demonstrated that it can go into a place where there are difficulties and can quickly get the situation in hand. . . . They have a very substantial staff . . . they can throw at a problem."[19] Tierney also knew by then that EDS charges, while higher than the two or three competent, in-house shops, were cheaper than most hired contractors. As prickly as the Texans were, the Social Security Administration needed them.

The matter came to a head in late 1971. U.S. Representative Bill Alexander, a Democrat from Arkansas, had sat through several days of testimony about the high-handed, audit-shy crack troops of EDS when he learned that his own state's Blue Cross was about to sign on. He wrote to Eliot Richardson, then Secretary of Health, Education, and Welfare, asking him to hold up the award until EDS saw the light. Richardson wrote back that no award would be made unless the contract provided for "the examination of all pertinent records."

Richardson had no idea he was strolling into a minefield. Three weeks older and wiser, he wrote again to Alexander to tell him the Arkansas contract had been executed before he became involved. The contract included access to EDS financial information that "substantially differentiates the new contract," the Secretary wrote. (In fact, the contract still didn't allow the government to audit EDS books.) Richardson reminded Alexander of the crisis facing Arkansas Blue Cross and "over-age-65 people in Arkansas."[20] The war was over, even though the skirmishing would go on for years.

The suspicions about Perot would linger. The press pointedly connected his victories over the Social Security Administration and his support of the Nixon administration. The left-leaning *Ramparts* magazine in 1971 examined his old-boy ties in Dallas to explain why Blue Cross would stand by him so loyally. From its interviews of board members, Ramparts reported that a Blue Cross director, a leading Dallas banker, had forced the controversial pact on a reluctant Blue Cross board to position EDS for its upcoming public stock offering. Beauchamps snaps, "That is not correct at all."[21]

The California journalists and the Washington bureaucrats were operating in Texas without local guides. For starters, public health insurance was an alien concept in conservative Dallas. The business establishment drew some comfort from the fact that "gummint" at least was letting "bidness" do the work. Leave it to the feds, they observed, to screw up by trying to confiscate property and to limit a man's God-given profits. Blue Cross and the federal auditors never did speak the same language. Back when the topic was a relatively simple question of where Perot ought to sit at the table, the government auditors were astonished to hear a Blue Cross middle manager break into a lecture on their "evil and untrusting minds."[22]

History exonerates Beauchamps. There was no mutual back-scratching evident in 1974, when Blue Cross terminated its contract with EDS. Beauchamps recalls,"I told [Perot] I thought a function like data processing belonged in-house once we had the capability. It was too important not to be flexible. . . . Perot wouldn't take no for an answer."[23]

Perot continued to play hardball. EDS bid against Blue Cross for the Texas Medicaid contract and won. Beauchamps wasn't particularly surprised. He had watched EDS sell to other Blue Cross outfits. "They were competitive enough that they left a good impression or a bad impression wherever they went. It's in the nature of being that forceful."[24] Beauchamps rehired EDS after its new internal computer operation wobbled into disaster. EDS worked for Blue Cross for another decade until a final, acrimonious split.

The truth was out about Perot. It wasn't only the revisionist theories of his success floated by *Ramparts* and other critical publications. The nation saw his extraordinary zeal in his 10-day flight around the world in 1969 trying to deliver Christmas meals and medicine to prisoners of war in Vietnam. The business community was put off by his no-prisoners assault on Wall Street as the would-be rescuer of duPont Glore Forgan, his first ill-fated attempt to join the establishment.

The nation saw him for the zealot that he was and chose sides. Perot-haters had more fun. His boldness made him an easy target. Every story about Perot in those years had the word *controversial* in it. The only suspense was whether the writer would attach the label to his politics or to his business style. Zealots lead with their chins.

Of course, Perot scored some points himself once the Medicare row was finally out in the open. Government, he cracked, "defines a horse as an animal with four legs, a mane, and a tail, but it doesn't care if it is a race horse or a mule."[25] Congressional tormentors like Naughton, he told reporters, "are attacking men who are Rembrandts, and they can't even whitewash a fence."[26]

But while EDS completed its initial public offering in 1968, Perot was uncharacteristically silent. Medicare processing was the heart of Wall Street's EDS story. Then, as now, numbers mattered less than a snappy and enthusiastic sales pitch—a way to remind investors that the Xerox machine once seemed outlandishly expensive compared to carbon paper. It was less of a stretch to sell EDS as the capitalist ally of social programs, the government's cost-effective friend. Perot knew the truth of this uneasy alliance a year before the initial public offering. (Mind you, Perot was prevented by law from saying anything about EDS that went beyond the official descriptions in the offering prospectus. Nor was EDS obliged to disclose government displeasure short of official action; the ultimatum was not delivered until 1970.)

Perot had immersed himself in prospectuses and stock tables. He found a pattern in the initial public offerings of some 21 high-technology companies. The underwriters, who sell stock issues and promise to buy unwanted shares, carved out a healthy margin of error for themselves. New issues in this market often doubled in price in a matter of weeks. Perot entertained a steady procession of investment bankers. Finally, a huge, fast-talking Italian from the Bronx, Ken Langone, offered to bring out EDS shares at $16.50, or 118 times its earnings per share.

Perot was not impressed with Wall Street. He learned that valuing stock was guesswork. Not only that, the offering that spelled out the deal seemed to him to be calculated to dissuade buyers. Perot wrote his own stirring account of the EDS start-up. Langone's lawyers, shrugging off his efforts, explained that the offering prospectus emphasized the risk so that investors couldn't sue them later.

Perot called a company meeting to discuss the public offering. The employees' shares, to be split 10 for 1, finally had a value. The 100 shares of stock Perot had handed to Mrs. Gunn would be worth $16,500 to start. He asked employees to come to a microphone to speak their minds for or against. There wasn't any rush to find fault with it. Perot himself pointed out the pitfalls.

Langone's firm, R. W. Pressprich and Company, brought 650,000 EDS shares to the market on September 12, 1968. That number represented only six percent of the 11.5 million shares in EDS, and it was a calculated gamble. With so few shares outstanding, a sell-off of a relatively small number could drive down the price. Still in all, the stock market was in a perfect froth over high-technology stocks, so limiting the offering forced investors to bid against each other.

EDS shares rocketed on opening day to $38, and climbed in 1969 to an astronomical $160, or 500 times its earnings then. Perot and the EDS treasury each netted $5 million in cash on the first day of trading. None of the employees could sell—the seven-year clock was still running—but they held as a group $25 million in stock at the first trade and $57 million at the end of the day. Perot's holdings, 9.5 million shares, were worth $200 million at the opening bell and a phenomenal $1.5 billion at the stock's height. *Fortune* magazine sent writer Arthur Louis to Texas to write about "The Fastest Richest Texan Ever."

CHAPTER FIVE

THE CULT OF EDS

The Medicare crisis was just what the doctor ordered. Blue Cross shops from Boston to San Francisco desperately needed help, so EDS suddenly had motivated customers. Better still, the muddle in the computer rooms suited take-charge Perot to a tee. A store in trouble can lock the front door until it catches up on back orders. Insurance claims processors have no such luck. No matter how screwed up the claims department is, people go right on getting sick, mailing in claims, and blissfully expecting to be paid. They write huffy letters when no check is forthcoming. Since complaint letters are new claims until they are matched with the originals, backlogs feed on themselves.

Faster computers are the obvious answer. But computer changeovers are fraught with peril even in normal times. One computer guru likens the challenge to driving a speeding car with four flat tires while simultaneously trying to change the wheels. Planning didn't help much. Perot captured the essence of the EDS's Blue Cross campaign in exactly 11 words: We want a teaspoon of planning and an ocean of execution. (Translation: 80-hour weeks and six-month hotel stays.)

EDS had major problems to solve first. The company needed thousands of engineers and operators. In a good month, however, an EDS recruiter could deliver a handful of data processing veterans. To hire inexperienced workers, EDS needed to beef up Behne's systems engineer development (SED) program to handle hundreds of trainees at once. Behne did it so well that recruiters for rival computer services firms created a lucrative black market in his SED class rosters.

Recruiters still strained to find the numbers of inexperienced people that EDS needed. Where would its recruiters find thousands of candidates who could deliver Perot's "ocean of execution?" EDS threw bodies at a computer installation until the machine was up and running. Still more bodies stemmed the tide of incoming claims. Finally, EDS untangled the backlog the only way it could be done, one claim after the next. Who could endure this regimen?

Uncle Sam was the answer. Hundreds of officers mustered out of the armed services every month in places like Camp Pendleton, Fort Bragg, and Pensacola Naval Air Station. Perhaps a dozen of them would be hard chargers stifled too long by the service bureaucracy and eager to prove themselves. A smaller number would share Perot's middle-American values. No one was sadder than Ross Perot to see the compulsory draft end. In his company's first flush of growth, the armed services were his farm club.

Each wave of new recruits made EDS more insular. They were men in their late 20s who dressed and acted the same. These service veterans inspired the criticisms of EDS as a lock-step, militarist organization. That observation missed the point; most of the new recruits were just as unhappy with bureaucrats as Perot. At EDS, they were individualists in a cult of the can-do. Nothing was impossible for men who wouldn't quit.

They made EDS a great company, but they also contributed to its flaws. Their elitism rubbed nearly everyone the wrong way. And they were surprisingly naive about the world outside their own rarified organization. Nevertheless, they racked up victory after victory in the Blue Cross campaigns.

Senior Vice President Jeffrey M. Heller earned his stripes in Harrisburg, modifying EDS software to process Medicare claims in Pennsylvania. He traveled a 220-mile circuit to program on rented computers in Harrisburg, Allentown, and

Philadelphia. "Sometimes we would be in Allentown," Heller recalls, "and the program wouldn't work because the machine wasn't big enough. We'd get in the car and drive to Philadelphia [to use a bigger machine.] We'd solve that problem and go back to Allentown."[1] Heller and the EDS advance team typically spent every waking hour at the task for as long as six months at a time.

The team of young ex-Marines and Army men fell back on service folkways to help them survive. "People come out of boot camp thinking they have done something special," explains Heller, a Marine Corps fighter pilot. "A little society develops within the group. The esprit de corps is pretty catching."[2] Heller's software modification team began calling themselves the "Mod Squad" after a television police drama of that era. The history of EDS was written by groups of men calling themselves the "First Wave," the "Dirty Thirty," or the "Wild Bunch," and finding relief in foxhole camaraderie from impossible tasks. The inevitable side effect was a certain swagger.

Almost from the start, EDS was stamping out fires of its own making. When EDS showed up in 1969 to take over the computer operation of Blue Cross of San Juan (Puerto Rico), the agitated locals locked themselves in the computer room. They shot staples into circuit boards and poured sand into disk drives. Says Gunn, "I don't think IBM ever got that computer operational again."[3]

EDS learned from its mistakes. From that day forward, the company planned its "transitions" as military operations. The customers' managers called their employees into one room to brief them about the changes and turn them over to their new bosses. Meanwhile, other EDSers slipped into the computer room to secure critical equipment and files.

San Francisco was EDS's MBA course in computer room takeovers. California Physicians Service, the state Medicaid processing agent, had 650 employees in 1969. There were 630 people in all of EDS at that time. Computer industry pundits predicted a disaster in the making for cocky EDS.

Even Meyerson and his Medicare crew were startled by the mayhem in San Francisco. They discovered that claims literally were disappearing through the cracks. One day the elevator refused to open in the basement of the Blue Cross building. Repairmen found a pile of claims in the bottom of the shaft. EDS officials guessed that clerks took the difficult claims with them on break. When the elevator door opened, the clerks dropped them into oblivion through the crack between the car and floor.

Labor relations were just as nasty. The California Physicians employees worried first about their pay and benefits. EDS learned to carefully evaluate the differences in pay and benefits and to craft a plan that bridged the gap. The EDS approach to pensions took some explaining. The company relied on EDS stock to supplement a modest pension plan. The reluctant converts in San Francisco pointed out, correctly, that stock was only paper until it was sold.

The second reaction was more visceral. The EDSers, Vietnam veterans decked out in dark suits, white shirts, and narrow ties, had landed in one of the hippest cities in America. *San Francisco Chronicle* columnist Herb Caen made the EDS dress policy notorious. Scores of employees clipped his column, "Space Age Company Has Stone Age Dress Code," and mailed it anonymously to their new masters lest they miss the point.

EDS recruiters passed off the dress code as an anomaly, but it wasn't. EDS accurately reflected the conservative values of its founder. Perot's notions of employment rights differed from California state law. If EDS found a computer operator asleep on the job in Texas, he was fired on the spot. California law required EDS to have a clear policy forbidding naps. Had EDS warned the employee? The state would force EDS to reinstate the drowsy operator because EDS hadn't followed proper disciplinary procedures.

The National Labor Relations Act proved to be an even ruder awakening. Until California Physicians, EDS had no concentration of hourly workers. Perot didn't want any then either, but California Physicians insisted that EDS take over its data entry shops, where platoons of clerks read doctors' bills and keypunched the data onto cards. As employment procedures go, "Do what makes sense" translates poorly in the tedious world of data entry. The clerks weren't particularly interested in the new freedoms they had as employees, since they still couldn't look up from their keypunch machines. They wanted to know their rights: how many sick days? How many breaks?

The outcome was predictable. The Teamsters forced an organizing election in a Southern California keypunch shop. An office worker's union forced the same vote in an EDS shop in Concord, California, just outside Oakland. Ex-Marine Patrick F. McAleer was managing the Concord keypunch shop. "I threw the first union organizer out of my office," McAleer says, "This guy from the National Labor Relations Board came in flashing a badge saying he wanted to see my files. I threw him out too. Jim Meler had to come over and bail me out. They were going to throw me in jail. I didn't know anything. In typical Marine Corps fashion I didn't want to learn."[4]

EDS won a split decision. The Southern California keypunch operators turned down the Teamsters, while the Concord operators, wives of longshoremen and autoworkers, voted the union in. Perot transferred the work and closed the facility rather than tolerate a union beachhead in EDS. The company added another rule: Locate data entry shops in white-collar suburbs where wives were friendlier to management.

Even as the personnel problems continued, EDS rolled right along with its turnaround. The Mod Squad started in San Francisco in February, the day after it finished up in Harrisburg. Senior Vice President Gary Fernandes arrived at a company apartment on Jackson Street, drew a bed assignment and linen, and turned out for work at 8 A.M. the following day. Fernandes can't say which day he arrived. "Days didn't make a heck of lot of difference," he says. "Through the Fourth of July weekend, it was seven days a week, 14 hours a day. It was total commitment. My wife and infant daughter joined me shortly after that. We didn't have a car. . . . I think I had one day off in that period."[5] Installation complete, Fernandes flew to Des Moines to start over again.

The processing system started up on schedule the weekend of July 4. By the end of 1969, EDS had unraveled most of the snarl. A year later, the personnel problems were largely gone. Twenty years later, California Physicians remains an EDS customer. "It was a major victory," says Chairman Alberthal. "There were critics who said EDS finally bit off too much."[6] EDS handled it without a glitch. Since there were no larger public health plans, EDS had proved itself capable of taking over any plan in the country.

EDS came away smarter about employee psychology, unions, and labor law. Low-key, likable Meler became an employee ombudsman. It was his job to deal with union organizing petitions, unfair labor practice, and other incipient revolts. Meler kept his bags packed. He participated in 150 takeovers over the next 15 years. "My backhanded compliment was 'Gee, Meler, I hate to see you show up,' " Meler says. "That meant there were problems. They were also happy to see me."[7] Union petitions cropped up repeatedly in the industrial Midwest, but EDS never lost another election.

EDS did not change its style of all-out attack, however. The first order of business was gaining control of Medicare payments regardless of the toll on workers. The new wrinkle was that Meler and other mediators were standing by to deal with the casualties. It was simply the nature of the beast. EDS couldn't afford to let the backlog keep growing. "It wasn't by science or skill that we made it work," Fernandes says. "It was sheer force of will."[8]

The troops drew strength from Perot. "Ross's greatest strength and his greatest weakness is that he does not understand there are things that can't be done," Fernandes adds. "He conveyed that to you. You expected if you were smart enough and worked hard enough there was nothing you couldn't do."[9] The heroes of San Francisco went on to bigger assignments and spread the gospel. Alberthal wound up running the San Francisco account in 1970 at the age of 26. Fernandes was running the Iowa Blue Cross account by 1971 at age 27 with less than two years in the company. Behind them came wave after wave of new hires.

The recruiting effort was very aggressive. Back in 1968 when EDS consisted of 300 employees, 1 of every 10 was a recruiter. The recruiting department had a clerk who did nothing but book airline seats and hotel rooms and a secretary who sat all day compiling and typing recruiters' reports. The recruiters had their hands on the throttle at EDS. Perot never asked them for budgets, or issued orders except to bring in as many good people as they could find. "The pressure was put on people in sales to get out there and sell some business . . . so the new recruits will have something to do," says Gary Griggs, EDS's chief recruiter in 1970, now a consultant in Princeton, New Jersey.[10]

Fortunately for EDS's sales staff, finding EDS workers was harder than finding new accounts. Before Behne's training classes came up to speed, EDS had insisted that applicants have five years of experience and topnotch talents. Says McAleer, who began as a recruiter, "the recruiter who came back with four [hires] a month was walking on water." Only one of 70 interviewees survived the written tests, spouse interviews, team interviews, and final appraisals by an officer. The EDS recruiting staff worked it down eventually to one in 30.

The recruiters' schedule was brutal. They interviewed prospects in their hotels for 10 straight days from Monday of one week through Wednesday of the next. They flew back to Dallas to catch up on their paperwork on Thursday and Friday, took Saturday off, and flew out again Sunday night to begin the ordeal once more. The alternate weekends at home undermined more marriages than they shored up. The recruiters came home from 10 days of hotel meals and continuous meetings wanting a home-cooked meal and some solitude. Their wives wanted a night out and conversation.

Most EDS executives had difficulty reconciling Perot's ideals of a family-oriented company with the reality of long hours and longer absences. The recruiters couldn't even make a pretense that they enjoyed a normal family life. Hiring single men was one answer, but Perot approached this radical idea warily. Would they disrupt the office? Would they hang in for the long term? McAleer, the test single man, finally broke the bachelor barrier at EDS.

The recruiters stood out in other ways. They were younger on average. They were more often military veterans, ex-officers. They were well paid by EDS standards. In addition to their base salary of perhaps $500 per month, they earned bonuses of $150 to $300 for each new hire they brought in. (By contrast, Alberthal was hired as a systems engineer in 1968 at the princely sum of $700 per month. He was still earning less than $2,000 a month in 1974 when he was appointed a corporate officer.) The recruiters also affected an "anywhere, anytime" esprit. Perot gave them their name, the "Wild Bunch," after the movie, and they loved it. Scattered across the country today as executive recruiters, bank officers, and corporate managers, they still hold periodic reunions.

The California contract was a watershed for the recruiters as well. The short-handed EDS managers did their best to convince the local employees to stay with EDS, but they quit in droves anyway. The recruiters were hard pressed to replace even a third of them at the start. Griggs led a tactical squad to San Francisco to beat the bushes. Recruiter Raymond Garfield, now a real estate executive in San Francisco, can still picture a Bay area home visit. The recruit's wife sauntered into the room, slouched against the wall opposite him, and sank to the floor cross-legged. "So," she remarked. "You're the guy who's going to put my old man in a white shirt."[11] Why should clothes matter? Garfield shot back. The husband signed on.

The affinity was stronger in places like Camp LeJeune and Fort Hood. The Wild Bunch started with the officers at those bases who assisted civilian recruiters. They were still looking for men prepared to describe their finest hour. They added some tests specific to military service. They wanted officers who were fed up with the creaking chain of command. Combat experience was a plus. As Griggs explains, "You mature in a hurry and learn a lot about men when you are responsible for lives in combat."[12] Combat veterans also were better risk takers.

Perot drove everyone, including the Wild Bunch, to try harder until they began making mistakes. One young recruiter had compiled a spotless record at Camp LeJeune. He culled candidates so carefully that almost every Marine he sent to Dallas was hired. His superior took him aside one day.

After a minute or two of praise, the manager remarked to him that he might be erring on the side of caution, eliminating candidates that the Dallas interview teams would have hired. McAleer observes, "Most of us coming back from Vietnam didn't have any trouble with that [failing]. If we screwed up, would anyone shoot us? I doubt it."[13]

Perot was a master at getting his recruiters to reach for the brass ring. Griggs was recruiting at Camp Pendleton and the other bases around San Diego. He was successful, but he was missing good candidates simply because he couldn't get around fast enough. He walked into Perot's office one day with a proposal. What if EDS advertised in base newspapers and service publications? Wouldn't fast-track officers flock to a seminar featuring the fastest, richest Texan yet? Perot tested Griggs's idea for hours and finally gave him a go-ahead. How will you begin? Perot asked. Griggs gave the wrong answer:

> "I said I've got to go find someone to write ads and work television for me." He said, "No, no. If you're not going to do this yourself, then we're not going to do it." I said, "Perot you're out of your mind. I don't know how to write ads." He said, "Well, you better figure it out." I did. I went to a printer who had done some work for us. I bought radio time. I went around with the *Fortune* magazine article in my hand to the financial editors of the newspapers and asked them if they would like a personal interview with Ross Perot. That's the quality he has. He wasn't going to let you come up with something and then pawn it off on someone else to do.[14]

Hundreds turned out for the seminars. Griggs and the other recruiters warmed up their audiences with tales of EDS and Perot. Then Perot took the floor, sometimes for hours. Perot can deliver a knockout speech to any group. In a sympathetic room, like the assembled Marine officers at Pendleton, Perot is awesome. He knew the last dark thoughts of these men in the evening and their first glum reverie in the morning. He was frustrated himself by a hidebound navy 15 years earlier. Perot held out to them a company with no seniority or politics, one that rewarded individual initiative and achievement, and stood for traditional values. The unspoken promise was standing before the assembled officers—the fastest, richest Texan himself. Almost everyone at the seminars crowded around the registry tables afterward. EDS still turned down most of them, but at last the company was bringing in recruits by the busload.

The Wild Bunch found itself in a tight, exhausting orbit with Perot. "He requires your full attention," says Rob Brooks, now a Dallas executive recruiter. "He keeps your adrenalin flowing because of his intensity." Once, when Perot expressed a craving for a chocolate malt, Brooks volunteered even though there was nothing open at 3 A.M. Brooks talked the hotel's night manager into opening up the kitchen so that he could mix the malt himself. "The word *impossibility* was not in his vocabulary," he explains.[15] Brooks excised the word from his as well.

Perot had an inexhaustible supply of challenges. Garfield learned how to produce recruiting videotapes. Then he put together a college recruitment program. When Perot turned to philanthropy in late 1969, the Wild Bunch served as his posse. They were available while the systems engineers often were not. Griggs staggered away with one philanthropic assignment thinking " 'This guy is nuts.' But the next thing you know you're sitting in a hotel room figuring out how to do it. . . . What other business in America would you find something like this happening? The average age in the company at the time was 28 years old."[16]

The life was too intense for the Wild Bunch to last. The average tenure in the group was approximately two years. One by one, they flamed out and fell out of the formation. Griggs reached his breaking point when EDS asked him to move once too often. He had parachuted into New York after Perot bought the duPont Glore Forgan brokerage. The movers were coming to pack up his belongings in Dallas when he was reassigned from New York to Los Angeles. He telephoned his wife to relay new instructions to the moving company. He spent three months on the west coast, four months back in New York, and then returned to Dallas. "I got word they were going to ask me to move to Miami."[17] He resigned instead.

There were no soft landings for the Wild Bunch. Since their technical skills were middling or nonexistent, they weren't transferred to other parts of the company. Garfield asked President Hart and Vice President Marquez to reassign him to sales. When they refused, he quit. They spent the better part of a day trying to talk him out of it. "When they couldn't, it was like I had the plague," he says. "I really resented that."[18] EDS had acquired the IBM syndrome. No one walks away from the best company in the world unless there is something wrong with him.

Garfield saw it differently. "I hope even though no one smiled and shook hands with me and said 'Good bye and good luck' that they all had some respect for what I had accomplished and for the decision I was making,"[19] he says. Of the 30 recruiters who formed the Wild Bunch, only two remain at EDS; and one of those, McAleer, quit and returned.

They put their stamp on EDS nonetheless. EDS in 1968 was 300 older professionals operating in a collegial style. After the recruiters had done their work in 1972, EDS largely was 3,000 computing newcomers in their mid- to late 20s. The management character was different also. The old EDS was a confederation of entrepreneurs. The new EDS, while hardly a bureaucracy, had a specific chain of command and had institutional recruiting and training functions. Even at the project level, EDS now had management tiers and staff specialists. The Marine and navy alumni accepted authority without question and waited for their moment of glory.

The recruiters spread the mythology about Perot and EDS. They were the apostles of the horseback newsboy. The service officers who packed hotel ballrooms outside Camp LeJeune came half expecting Perot to walk on water. Of course, Perot was the master of symbols. Perot also gave the Wild Bunch its slogan: Eagles don't flock. You have to find them one at a time.

Perot has never ducked the fact that he owes his success to the indomitable, industrious EDS employees. He is fascinated by this group and its accomplishments. He described them in this speech delivered some years ago to the Grand Rapids, Michigan, Junior Chamber of Commerce:

There are no geniuses in this group. In terms of mental capacity they would probably be ranked slightly above average. One characteristic stands out: These people are honest. They do what they say they will do. This causes other people to trust them. This creates an opportunity for these people to lead. Never forget trust is fragile. It takes years to earn. It can be lost in an instant. It must be re-earned each time you have contact with another person.

Another characteristic of these successful people is that they have a great deal of self-discipline. They are able to stick to the task at hand. They realize that the more successful they become, the more unpleasant the tasks will be that they have to perform.

Toughness or resilience is probably the most dominant characteristic I have observed in this group. These are people who have the ability to lock onto a problem and pursue it through many disappointments and failures to a successful end. On occasion I have felt that the dominant characteristic of these people was simply that they couldn't recognize when they had failed, refused to quit, and went on to succeed.

Again and again, you will find their brilliant business careers built squarely on the rubble of their early failures. They turned their early failures into learning experiences. . . . As you watch them make decisions in machine-gun fashion, you would first conclude that they are making intuitive decisions rather than carefully thought-out logical ones. In fact, these people are bringing the sum of their total experience to bear. . . . Their early successes, failures and disappointments are all focused on the problem at hand. . . . As a group, these people are extremely competitive. They love to finish first in whatever they are doing.

If you learn to do something better than anyone else you will find that financial success comes as a byproduct. . . . Making money has never been one of my goals. . . . If we had set out to use EDS simply as a vehicle to make money, I don't think we would have been successful at all. Instead we set out to build a great company made up of great people. . . . Don't expect the financial rewards to come quickly or easily. You would probably consider me to be quite successful at an early age. It took me 15 years to build up to an income that exceeded our family's monthly needs.[20]

Perot's contribution? Love. "I hope it's apparent to you that the people in EDS have a very special place in my life. Next to the people in my family, they are the very best part of my life. I don't just like the people in EDS. I love [them]."[21]

Perot's protestations of love ring hollow today in light of his new company, Perot Systems, and his bitter struggle with these same employees. But leadership is ephemeral—immediate and visceral. He believed what he said that day. His employees believed him too.

CHAPTER SIX

WRITING THE BOOK ON LEADERSHIP

Disclaimers first: There are no foolproof checklists, no 10 steps to effective leadership. We can learn the tricks of the trade by studying Perot, but leadership is not a state of grace. It is a relationship built on trust, respect, and affection—hard to gain and easy to lose—as we have seen. Even Perot lugged his toolbox to work every day to patch and repair, strengthen and extend his hold over EDS.

There can be no more doubt that he is a master mechanic. He has molded two disparate groups into efficient business organizations. The first, a loose confederation of professionals, was a skeptical and independent crew. Yet we remember Anne Ellis shoving her briefcase under the gate at Great National in the middle of the night and scaling a 10-foot fence. The second group, the young Vietnam veterans, was more malleable and awestruck. But awe can't sustain followers living in hotels for months at a time and working 80-hour weeks for niggardly salaries.

Perot-style leadership is dangerous when the issues are complex. He worked his wonders by purging compromise from the heads of his followers. He gave them black-and-white choices. EDSers sometimes found themselves crossing the boundaries of fair play for the sake of the mission. And Perot's influence faded as EDS grew and developed its own identity as an organization. Nevertheless, thousands of fervent followers turned Perot's vision into the thriving enterprise that is EDS.

Perot began turning his recruits into followers during the laborious interviewing process. The long application forms, the home visits, and the team interviews seemed designed to discourage the candidate, but the ordeal had a hidden purpose. In the classic recruiting story, Jim Messerschmidt, the other Wild Bunch survivor, was squiring an applicant around the EDS computer room on Mockingbird Lane. Computer shops in the 1960s were usually Crisis Central, so the spotless, orderly EDS room ordinarily was impressive. Then Messerschmidt opened the door to an adjoining classroom and threw on the light switch. There was a programming team sprawled out on cots in the debris of fast-food dinners. According to the apocryphal version, the horrified applicant barely stayed long enough to collect his things.

Every EDS job applicant confronted the unspoken question: Am I prepared to make this kind of commitment? The candidate had subconsciously accepted the challenge before the offer came. The offer was presented as a badge of honor. "Once you got in you felt like you were a member of a very elite club," says recruiter Brooks.[1]

In a sense, Perot's Eagles were already members of an exclusive club when they turned out for recruiting seminars at Fort Dix. They had conservative values for the times, and modest backgrounds. The United States wasn't supposed to have social classes, but college men in the early days of the Vietnam War had a choice of whether they wanted to fight. Privileged young men sat out the war in National Guard companies or divinity schools. "Squares", as well as kids from the ghettos and farms, went to war.

From these prospects with traditional notions of duty and honor, the Wild Bunch sifted and winnowed further to arrive at a small group of believers, joiners, and doers. The job applicant who asked too many skeptical questions never heard from EDS again. The candidates who survived shared Perot's Norman Rockwell vision of America.

EDS applied a kind of reverse snobbery. Tiny St. Mary's College of the Plains in western Kansas was on the EDS recruiting circuit. The Harvard Business School was not. The rationale assumed that morals and the work ethic were more alive in Kansas than in Cambridge. It also assumed that men and women from modest circumstances had more to prove to themselves and to the world than Harvard MBAs. The Vietnam vets fit that mold. They found themselves well behind their contemporaries who had gone on to careers, sideburns, and paisley ties.

Charismatic groups, by definition, are set apart by their beliefs. In the theories of early 20th century German sociologist Max Weber, a charismatic leader draws his power from people who share his values and trust the leader to act on them. In contrast, bureaucrats draw their authority from a system of government. The two approaches are the opposite poles of power. Bureaucrats issue commands and maintain order. Outside the castle gates, charismatic leaders make appeals and accomplish change. Weber didn't win many converts to his scientific theory of *charisma,* and the word fell into common use to describe vaguely an extraordinary emotional appeal. Modern attempts to explain it still begin with the process of change, however. Charismatics have a mission.

Was EDS such a group? Of course. Every start-up is trying to carve an existence for itself out of the status quo. From the start, Perot used IBM to define EDS in opposition, just as he is using EDS today to define Perot Systems. Perot carries it a step further. EDS and Perot Systems were not only better mousetraps, in Perot's mind, they were models of how companies should deal with people.

> At EDS we are dedicated to dealing with each person as an individual. There is only one class of employees at EDS. We do not tolerate one person looking down on another. We strongly discourage an atmosphere where one person would look up to another as more important because we think that stifles free, open communication. Instead we try to maintain an environment where each person deals with each person in our business as a full partner. . . . We constantly work to prevent company politics at EDS. We want men and women who would not stoop to build their careers at the expense of others.[2]

Naturally EDS attracted some political animals anyway. It wasn't just prestige on the line. Perot periodically dangled plum assignments. Thousands of shares of incentive stock often rode on the selection of project leaders. Elbows and feet flew furiously at times. EDS's project orientation kept the competition from being destructive. The executive running the California Medicaid account seldom dealt with the man running the Army VIABLE computer system.

Perot kept infighting to a minimum. No one doubted his commitment to a politics-free EDS, so nothing happened until he turned his back. Since he could pop up anywhere in the company, talking to anyone from clerks to management peers, blatant manipulation by EDS managers was risky business. The managers who dealt with Perot and saw how effective his style was didn't need to be policed. Perot says, "If I trust and respect you, you're going to get a whole lot more out of me. How do you get that? You earn it. You can't write the official memo, 'From now on we're going to trust and respect each other.' What are you going to do the day after the memo? Hit him over the head with a hammer?"[3]

That isn't to say that Perot did not horsewhip EDS managers vigorously and often. When Perot breezed into a distant EDS facility, the outcome was predictable. He would lose his escort as he made his way through the building schmoozing with employees and checking doorsills for dust. "The day would be over, and you would get a flogging the likes of which you had never received in your life," says Richard Shlakman, EDS general counsel. "Then you'd get among your people and find they were the most pumped-up, energized folks you could find." [4]

Consider computer operator Lawrence Clifton's first encounter with him in the early 1970s. Perot bounded into the tape library in New York where Clifton toiled, stretched out his hand, and exclaimed, Hi, Larry, I'm Ross Perot. Clifton's jaw dropped lower when Perot congratulated him on his recent marriage and asked him if he had any furniture. Clifton answered that he had a bed and a dining room table. Perot instructed him to get with his account manager and work out a no-interest loan. Those few minutes remain a vivid memory for Clifton.

It's this aspect of leadership that trips up those who are looking for a formula. Humans at an early age learn to distinguish feigned concern from the genuine article. Lonely or not at the top, leaders are surprisingly successful in relationships. Warren Bennis cites a survey of corporate chiefs in his book, *Leaders,* in which "almost all were married to their first spouses. . . . They were also indefatigably enthusiastic about marriage as an institution." Taking questions at speeches, Perot quips that he has no answer for this one: Why in the world did Margot marry you? Similarly, Winston Churchill said of his wife Clementine, "For what could be more glorious than to be united with a being incapable of an ignoble thought?"[5]

EDS employees could not detect a difference between the Perot who held press conferences to announce multimillion-dollar gifts and the man they met in the office corridors. Perot has helped thousands of people inside and outside the company, and without public fanfare. He readily agreed to reassign Penny Pasquesi from Europe to Chicago so she could be with her dying aunt who raised her. After she arrived, he telephoned her and sent her notes and flowers.

The homecoming of Americans held hostage in Tehran illustrates his thoughtfulness and his savvy. Perot had buses standing by on the tarmac at Dallas–Fort Worth International Airport so that Chiapparone and Gaylord could reunite with their families privately. Then the group drove to an airport concourse where 2,000 fellow employees celebrated with the rescued and the rescuers under banners reading, "Welcome Home Paul and Bill."

Perot never passes up public opportunities to make heroes of his people. He often speaks of Meyerson's role in snatching away a $10 billion U.S. Army contract from IBM. "Our 15 guys were saying well, we probably can't win, but it will be a great experience. Now this is leadership, and this is what the future is all about. Mort walked to the front of the room, and he wrote down out of his head the seven criteria we would be judged on two years later.

"He didn't say, 'Hey you guys are a bunch of wimps. We've got to work on your manhood.'

"He wrote it down and he said, 'Look, there's only one issue to focus on. We're going to be judged on seven criteria. Two years from now when the dust clears, we're going to beat them . . . seven to zero. That's the day we won.'"[6]

The story, alas, is almost all myth. There were five evaluation criteria. The army didn't identify them until after the competition. EDS's bid was initiated in the ranks in Washington. Top management became enthusiastic some time after the fact.

Perot relates these stories as gospel. To illustrate the grit of the average EDS engineer, he tells of the trainee who saved the day in a crucial test of a computer system in Washington. The EDS team was scattered throughout the building and had difficulty communicating. The hero of the day ducked out to borrow walkie-talkies from a government agency. The rest of the story? The "trainee" was a retired military officer with 24-karat connections in Washington. Shlakman doubts that Perot remembers the caveats. "He gets to the point where he believes every word he says."[7]

The stories are only a piece of his communications genius. Consider the nicknames. The tag "Wild Bunch" began as sport between the hardworking recruiters and their joshing, admiring boss. But the pet names have a psychic kicker. The Mod Squad and the Sunshine Boys were, by virtue of their names, unique groups with uncommon qualities. Perot also equipped them with a full repertoire of aphorisms should they find themselves indecisive. (Of course, EDSers aren't indecisive. The first one who sees a snake kills it. And champion snake killers watch their step; they are never more at risk than at a moment of great fortune.)

Perot collects aphorisms and recycles them. Perot heard this one from a West Virginia construction worker and wrote it down on the back of an envelope: "There ain't many hunters left, but everyone wants the meat." Many of his best GM taunts were first uttered by his victims. Retired GM President F. James McDonald first observed that the United States won World War II faster than GM could put out a radical new small car.

Perot underscored the historic significance of EDS groups and their work. Meyerson's Medicare programmers wore red jumpsuits to signify the importance of their work to the company. The first EDS employees to arrive at GM—they were nicknamed "the First Wave"—were presented with crystal eagles bearing that legend and the significant date. One more EDS aphorism: We reward our people for their achievements while their brows are still wet from the effort.

Perot also led by example. No one at EDS doubted Perot's willingness to fight to win. They were quite prepared to do as he did. Even green recruits who had little contact with Perot watched men like Meyerson and Alberthal master seemingly impossible assignments. Persistence and valor are contagious. Barry Posner writes in his book, Leadership Challenge, "Answering the summons of adventure lifts our spirits. There is something about being invited to do better than we have ever done before that compels us to reach down deep inside and bring forth the warrior within."[8]

Perot has a more graphic explanation: "The world is full of morning glories that fold up at night. Don't be one. . . . Let's use boxing. You can lose the first 14 rounds but you deck your opponent in the 15th round you're champion of the world. . . . Maybe you can't outbox him, but maybe you're in better shape than he is. Sooner or later he won't show up. I've had that happen again and again and again in my business career."[9]

Perot honored the rules at EDS. "We never ask anyone to do what we haven't done before and wouldn't do again," he says. "That's a pretty fundamental rule in leadership. . . .

"It's very important when you bring young people in to give them a set of rules. . . . Most big organizations in our country don't have a company philosophy. They will tell you they do, and they'll pull something out they said in a speech. But does the average guy down on the floor know it? If he doesn't know it forget it. . . ."

"There are no penalties for honest mistakes. . . . Go for results and not procedures. . . . I'm an old guy, and that doesn't sound too good to me anymore. But it's what you did lately that counts in business, right? There's no reward for staying alive. . . . And don't ever ask your people to do something stupid. I have asked EDSers to do the impossible, and they have never let me down. . . . If you want the best from your people, give them an impossible challenge but not a stupid challenge. . . .[10]

"The best advice I can give you there is treat them like you treat yourself. Things you don't like, they don't like. You don't like to be jerked around; they don't [either.] You don't like to be talked down to [and] they don't [either]. You would rather work with somebody rather than for somebody. So would they. You hate people who come in and pound on your head after you gave everything you had and failed. . . . It's that simple."[11]

Last but not least, Perot lightened his troops' burden with humor. His own comedic accomplishments seldom rise above gentle teasing, but he loves jokes even when he is the butt of them. Perot had a habit of scolding recruiter Griggs for favoring the Marine Corps over the other service branches. Griggs plotted his revenge. He asked an acquaintance in the Marines to ship him several boxes of Marine Corps mementos. He recruited Perot's secretary to tip him when Perot left town on a trip. Griggs swept in, boxed up Perot's considerable collection of navy memorabilia, and replaced them with Marine Corps totems. Griggs's phone rang early on the morning Perot returned to the office: "Griggs, get up here!" he bellowed, laughing. Perot loved it.

Every year EDS employees plotted a stunt to pull on Perot during the joint celebration of EDS's anniversary and Perot's birthday. One year they dragged him into the parking lot to suit him up in armor and mount him on a white horse. Another year, they presented him with a truck-mounted portable toilet. It was a punchline to some inside joke that is either lost to history or unrepeatable. Finally the parties got out of hand, and Perot stopped them.

The pranks sound vaguely like navy hijinks. They did have a root in the sort of male bonding that happens in barracks. Keane Taylor was a favorite target of jokes because of his quick temper. Perot called Taylor in Europe one December with an urgent and mysterious request to return to the United

States. The Taylors were just heading out the door for a skiing holiday. "I think, great, I've got to go into the other room and tell my wife and kids to forget about me," he says. Perot lingers on the phone. "Then I'm thinking he knows I'm going skiing. He busts out laughing."[12]

Women were strangers in a strange land at EDS. Perot needed a gender translator during a particularly puckish moment in the mid-1970s. He had invited the professional women of EDS to a luncheon and placed a gaily wrapped present on each place. The women opened them to discover an odd contraption—a plastic ball with a clip attached. Perot pressed his guests to guess what the gift was. His guests were stumped. Finally one guessed correctly that it was a skinny-dipping clip, a float to hold the swimmer's suit after she had shed it in the water. Perot roared with laughter. His guests laughed politely.

The first time that Portia Isaacson applied for a job at EDS, this pioneer of personal-computer retailing was told the company didn't hire women in technical positions. Perot hired her some years later to help lead EDS into microcomputer markets. She hired a retired army colonel as her aide and sent him to EDS meetings. "I didn't fit in too well," she says.[13]

"Is it smarter to have me love my work or hate it?" Perot asks. "All over corporate America we have environments where people just hate to go to work. Work should be fun. It should be like sports all day everyday. You have a competitor out there, and everybody in the place ought to be aimed at beating him. Everybody ought to be dead aware of whether we are winning or losing, because then the competitive instincts of our people take over, and believe me they are very strong."[14]

That begs the $64,000 question. If working for Perot is like playing in the Super Bowl every day, why has no one lasted in the inner circle? Long-time aide Merv Stauffer shocked the company when he quit Perot in 1988 and returned to EDS. Intensity is the obvious answer. Few people have the constitution to play daily Super Bowls.

Intensity is not the only hardship in the Perot inner circle. Perot often does not listen. Once Perot distills the challenge to a pithy, eight-word catechism, he didn't want to hear nuances. He uses his debater's skills to present the question to his subordinates in stark black and white. He wants action, not argument. "It is not the critic who counts," he would quote Theodore Roosevelt. "The credit belongs to the man who is actually in the arena, whose face is marred by dust and sweat and blood; Who strives valiantly and comes up short again and again; Who . . . knows in the end the triumph of high achievement and who, at the worse, if he fails, at least fails while daring greatly."

Perot's code phrase for one of these impossible missions was the summation, "Doncha see?" Shlakman drew the task of winning landing rights from the Soviets for Ross Perot, Jr., during his helicopter flight around the world. Shlakman tried to point out that the Kurile Islands off Alaska housed sensitive Soviet military installations. Tell the Russians the flight is sporting event, Perot replied. The Russians love sports, doncha see? "Every time he asks you to do something that was rolling a large rock up a steep hill," says Shlakman, "you'd get that oversimplified approach and that sentence, 'Doncha see?' I learned to hate that phrase."[15]

More often than not at EDS, Perot's simplified view proved to be the right one. He had a legendary knack for finding the one salient question in a complex issue. His chagrined subordinates knew he could puncture their presentations at will. Says McAleer, "He is uncanny at that. I don't care how well you have prepared. That was the thing that drove us all nuts. You would think you had it all covered. First question, Bam."[16]

If EDS executives persisted in being wrongheaded, Perot used his rhetoric on them like a razor. Vice President James Buchanan on a number of occasions saw Perot's ears redden, a certain sign that Perot had exhausted his small store of tolerance. "It just made you determined never to get caught in that predicament again," Buchanan says. "You always knew he was right."[17]

In theory, EDSers had a standing invitation to puncture his ideas as well. In practice, there was no doubt about whose company it was. Recruiter McAleer protested when he was asked to stand watch in the computer rooms on nights and weekends. He didn't know anything about computers. Tell Perot it's a dumb idea, he said. Perot called him on the carpet. Only one person decided which ideas were dumb and which weren't. McAleer began standing watches. EDS executives learned to watch for the signs that further argument was pointless. Griggs disarmed Perot with a stock joke: "I suppose we're going to put it to a vote of the majority shareholder."[18] Naysayers waited a long time before Coach Perot called their numbers again.

The elite club at EDS kept Perot out of trouble. The vets overlooked his penchant for putting his values to work at EDS in ways that were extreme, if not illegal in many states. Infidelity was grounds for dismissal, for example. "His wife has a lifetime contract," Perot says. "If she can't trust him how can I?"[19] Sexual harassment was dealt with harshly in chivalrous EDS. "Two, three times a year I get a letter and we pounce right on it," Perot says. "It's handled by me personally. I've always said anyone messes with the women in this place, I'll kill them."[20]

One secretary lost her job at EDS because the FBI came to question her about a former boyfriend apparently under investigation for drug dealing. EDS used polygraph examinations to settle cases of alleged misconduct. If the evidence suggested guilt, but couldn't prove it, the suspect was fired for refusing to submit to a polygraph test. Employees who endured did so partly because they were like-minded and partly because Perot was Perot.

Much harder to take was Perot's tendency toward micromanagement. Within the boundaries of their assignments, the recruits were free to "do what makes sense" as long as they could defend their judgment. But Perot couldn't always keep his compulsive side in check. When he swung into action, the hapless manager could only step back and hope Perot wouldn't trample his pride too much. Perot once picked up the telephone himself to complain to the *Dallas Morning News* about burying EDS earnings in a table. The next day the chastened editors ran the earnings report as a story, and Perot fixed a look on his public relations man, Jerry Dalton, as if to say who needs you? Perot always had the edge. Some of us are billionaire folk-heroes, and some of us aren't.

EDS executives learned that some tasks, particularly those that presented a face of EDS to the public, were undertaken at their peril. Woe to the writer who offered to prepare a speech or ghostwrite a letter for Perot. Even landscaping was his province. The golf nuts at EDS were terrified back in 1974 when the company was building its new headquarters on Forest Lane in Dallas. The site was an 18-hole golf course, and the objective was to save as many of the greens as possible. Nine holes were gone and Perot was penciling another three into oblivion. Six holes worked fine if you played three rounds, he insisted. The traditionalists won the argument.

EDS's PR manager Wright makes the point more graphically. Leading a visitor to his window overlooking the green expanse of the Forest Lane campus, Wright pointed out a specific bush beside the drive. Perot had ordered its planting to cover up an electrical connection box. Perot found it difficult to delegate landscaping decisions. "Your leash was never very long, no matter what was said," says Wright.[21]

So what were the options of EDS managers whose lot it was, using Teddy Roosevelt's words, "to fail while daring greatly"? They could enlist Meyerson, William Gayden, or Tom Walter, three senior executives capable of dissuading Perot when the moon was right. Or they could plunge into the breach and hope for the best.

Perot twice set out on impossible missions, as we shall see. Both times Perot was implored to help save institutions. Wall Street needed his money to prop up the ailing duPont brokerage in 1971, and GM wanted somehow to capture EDS's will to win. Perot, seeing that the ossifying institutions needed more, proposed radical surgery. The institutions decided they didn't need Perot's help that badly. Absent a compelling crisis, as Weber observed 60 years ago, bureaucrats always win.

Weber argued that bureaucracies were the higher order and that charismatics would eventually fade from the landscape. The opposite happened. Churchill, Hitler, Gandhi, Khoumeini are but a few of the charismatic figures of the 20th century. Weber's critics also were nonplussed that Churchill and Hitler could be explained in the same terms. But there's nothing inherently good or evil about strong leadership, just as bureaucracies are not by definition moral or immoral. Opposite poles of the power continuum, leaders and bureaucrats seem to take turns as the transgressors of the hour.

In American big business, bureaucrats are ascendant. Harvard Professor of Management John Kotter writes that management is prone to inertia. Systems of checks and balances become means of avoiding decisions and ducking blame. Management's sampling techniques, "reality checks" in Kotter's words, fail too if they provide old answers to new questions. Leaders use their intuition to find sexy new answers. But leaders require everyone to accept it on faith that the question needs answering. Kotter writes, "Both management and leadership are probably always needed to some degree because either in isolation can become perverted."[22]

Weber's critics found a final flaw in his work. The social theorist assumed that charismatic groups were transitory by nature. If they grew and prospered, he reasoned, they would fashion their own bureaucracies to deal with the "routinization" of their mission. Regardless, he argued, they could not survive their leaders' departure. Obviously, EDS grew and prospered and kept its charismatic fervor. And it survives Perot, although GM was terrorstruck that it would not.

Perot and EDS staggered through much of the 1970s coming to grips with Perot's distaste for middle management. There are only two classes of people in Perot's black-and-white world, leaders and followers. He tolerated the managers who stood between him and his troops only if they were faithful surrogates. Middle managers who failed his exacting standards of leadership got the lash.

Worse, EDS middle managers who are not Eagle material often became turkeys. Even today, the company struggles to find ways to retain and motivate the average managers who turn on the lights and do the work. It's the Eagles at EDS who are showered with glory or stock awards.

The duPont Glore Forgan debacle began Perot's conversion. He was forced to delegate. "Everyone who has studied my business career has marveled at the fact that I surrounded myself with people who are more talented than I am," he boasts. "I remind them that when you're not that smart it's the most natural thing in the world. I knew I needed help. [Suppose] the boss is the smartest person in the world, and no one else can do the job as well as he could. It's very difficult to turn it over to other people, but you cannot multiply your effectiveness except through other people."[23]

Meyerson became Perot's balancing half. Shlakman was struck by the elegant division of labor between the two. EDS gathered its top 200 executives on a Saturday after the GM deal was announced. These were nervous people. They looked to Perot and Meyerson for reassurance. "It was absolutely a fascinating study in the character of the two men," the attorney says. "Every single question that concerned the common EDS employee, Ross became passionately interested in. . . . Every question that dealt with the executives, the men in that room, Mort immediately wanted to make sure the right provisions were there."[24]

EDS middle managers had a champion when Meyerson became president in 1979. There were plenty of bruises in store for EDS before then. DuPont would introduce the EDS innocents to the real world.

CHAPTER SEVEN

THE LIMITS OF CHARISMA

Once Perot made his fortune, one particular misunderstanding cropped up time and again. What solicitors had in mind when they asked Perot for help with their philanthropic projects was a check, certainly, and a public appearance or two, perhaps. But Perot doesn't believe in halfway measures. To him, it was a short step from joining Roger Smith as his latest import fighter to comparing notes on GM's shortcomings with union members and car dealers.

The duPont Glore Forgan debacle also began with Perot and his petitioners operating on different wave lengths. The New York Stock Exchange wanted Perot's money to shore up the sick stock brokerage. Perot was interested, but he had a laundry list of his own objectives, including some idealistic ones. Both the NYSE and Perot quickly realized their joint error, but it was too late. We have already seen that Perot can't reset his moral compass to suit the business situation. Unlike the Social Security flap and the Iran rescue, which ended well, Perot rode his principles right into the dirt at duPont. And as a result of his embarrassing fall, EDS began insulating itself from its charismatic leader and his magnificent tangents.

The NYSE knew how to win over Perot. Attorney General John Mitchell, Treasury Secretary John Connally, and White

House aide Peter Flannigan all phoned Perot on the same morning. If duPont failed, they stated gravely, it could touch off a panic that would bury Wall Street, perhaps forever. Would Perot help? Of course he would. Perot lent duPont $10 million. "As long as there is a Wall Street," an emotional NYSE Chairman Bernard J. Lasker proclaimed on the eve of the duPont bailout, "we will owe a tremendous debt of gratitude to Ross Perot."[1]

The Wall Street-Perot romance soured in a matter of months. Undoubtedly, Perot told his petitioners from the NYSE what he had in mind for duPont. Surely the exchange officials kept nodding. They desperately needed cash to shore up failing members. They hoped that Perot would be a good sport if duPont went under. After all, the Street had handed Perot all that money in the first place.

Instead, Perot used duPont as both a soapbox and a demonstration program. Perot wanted Wall Street to be a Rockwell tableau of wise men in sober black suits rationing investment capital to deserving American industry and building wealth for hardworking, thrifty Americans. That's what Perot had expected to find when EDS went public. What the stock market really was, he learned in horror, was a sweating, shoving mob of gunslingers, young men with MBAs and long sideburns searching for the next "concept" stock to jump on. Perot didn't cotton to gambling. He remembered the questions put to him after he gave a speech to Missouri school teachers at the height of the 1960s stock boom. The audience pumped the fastest, richest Texan for stock tips! "They wanted to shoot dice," he says. They were willing to risk what Perot called "fruit-jar money."[2]

The brokerage failed in part because he tried to remake it in the mold of the paramilitary EDS. As Perot cracked down on duPont salesmen, entire branch offices defected. At the same time, Perot lectured long and often on the Street's shortcomings. His ideas were good ones, but they didn't win converts or business. The Street didn't take to the righteous outsider any better than GM would 15 years later. Lasker's eternal gratitude notwithstanding, brokers practically cheered when Perot placed the brokerage in Chapter 11 bankruptcy protection in March 1974.

How many people would take on the burden of reforming Wall Street or GM? It's no wonder that a steady procession of supplicants misjudged the sharp point that Perot puts on his philanthropy. His credentials are impeccable. He has given perhaps $200 million to charity over the past 25 years. His interest dates back to a boys' home in Dallas in the mid-1960s— before he became super rich. James Just, one of the first dozen EDS employees, was the company's first charity point man. His sister, Bette Perot, runs the Perot Foundation today.

Often, Perot swings into action without being asked. When a Dallas policeman was paralyzed in a skiing accident in 1988, Perot sent his jet to Colorado to bring him back to Dallas and told the policeman's doctors to spare no expense. Perot came to the aid of his neighbor's son, hurt in a car wreck. He helped the parents of a youth swept away in a flash flood, wives of POWs, the parents of two girls murdered in a small Texas town, the mothers of Vietnam casualties, his uncle Henry Ray, and his first skipper aboard the Sigourney, to name but a few.

He has helped literally thousands of people, providing them everything and asking nothing, not even recognition. Bette Perot is supervising several of these cases at any given moment. As Perot explained it in 1968, "Making all this money is partly an accident. I could have put the same amount of energy into a corporation that made steel forgings but I would have been in the wrong place at the wrong time. I had the opportunity to be in right place and I have an obligation to do something creative."[3]

The problems start when solicitors bite on Perot's "aw-shucks" pose. Perot doesn't consider EDS an accident. Far from it, EDS is a triumph of Perot's ideas over convention. He has few qualms about injecting those ideas into philanthropies as a condition of his support. A case in point is his aid to the University of Texas Southwestern Medical School in Dallas. Perot offered millions of dollars and his influence as a patron of the school. He had a laundry list of conditions. Among them: The school must charge nonresidents the same tuition as residents. State officials complained about subsidizing the education of non-Texans. Perot wanted the school to attract the brightest minds to Dallas so they would start bioscience companies. The legislature acquiesced.

Perot had an ambitious agenda for duPont. First, he thought he saw a lucrative new field for EDS. Wall Street was choking on success in those days; everyone wanted to make a killing in the market. Before computers, a daily volume of 15 million shares brought Wall Street to its knees. Runners, clerks, and cashiers were hard pressed to get the money to the seller of the stocks and the certificates to the buyer. The NYSE was closed on Wednesdays at one point in 1968 so that the clerks could catch up. Of course, that only made Tuesdays and Thursdays worse.

Perot had a better idea—EDS. He swapped 100,000 shares of EDS in 1970, then worth $3.8 million, to take over duPont's back office under a facilities management contract. Perot also cajoled the NYSE into hiring EDS for $250,000 to study computerization of the exchange. EDS had a beachhead on Wall Street.

Even Perot had misgivings about the next step, taking over the crippled brokerage itself. He had ample warning. When brokerages aren't able to exchange certificates and money in the alloted five days, Wall Street calls the result a "fail." DuPont had an epidemic of fails on its hands. DuPont originally asked Perot for a $5 million life-support loan. In the middle of negotiations, duPont raised the amount to $10 million. Barely two months later, nervous New York Stock Exchange officials returned, sullen duPonts in tow, and asked for more capital. Ultimately, the missing securities, bad debts, and uncollected dividends in duPont's back office amounted to $42 million.

The duPonts were one reason Perot didn't break off negotiations to buy 90 percent control of duPont. The scions of the most famous dynasty in American business were the perfect patrician foils for populist Perot. Lazard Freres partner Felix Rohatyn represented the NYSE in the negotiations. As he told writer John Brooks, "The duPont representatives seemed to be arrogant without having much to be arrogant about. There was an air of sullen defiance."[4] Perot shot back contempt. Later he would say there wasn't enough management talent at duPont to lead a group of monks in silent prayer.

Perot put the question to Meyerson. If he put up the money would Meyerson run duPont? Meyerson, then 33, was thrilled by the prospect. He moved to New York in May 1971. The two were going to show Wall Street how it was done.

From the start, Perot had used his charitable millions to advance his social agenda. His first two major gifts prove this point. He gave $1 million to the Boy Scouts of America to take the program into the ghettos, since scouting had worked wonders for the young Perot. He gave $2.4 million to the Dallas public schools to fashion remedial programs for black and Hispanic students and to provide hot breakfasts.

DuPont also fit the philanthropic pattern in its scope. Perot doesn't think small in matters of charity. He demanded his money back from the Dallas Arboretum and Botanical Society in 1988 when it cut back its ambitious plans for a lakeside garden. If it wasn't going to be world class, Perot complained, he didn't want to support it. The society struck a deal. The arboretum could keep the $2 million that Perot had already given; he would keep the remaining $6 million of his pledge.

Another world-class project in Dallas has put a chill in the air between the city and its best-known benefactor. Perot rescued a local symphony hall project in 1984 with a gift of $12 million. He had more conditions. The city must name the hall after Meyerson. And to make sure that it was world class, only Perot and Meyerson could approve changes in the design. The hall's architect was I. M. Pei, an exacting man with a history of cost overruns. After he built the superexpensive Dallas city hall, wags dubbed him "You Will Pay." The $50 million hall didn't seem so extravagant in 1984, when Dallas was booming. It cost $100 million when it was completed and opened in 1989 in the middle of the worst local economy in recent history.

Wall Street cooled quickly on the duPont saviors, Perot and Meyerson. The Texans stood out like missionaries in their dark suits, white shirts, and narrow ties. Meyerson was careful not to purge duPont executives, or ask them to honor the EDS dress code. But the duPont brokers detested the changes he did make, such as banning alcohol during business hours. They also suspected that the EDS people assigned to them as administrative aides were spies.

Perot lent credence to the espionage theory. He sent securities attorney G. Michael Boswell to look over Meyerson's shoulder. Boswell would observe during the week and return to Dallas every Saturday to brief Perot. Says Boswell, "There was a culture clash you wouldn't believe. Part of my job was to sort out what that clash was and to build a bridge. A lot of that went away as we went forward. It never was an easy relationship."[5]

Meyerson and the EDS managers found it impossible to overlook the difference in work habits. "Brokers work six-hour days," says recruiter Gary Griggs, who came along to Manhattan. "No one at EDS works less than 60-hour weeks."[6] Meyerson scheduled an 8 A.M. meeting so that duPont employees would make a flying start at the day. Instead they slouched to their desks and telephones grumbling, and the meetings died off.

The reluctant converts made other adjustments. The brokers learned to toss their lunch-time martinis into the potted palms at the first sign of a crewcut. Some switched to camouflaged cocktails, such as a vodka and tonic without the lime. Perot acknowledged the culture clash. "One of our philosophies is that we fire people," he says. "We fired those who thought our objectives were too Boy-Scoutish and would not support them."[7]

For the first time in his life, Meyerson was overmatched. Brilliant and urbane, Meyerson presents himself with a becoming self-consciousness, a slicker "gee whiz" version of Perot's "aw shucks." His origins are equally humble. His grandfather was a Russian emigré who rode the train west to Fort Worth. Meyerson studied philosophy and art at the University of Texas. He was introduced to computers over a bridge table in the army, where he was a colonel's aide.

Meyerson's tastes are baroque and modern in turn. He travels to Europe to attend his favorite concert halls in Vienna and Amsterdam. (The Dallas hall modestly aims to be their equals.) But his taste in furniture runs to chrome and glass. He remodeled a utility power station in 1988 into a startling work of industrial chic. The crane that once moved 20-ton equipment still hangs in the Meyerson living room as a conversation piece. He remodeled the third floor of the building into his private concert hall, complete with adjustable sound baffles and six-foot stereo speakers. Passersby are likely to hear Joni Mitchell blaring from the Meyerson home one day and Gustav Mahler the next.

Meyerson was unable to charm his way into the small, exclusive club that was Wall Street in the early 1970s—at least while Perot was blasting Wall Street for its shortcomings. Perot had moral leverage. He could call up Morgan Stanley or Lehman Brothers and chew them out for skipping duPont in the underwriters' latest syndication. The old-line houses would bring Meyerson in for one deal, and then his phone wouldn't ring again.

Meyerson tried hiring Wall Street regulars as guides, but this strategy failed too as he made a series of bad hires. His experts quit abruptly, or came aboard and did nothing. The turmoil strengthened the conviction in the duPont ranks that the "Texas Mafia" didn't know what it was doing.

Perot was no small part of the problem. Griggs was sent to California to turn around a brokerage operation there. Griggs stopped dressing conservatively. "That's how we turned that [office] around," he says. "People thought I was a human being." Perot was not impressed when he bumped into Griggs in New York. He made it clear that real men didn't wear blue shirts. He called Meyerson on the spot and said "I'm here with Griggs and I don't know whether to kiss him or shake his hand."[8]

Perot was making bigger waves. He chided the Street for its bankers' hours. "The New York Stock Exchange should never close its doors," duPont sermonized in its advertising. DuPont ads also struck a populist theme: "For 38 years of my life, I was a 'little guy.' There are so many of us. We are America."

He railed against the gunslinging mentality on Wall Street. DuPont promoted a conservative pyramid portfolio in which 70 percent of the client's holdings was invested for safety and yield, 20 percent for cyclical market opportunities, and 10 percent for speculative growth. He remarked pointedly on NBC's "Today Show" that investors would do better if brokers were paid for results rather than sales.

Perot uses an even more conservative approach for his own money. All of Perot's billions are invested with capital preservation in mind. Only investment income is used for risky investments. Of course, the $200 million or so generated annually by Perot's fortune allows plenty of risk taking.

Perot broke duPont in a bold gamble on the abilities of his Vietnam vets. Securities sales plunged after the demise of the great bull market of the 1960s. Other brokerages were laying off salesmen and closing offices to cut their expenses. Perot thought his competition was being cowardly and short-sighted. Instead of retrenching, duPont would gear up. Borrowing several pages from EDS, it would hire 600 ex-military officers in a 60-day period. (ROTC officers enlisted and resigned en masse during May and June.) He would send them to a training academy in Los Angeles where they would study salesmanship in the mornings, and in the evenings, study for their stockbrokers' licenses. In between, they would make cold calls for the United Way just to sharpen their telephone skills.

The recruiting program created more controversy on Wall Street. The recruits were asked to sign a contract obligating them to work off their training costs. If they quit right out of school, the recruits owed duPont $25,000. The "lazy" Wall Street regulars sent up another cry. The only way Perot could keep registered representatives was to chain them to their desks.

The recruiting push fueled more discontent inside duPont. Regulars read the mass hirings as a latent pink slip for themselves. Perot's efforts to teach telephone courtesy and good work habits to the brokers already were rankling. He pushed the brokers to stay on the phone all day prospecting for more business. He made the duPont brokers work nights and Saturdays. The message flashed around the duPont grapevine: If you don't like the new work ethic, the door swings both ways. Says former duPont broker Alan Aldridge, now a securities executive in Los Angeles: "Many of the brokers took offense at that statement."[9]

Good stockbrokers already know how the door swings. Only a minority of registered representatives have the moxie and the connections to make it big in securities sales. Those who do, often present themselves as a package deal: Love me; love my quirks. The brokerage firm grins and bears it usually because the star salesman can take his clients with him when he walks out the door. Back in the early 1970s, A. G. Edwards and Sons played Avis to duPont's Hertz in the Midwest, the heart of duPont sales network. Edwards profited greatly from Perot's miscues at duPont.

In Decatur, Illinois, in the summer of 1973, the branch manager and 10 salesmen crossed the street to join Edwards, leaving only the secretaries behind. James Lundquist, now an Edwards vice president, was assigned to the Decatur office temporarily to help salvage the business. He returned to his home base in Springfield so disillusioned and vocal that his manager fired him that very day. Lundquist joined the Edwards office in Springfield. The Chapter 11, he says "was just a matter of time. I could see it coming."[10]

Perhaps Perot's cures would have worked in better times. The military men did better on average than typical beginning brokers, by most accounts. Perot also scored some successes with specialty products. National sales manager, Stu Greenberg, was working up life insurance plans in partnership with John Hancock. The range of investment products allowed duPont brokers to address all of the financial management needs of middle-class families. Prudential-Bache and other brokerages would try a similar approach a decade later.

But selling securities in the early 1970s was like farming without rain. The hysteria of the late 1960s had turned into a bloodbath by 1970. On April 2, 1970, EDS shares shed $60 to close at $90. Predictably, the media raced to describe Perot's $500 million haircut as the largest daily loss ever. The news got worse. Penn Central and Lockheed were going broke. The end of wage and price controls touched off a wicked price spiral. Says Boswell, "We did study after study showing we could make money if the trading volume just hit 12 million shares per day."[11]

EDS's Wall Street bonanza never panned out. The long, slow afternoons on Wall Street cleared up the back office muddle in a flash; clerks had plenty of time to complete sales, so automating Wall Street was no longer urgent. The NYSE adopted some of the recommendations in the EDS study of a computerized stock market, but not the one closest to Perot's heart—to hire EDS. Perot landed only a few other brokerage accounts. EDS signed one account, Walston & Company, by investing $4 million in the ailing firm. Meyerson and top EDS lieutenant, William K. Gayden, took seats on the Walston board.

By summer 1973, the NYSE was knocking on Perot's door asking him to inject an additional $17.8 million in duPont. By then, Perot had $93 million on the line, and the brokerage business was worsening by the day. Perot and Meyerson needed a creative answer.

They found one. DuPont would move its sales offices into Walston, and Walston would move its back office—and capital—into duPont. The sales operation, duPont & Walston, would guarantee the back office, duPont Glore Forgan, sufficient revenue to break even. Since duPont couldn't lose money, the arrangement meant its capital was safe.

Of course, the capital was safe only so long as the combined sales organization could meet its obligations. Neither firm spent much time spinning what-if scenarios. Both faced serious problems. Walston was marginally better off than duPont, but its future was less secure. The Walston family, unlike Perot, didn't have deep pockets. Meyerson won an agreement in principle from Walston's 20-man board to enter a business realignment with duPont. The realignment was another creative wrinkle. Under Delaware corporation law, it didn't require shareholder approval. The Walston board set a meeting on Sunday, June 30, to approve the deal. The exchange had ordered duPont to bring its capital into compliance by July 1.

The Walston family rallied opposition. All day Saturday, the brothers hammered away on what was unknown about the deal. They later claimed in a lawsuit that they weren't told that duPont was under exchange orders to raise its capital. They also argued that duPont had concealed an exchange study that predicted the combined operation would be broke in eight months, an eerily accurate forecast.

When the board convened the next morning, the duPont camp was in charge. The chairman of the board, a Walston employee, sided with Perot. The Walston brothers controlled 10 of the 20 votes. Accusations began flying. The family accused the duPont executives and their allies of sharp dealing. The duPont camp thought the Walstons were reneging on the agreement in principle. Indeed, Meyerson already was putting the realignment into effect.

Lunch came and went. So did dinner. The two camps spent most of the time in caucuses. They could manage nothing in joint meetings except impassioned speeches and bitter debate. Finally, in the early hours of Monday morning, director George U. Robson, a Walston loyalist, excused himself and returned to his hotel. The septuagenarian was recovering from a heart attack. "They finally wore George Robson down," says Carl R. Walston. "He was a very, very sick man."[12] The chairman called for the vote. The Walston camp requested that Robson be allowed to vote by telephone. The answer was no. The vote was 10 to 9 in favor of the realignment.

Meyerson had recruited industry veteran Walter Auch to run the sales network. Auch counseled against the consolidation. "I said you can't breed two dogs and get a racehorse," he recalls.[13] He was right. Emotions ran high and sales volume low. The Walston brothers were fired in August. Key executives left. In Hartford, Connecticut, 14 Walston brokers walked out en masse.

The stock market got worse, thanks to the Yom Kippur war and the oil embargo. Not even Perot could turn the sight of gas-station lines into a Rockwell painting. Perot pulled the plug on duPont and Walston, the sales arm; Auch and Meyerson traveled to Dallas to convince him. "He said, 'I want to ask you two questions,' " recalls Auch. " 'Can you assure me that the clients aren't going to be hurt? And will you see to it our guys are relocated?' "[14]

It was an orderly transition. All of duPont's 146 branch offices were put up for sale. The brokers, clients, and accounts went with the real estate. It took four months and cost Perot $16 million in additional operating losses, but no one else lost money. One of the big buyers was A. G. Edwards.

That left the backshop, duPont Glore Forgan, with very little business; but Meyerson still wanted to press on. Boswell and a handful of ex-EDS executives staged a palace revolt. They went first to Meyerson. When Meyerson refused to consider closing down, the group went to Perot. "Meyerson still doesn't like me, but I was working for Perot not him," Boswell says.[15]

The duPont board met in a final stormy confrontation in the Regency Hotel that March. The meeting crackled with anger but the outcome was inevitable. DuPont filed for Chapter 11 bankruptcy protection. Meyerson and Perot slunk back to Texas in defeat. Only *Barron's* managed a note of praise in the gleeful chorus of I-told-you-sos. "His concept of total asset management for those of small or moderate means represented a badly needed return to basics which Wall Street, at great cost to itself and investors, had forgotten during the go-go years."[16]

Perot had one final humiliation in store for him. The trustee in bankruptcy, J. Winthrop Allegaert, took over the Walstons' suit on behalf of the bankruptcy estate. Perot paid $6 million to settle the suit out of court, enough to assure creditors of being repaid in full. Allegaert today says that his suit was just business as usual in bankruptcy court. The Walstons find it hard to be that magnanimous even 15 years later. They still want a day in court for the shareholders, who recovered nothing. Says Jack H. Walston, "It was the most awful experience of my life."[17]

Perot wasn't any happier about this final loss. Richard Shlakman remembers a long silence on Perot's end of the telephone conversation in which he and attorney Tom Luce presented the settlement deal to him. " 'Jimmy Hoffa's attorneys don't settle. They win and he's a crook. I'm not, and my attorneys want to throw in the towel. Maybe I need Jimmy Hoffa's attorneys,' " Shlakman recalls.[18] Shlakman and Luce had worked night and day on the settlement.

DuPont cost Perot some $60 million after taxes and stripped him of his last romantic notions about Wall Street. He still knocked lazy Wall Streeters in a *Barron's* interview in 1987. He says, "This is a great business to work in but a terrible one to be an owner in. Where else are there so many mediocre people with absolutely unbelievable incomes?"[19]

Both Perot and Meyerson seemed to lose faith in EDS and themselves after duPont. The company now had plenty of competition and much slimmer profit margins. Congress seemed ready to enact national health insurance. The uncertainty froze the Medicare business. Perot worried that the rising tide of minicomputers and personal computers would swamp EDS's giant informations factories. In short, EDS was adrift.

Perot tried another start-up. He assigned a young systems engineer, former Naval Academy middie Joe Glover, to size up the young personal-computer business. Glover visited Microsoft, then a two-man software house, and discovered Apple at a trade show manning a single folding table. "Even the most visionary measure of the micro industry didn't imagine a $70 billion industry," says Glover. "Ross saw that. He could truthfully say he was not surprised."[20]

To learn more about small computers, Perot visited Portia Isaacson at her computer store in suburban Dallas. Isaacson, an early computer retailer, was an apostle of distributed data processing, networks of minicomputers and desktop computers that would be more flexible and reliable than giant central computer installations. Perot hired her as an EDS Fellow and instructed her to spread the gospel inside the company.

And when Lloyd Haldeman resigned as director of the Dallas Symphony to return to his entrepreneurial roots, Perot was on the phone to him within hours. Perot convinced him to bring his idea to EDS. The result was Inovision, a catalog purveyor of advanced electronics and video cassettes, a precursor of the Sharper Image. Perot also launched a minicomputer company aimed at small businesses, and computer training classes on videotape. This constellation of start-ups, Perot told his troops, was the new EDS.

The old EDS was not amused. Isaacson had good attendance at her lectures on micros and minis until she became an EDS Fellow. "The minute he hired me, no matter what my title, I lost every ear in the company," she says.[21] Clearly EDS had developed a set of interests independent of its charismatic leader. The old EDS set itself in opposition to the new businesses.

The new EDS also failed because of its timing. It was much too early. When Inovision began marketing videotapes in the late 1970s, only 250,000 homes had VCRs. Personal computers didn't amount to much of an industry until IBM entered it in 1981. By then EDS was already dismantling the start-ups. It had traveled as far as Perot's charismatic, intuitive leadership could take it.

It now needed management. Fortunately, Meyerson had absorbed the lessons—and bruises—of duPont and was ready to provide that management. From 1979 on, EDS revived as a growth company. The *Wall Street Transcript* three times voted Meyerson the most outstanding CEO in the computer-services industry. He wasn't the CEO, in fact but only because he declined the honor each time Perot offered it.

Meyerson provided the creative grease between Perot and the real world. He turned his fertile mind to solutions that allowed Perot to hold on to his dogma and allowed EDS to adapt. Consider the parable of feeding at the same table as shareholders. Perot froze his salary at $68,000 once EDS went public. He would live or die with his stock holdings, just as the rest of EDS shareholders did. His decision effectively capped EDS executives' pay however. By 1979, the Eagles were woefully underpaid. The solution: Perot stuck with $68,000, but everyone else got a raise. The sad fact remains that stock ownership motivates no one when the shares are falling in value.

In 1978, EDS was far enough removed from its charismatic roots to hire a survey team to study morale and turnover.

Turnover, a problem for EDS even today, also flew in the face of Perot's notions of the ideal workplace. But newcomers have always struggled to adapt to EDS's rigid culture although they tend to stick once they have survived five years.

EDS also let its employees decide how much of the dress code they wished to keep. A conservative group, they blessed pastel shirts and allowed a few other minor changes but still outlawed facial hair. In 1984, the company began conducting leadership training classes for account managers. By then, most of the company's 14,000 employees had had little direct contact with Perot.

Meyerson brought a human touch to middle management. He gathered the Medicare managers at a sales meeting in a Dallas airport hotel in the late 1970s to hear two outside speakers. Both wondered if they had wandered into a convention of FBI agents. They urged the EDS managers to loosen up. In Meyerson's summation that night, he echoed the speakers' themes. Maybe EDS would win more friends and contracts if its managers looked and acted more human.

The EDSers faced a quandary that night. Obviously they must appear looser for the next day's session, but how loose? Most settled on jackets and open shirts. Jeff Heller strolled in wearing boots and jeans with a bottle of Lone Star beer in his back pocket. Meyerson was equal to the occasion. He defined *loose* as perhaps a bit more laid back than tieless and a bit less so than ranchhand duds.

That isn't to say that Meyerson abandoned EDS's entrepreneurial roots. Account managers still had complete responsibility for completing their missions and great latitude in how they went about it. EDS had no seniority and minimal bureaucracy. Meyerson could tolerate meetings and memos, but he certainly didn't encourage either.

And Perot was still around, his white charger prancing in the courtyard and his lance leaning against the door. Company employees still regarded him as their spiritual leader. He was still out there waging holy war and taking no prisoners. Only now he left EDS at home in capable hands.

CHAPTER EIGHT

THE CRUSADES

Ross Perot vs. the Texas education establishment seemed to be a hopeless mismatch. Education had an entrenched state bureaucracy, unions, professional and trade groups by the dozen, and large payrolls in every town and city in Texas. Perot had only his persuasive gifts and the state's moral obligation to provide adequate public schools. In fact, Texas schools were among the worst in the nation, but no reformer had been able to expose the special interests who defended the status quo. In a few scathing asides in his crusade for better schools, Perot had them shivering in their skivvies.

Football coaches, those potentates of small-town Texas? Rip! "I thought I was living pretty well until I found out that high school football players have towel warmers," Perot quips.[1] The vocational education lobby? Perot skewers it with a homely example of teenage boys scheming to get out of classes: "We realize we can have unlimited absences going to livestock shows . . . so we buy a chicken. I have a documented case of one boy . . . [traveling] 35 days across Texas with a chicken. Everyone wants to know why the boy came home? The chicken was worn out. A chicken can only take so much travel."[2]

Fiscal restraint? "You know how much it costs to keep a person in Huntsville [state prison]? More than it would cost to send him to Harvard. When I tell businessmen that, they say, 'Well, just send them all to Harvard then.' "[3] Populist prejudice against special classes for bright kids? "They said, 'No, no. That's elitism. . . .' I said, 'Fine, let's put the fat girls on the drill team. Let's let everyone play quarterback.' "[4]

Texas school reform in 1984 was an awesome display of Perot's iron will and razor wit. He fought off an army of special interests. He cajoled $3 billion in new spending from a notoriously stingy legislature to provide better pay for teachers, smaller classes, and preschool programs. As his reform legislation passed, one senator remarked plaintively, "Literally one man said this has got to be done, and we did it."[5]

As stunning as his victory was, Texans went straight back to losing the war. Voters threw out the appointed board that Perot counted on to police the bureaucracy. Bureaucrats dragged their feet, instituting controls on themselves. Angry teachers wore red dots on their wristwatches in 1986 in protest against Governor Mark White, who appointed a select committee on education reform with Ross Perot as chairman. White was crushed in the election that year. The legislature waited five years to give teachers another raise. None of these reversals diminished Perot's accomplishments. Even critics admit that Texas schools would be in much sorrier shape today if he had not conquered Austin in 1984. A deep recession in Texas was a major factor in the derailment of both school reform and White's reelection.

In hindsight, however, Perot's singlehanded crusade was a mixed blessing. As he had in Texas War on Drugs 4 years earlier, he oversimplified the problem and failed to build a consensus. Leave it to me, his actions told his fellow Texans, and they did. Neither he nor they expected the fixes to come unstuck. The parents who yelled "Tell 'em, Ross!" from the sidelines still didn't vote in school board elections. Football pep rallies continued to outdraw Parent-Teacher Association meetings by 10 to 1. Perot-style champions appeal to us because of our apathy. We like quick fixes and simple answers. The fact remains that we are powerless against the system in

America only because we don't care enough to participate. Then again, our apathy is not Perot's doing.

Perot would love to cure us of it. Inside EDS, employees who groused about current events in the presence of their boss had to be prepared for the consequences. Well, *DO* something about it, Perot would instruct them. It was one of the glories of working for EDS. Many companies encourage civic involvement, but few turn it into a religion, as EDS still does. EDS troops didn't need to be reminded that one man can make a difference. No matter who called—GM chairmen, Texas governors, or average citizens—Perot was ready to go. At times it seemed as if the petitioners formed a line outside his door.

Governor Bill Clements called in 1978 to enlist him in a Texas war on drugs. Perot threw himself into the job the same way he tackled the sale of an IBM 7070 to Southwestern Life. He soaked up every fact he could find about drug abuse. He came to two conclusions. First, Americans were too blasé about marijuana. It was harmful, and tolerance of it sent the wrong message to kids. Public opinion needed to be turned around. Second, Texas was woefully lax on drug pushers. The state needed to send a different kind of message to law breakers.

Perot found his volunteers at EDS. He drafted EDS attorney Rick Salwen to rewrite the Texas criminal code. Salwen had heard Perot speak to a school group and had offered his support. Salwen and four other EDS employees lobbied the bill through the legislature. Perot tackled the job of turning public opinion against drugs. Using his own money, he began an exhaustive tour of hearings and speeches.

Salwen developed a package of six bills. He wanted pushers to serve mandatory jail sentences, stores to restrict sales of paint and glue, and druggists to report every sale of restricted pills to the state police. He wanted wiretapping authority for the police and more. Perot responded in form when Salwen presented the legislation to him. Perot told Salwen he should go to Austin to get the legislation passed. Salwen tried to protest. "He said, 'Use my name. That will get you in the door,'" Salwen says. "'If you are a halfway good salesman you'll get it done.' He was right. Even the lawmakers who didn't like Perot let me in to hear what Ross Perot's lawyer had to say."[6]

Salwen met quiet resistance. Pharmacists, drug companies, trial lawyers and civil rights advocates opposed parts of the bill, sometimes violently, but they didn't dare to raise their voices. "It's pretty hard politically to oppose them and have someone suggest you're soft on drugs," says Representative Terral Smith (D-Austin), who opposed the legislation for practical reasons. "I thought that we ought not to pass bills that increased prison population if we didn't have prisons to put them in. They were very naive in many ways. . . . Salwen would make comments like, 'If you just put these laws on the books they'll quit selling drugs. You don't need more prisons.' "[7] Smith bottled up the bill in subcommittee until Salwen agreed to drop mandatory sentencing.

But Perot wanted laws so stringent that most dealers would not dare sell drugs to children. The state would send the remainder away forever. He crowed that they were going to chase drug dealers right out of Texas. Salwen's forces reintroduced it on the floor. "I thought a deal had been struck and they should have stuck with it," Smith says.[8]

Not all problems can be reduced to a pithy call to action. The reformers learned that risk is relative in Dallas minority neighborhoods, where gunfire punctuates evenings. Minors are recruited to exchange drugs for money so that adult dealers can avoid arrest under the state's tough laws. Dealers and runners have a clear understanding. The young workers are maimed and killed as object lessons on the dangers of skimming. Since the drug trade is one of the few growth industries in south Dallas, dealers have little trouble recruiting replacements. They're quitting school at age 14 to run drugs.

Perot's response in 1989 is even simpler and more extreme. "You can declare civil war and the drug dealer is the enemy," he says. "There ain't no bail. . . . [Drug dealers] go to POW camp. You can start to deal with the problem in straight military terms. We can apply the rules of war."[9] Once again, his answers are appealing—and dangerous. He is voicing the frustrations of middle America. How satisfying it would be to move from house to house in drug-infested neighborhoods and to lock up dealers behind barbed wire and gun towers. How dangerous it is to impose the tyranny of the majority.

Perot knows firsthand that enthusiasm can turn into abuse. A major drug trial was unfolding in 1979 in Tyler, Texas, as Perot began his war on drugs. Two undercover police officers were star witnesses for the prosecution. In the middle of the trial, their car was firebombed and one was wounded by a shotgun blast. At their next court appearance, they were flanked by unsmiling men in business suits and sunglasses. Reporters traced the guards back to Perot, who issued this statement through EDS public relations: "A trained, armed team is now protecting both officers. . . . This same level of protection is available to any law enforcement officer in Texas."

Unfortunately, the two cops were doing more than their duty. They confessed in 1981 that they had firebombed their own car and falsely accused a nightclub owner of the shotgun blast. The courts threw out almost 200 convictions based on their testimony.

The second thrust of Perot's war on drugs was more successful. As Salwen notes, "The best return was on educating the parents of white middle class kids on the dangers of drugs."[10] The war on drugs opened a permanent office in Austin to push drug education. Perot recruited General Robinson Risner to run the Texas program. Perot first met Risner as a returning POW. When he retired from the Air Force, he mentioned to Perot that he would like to work against drugs. The pair flew to Washington in the early 1980s to convince Nancy Reagan to join the fight. As a result of the two-hour meeting, the First Lady began her "Just Say No" campaign. Education efforts like hers have put drug use on the decline among children outside the ghetto. Perot is not happy with his partial victory. "Just Say No" is painless public relations, he snarls. The White House wouldn't buy his package of tough antidrug laws.

Perot doesn't approach his crusades intellectually. He becomes an advocate for an aggrieved group—for the POWs, the forgotten pawns of the Vietnam War, parents frustrated by the spread of drugs, or autoworkers losing their jobs to foreign competition. That's the classic formula for charismatic leadership: needy groups, compelling values, and uncaring officialdom. He becomes the group's champion. He goes to war for them, all or nothing, friend or foe.

In his campaign for better schools, he wanted nothing to do with half-hearted measures. "If the child is not going to get the maximum benefit, who wants it? We had to fight unbelievable battles."[11] Some officials do care, and some compromises are necessary, but Perot rolled right over them.

The Perot committee's report was a revolutionary document. He wanted schools open from 7 A.M. to 6 P.M. for on-site day care. He wanted three years of preschooling for disadvantaged children, à la the federal Headstart program. He wanted classes no larger than 15 kids for kindergarten through fourth grade. The price tag was $8 billion, but he was right on target. The street child is beaten before he starts; he is too far behind children from nurturing homes, Perot says.

He wanted recognition and merit pay for good teachers. He wanted to hold school districts accountable by publishing comparative test scores and such management measures as expenditures per pupil and the ratio of administrators to teachers. Charles Beard, president of the Texas State Teachers Association (TSTA), traveled to Lamar University in Beaumont to hear Perot speak. "The guy said everything I wanted to hear," says Beard. "So much of it we had been trying to make happen for a long, long time."[12] Perot lost the teachers' support as he pressed his reform, friend or foe. The teachers balked at the literacy and competency tests they were required to pass to remain teachers.

"He turned it into a Ross Perot committee instead of a select committee," says Raymon Bynum, a committee member and then head of the Texas Education Agency. "When he started out there was plenty of blame for everyone. He ended up blaming the problems on state Board of Education, TEA, local boards, and administrators."[13]

The realization sank in for Beard, Bynum and other insiders: Texas school kids had a champion. The education establishment had a foe. "The dumbest folks in college are studying to be teachers," Perot told a joint session of the legislature as the reform legislation came to the floor. "A losing [football] coach is going to get fired or made a principal. . . . There's no place for compromise." He quoted Winston Churchill, "Never give in. Never give in. Never. Never. Never."[14]

Of course, Perot was mostly right about the establishment. Says John Cole, president of the Texas Federation of Teachers:

> He realized that the major problem in education is that it is a government-sponsored monopoly. The only incentive for administrators is to provide a quality enough day care to keep parents off their backs while they keep taxes low. Why should you bust your butt to produce a well-educated child when the school district is going to get its money whether the kid graduates as an illiterate or goes on to Harvard?[15]

Cole's union supported reform to the end, even though Perot attacked the teachers' unions as a group, without acknowledging the support of Cole's. The kids' champion didn't have the time or the inclination to recognize those inside the system who also wanted to see it work.

There's some question about whether Governor White and the state leadership actually wanted this much reform. Traditionally, special committees are appointed in Austin to duck issues rather than to force them. White had promised schoolteachers a raise during his 1982 campaign. The legislature had balked in 1983, deciding that more pay for teachers was throwing good money after bad. White and Lieutenant Governor Bill Hobby tried to rein Perot in, but the crusader instead converted them into fearless reformers. Perot brought out the warrior in them.

Austin had chosen up sides when White called the special session in June. As capably as Salwen steered the drug legislation, school reform was no job for amateurs. Perot counseled school reformers:

> Do it in a special session. All the really good, expensive, high-powered lobbyists don't have anything to do. We hired them.

The ones we didn't need we hired defensively just so no one else could get them. We couldn't have won without them.[16]

Bynum says he was shadowed by Perot lobbyists. "I couldn't leave my office to go to the capitol. Certain individuals would show up and might even walk into a senator's office. . . . When Ross Perot decides to win it he doesn't care much who he runs over."[17]

Victory in hand, the state began pulling punches right away. The dreaded literacy test turned out to be a snap. It washed out only 600 teachers, or less than 1 percent, but it cost reform much of its good will with teachers. It probably cost Governor White his job in 1986. "Teachers were scared stiff," says Cole. "The psychology of teachers is low self esteem. You're not worth much is the message teachers get. Subconsciously they have bought into that."[18] The state never got around to testing teachers in their areas of expertise. The official reason was the expense of formulating all the tests. The real reason was economics of a different sort. The state didn't want to wipe out the thousands of football coaches teaching math and science. It couldn't afford to hire qualified replacements.

The statistics remain awful. Texas ranked 43rd among the 50 states in high school dropout rates at the end of the 1980s. Fully half of Hispanic children in Texas fail to finish school. The state's Scholastic Aptitude Test scores are improving, but Texas ranked 46th of the 50 states in 1988. The results are skewed somewhat because Texas gives the test to all students while other states restrict it to college-bound kids. Cole says ruefully, "I once tried to make a case that we didn't do that badly compared to states that test more people. What I found out was we did."[19] It's too early to call reform a failure. Test scores and retention should improve markedly once a majority of elementary school children have had the benefit of preschool training and smaller class sizes.

Reform played its cruelest trick on poor districts. The state picked up the tab for reform measures at first, but gradually shifted the burden back to local government. After five years of reform, added costs amount to $350 per child. According to lobbyists for rural school districts, the increase in state spending per pupil amounted to $20.15. The Texas Supreme Court recently ruled that the state's school aid equalization formula was unconstitutional because it was unfair to poor school districts.

Perot didn't intend to penalize poor districts. He was the special champion of Hispanic and black kids. He saw that Texas schools often expected disadvantaged children to fail. At one point, the Perot committee played with the idea of issuing education vouchers to disadvantaged parents. If the inner-city public schools were operated as dumping grounds, the parents could use the vouchers to take their kids elsewhere.

The recession knocked reform to its knees even in affluent districts. The TSTA's Beard says 900 of the 1100 school districts in Texas cut or froze pay levels in the 1987–88 school year. Reform moved Texas from 27th in average pay to 24th among the states. Five years later, the state had slipped back to 27th. "I don't think Ross Perot intended ever for that to happen," Beard says. "I wish he was on the scene to be a player in that struggle."[20]

Perot attacked the education establishment at its head. Perhaps there was no other place to begin the revolution in a bureaucracy as large and inert. Even Commissioner Bynum, who retired after the reforms, agrees. He says, "In some cases, the tactics may have been necessary, not desirable, but necessary."[21] The revolution stalled because it never shifted out of this top-down mode.

Local boards went right on compromising. Consider the local mandate to identify and reward excellent teachers. What happens when the district has 75 superior teachers and a budget that won't stretch past 50 of them? Which will it be, 25 demoralized teachers or an auditorium full of angry taxpayers? Not even Ross Perot could continue the war in all 1,100 Texas school districts.

Perhaps he misunderstood the need for 1,100 revolutions. He counted on a forceful, hand-picked board of education to prosecute the reforms, but the education special interests mounted a counterattack. State officials ducked the issue by putting it on the 1986 ballot as a referendum. The board seats reverted to elected positions. The first chairman of the elected state board, a Lubbock stockbroker, ran on an anti-Perot platform. Perot came out of retirement twice to fight for the reforms, but lately he has been declining invitations. Perot's specialty is the commando strike. He has little appetite for trench warfare, and less experience.

Top-down management worked just fine at EDS. He ran the company in a way that made compromise impossible. His managers at EDS weren't allowed choices. They had to swallow hard and do what's right, no matter how painful the consequences. Death to expediency. Because EDS executives were selected for grit and discipline, they seldom complained. More often than not, they couldn't wait for the next call to glory.

And glorious quests they were. Head recruiter, Gary Griggs, will always remember a Monday morning meeting in 1969 between Perot and the advertising executives of J. Walter Thompson. Perot was going to underwrite full-page newspaper ads in the 50 largest cities and a 30-minute television program to publicize the mistreatment of American POWs.

Griggs was in his late 20s at the time. He recalls:

> We meet in the lobby and there's [astronaut] Frank Borman. I'm thinking, "My God, that's Frank Borman." We go up to the board room and Ross tells them what he wants. They bring in the art director, the director of this and the director of that. They tell Ross it's going to take six months. Ross says, "You don't understand. I want this done now." They look at him and say "we can't do that." Ross says, "If Griggs here can do it, why can't you?" I'm sitting there thinking "What did this guy just say?"[22]

Griggs placed the ads in six days and went on to produce a televised "Town Hall Meeting," starring Borman.

EDS loved these crusades. Perot sent Wild Bunch recruiter Garfield to Lubbock in the early 1970s to help out in the relief effort after two tornadoes struck the west Texas city. "This was my first chance to do something that was humanitarian," says Garfield. "I was excited to be a part of it. . . . It was like a vacation. It may have been night and day but it was kind of like a plum to be asked by Ross to do something like this."[23]

Les Alberthal became a part of the company legends just before Perot flew to Vietnam in 1969 to attempt to deliver Christmas presents to the POWs. He had the task of loading 35 tons of food and medicine into a Braniff 707. The Flying Tigers staff in Los Angeles thought it was impossible to complete the job in the time that Alberthal was given. The warehouse manager told him, Don't sweat it. You send this Perot fellow to me and I'll make him understand. No, Alberthal answered, I'm afraid it's you who doesn't understand. Alberthal's wife flew in to help. The plane got off on time.

Perot turned the spotlight on the American Red Cross after the North Vietnamese told Perot that they would accept the gifts only if they were mailed from Russia in two-kilogram boxes. Perot asked the Red Cross officials on the plane to assemble volunteers in Anchorage, Alaska, to repack the supplies. Says retired Red Cross director Enso Bighinatti, "We rolled up in this blinding snowstorm. The hangar doors opened and there were a thousand people in there waiting for us."[24]

Boy Scouts, church members, and military men pitched in to repack the plane in a single day. Retired Dallas Red Cross worker, Ralph Shannon, remembers an engineer sitting on a table and leading hundreds of volunteers through the steps of folding a cardboard box. "I have been working with volunteer efforts my whole career," Shannon says. "That was one of the best efforts I have ever seen."[25] Perot's supreme confidence is contagious. Anything is possible.

Even reforming GM was possible in Perot's mind. He did not reject General Motor's overtures out of hand when Salomon Brothers Chairman, John Gutfreund, flew to Dallas in February 1984 to discuss a merger of the companies. The Salomon bankers and a small group of General Motors financiers conceived this wild idea in New York's Plaza Hotel in early 1984. It was codenamed "Project Plaza" to keep the identity of EDS secret. Since Perot still owned 45 percent of the stock, a decisive no would have sent Gutfreund and Project Plaza packing.

Perot and Meyerson flew to Detroit some weeks later. Roger Smith ushered them into a waiting helicopter to show them GM's massive facilities around Detroit. Perot looked down on dozens of parking lots, each packed with the cars of ordinary American working men. The discussions continued at EDS in Dallas, but Perot was already hearing cannon fire and breathing the heady scent of cordite.

Supposedly the decision to sell to GM belonged to all 28 EDS officers and directors. Perot called them together and asked what they thought. They raised objections. "Most of us did not want to sell," says Alberthal. "We didn't see any net benefit." Fernandes pointed out the obvious risks. How many senior executives of companies acquired by EDS were still on board? None. "Ross was intent on selling," Alberthal says. "It was obvious that's what he wanted to do. Owning the percentage of the company he did, that's what happened."[26]

Five years later, some EDS executives think Perot had a hidden agenda. They note that Salomon had prepared a strategy paper for the company in 1980 identifying the sale of EDS to a corporate giant like IBM or AT&T, as one means of delivering results for EDS shareholders. They noted that Felix Rohatyn joined the EDS board in 1982 and left it after the merger two years later. Rohatyn's Lazard Freres advised EDS during the acquisition. Was it a coincidence? Alberthal continues: "It is my understanding that there were discussions among Ross, Mort and [Bill] Gayden that we . . . wouldn't be able to grow [in sales] at rates we had been growing. I've gotten enough feedback to know that that was where the concept of selling was hatched. I don't know what was said."[27]

The money was important, but it wasn't Perot's only motivation. He knew the risk he was running. In his discussions with Smith, he went over all the potential problems. He thought he could write an airtight merger agreement to handle them. Even his own family was urging him not to sell. He probably would have listened if there was nothing on the table but money.

It was the other facets of the deal that swayed him. EDS would grow instantly by $3 billion and thousands upon thousands of employees. Meyerson had been scouting corporate America for just such a customer as GM. EDS wanted to show big corporations the advantages of integrating their computer systems into a single, global network. "Systems integration" could become a lucrative, new field for EDS—and fat stock awards for Perot's Eagles.

The Vietnam veteran crop of EDS officers never made the huge stock profits that their predecessors earned. GM itself would open up hundreds of new opportunities for the Eagles. Then there were all those cars in GM parking lots. He could help Smith turn GM around. He could help American industry beat the Japanese. Perot sought out the skeptical Fernandes after the meeting to tell him why the GM-EDS deal would be different. Doncha see?

Meyerson gathered the EDS management team in Dallas on Saturday, June 30, 1984. No one told duPont war stories. Perot was not second-guessed at EDS. When he pointed with his sword, his Eagles charged, confident in him and themselves. Meyerson went around the room: Heller would go to Detroit—Meler too; Fernandes and Alberthal would stay. The chosen were thrilled at their new assignment. They gave themselves a name. They were "The First Wave."

CHAPTER NINE

MIXING OIL AND HOLY WATER

Few mergers looked better on paper and worked worse in practice than the GM-EDS "alliance." It seemed like Christmas for everyone at the negotiating table. Perot had $900 million in cash and kept control of EDS. Not only that, but EDS would land GM as a customer, the largest computer services contract in history. Perot had made it painfully clear in his negotiations with Roger Smith that his company was to stand apart from GM.

Smith was eager to oblige. He wanted his GM middle managers, a group he scorned as the "frozen middle," to see shock troops in action. The two joked that Perot had Smith's permission to shoot the first GM functionary to turn up in Dallas with a GM procedures manual under his arm. Smith promised to send Perot a water pistol to use on him.

Salomon Brothers investment bankers had reason to pat themselves on the back. The deal had looked like it would fail because of Perot's refusal to give up the incentive stock awards that motivated EDSers and bound them to him. How could GM buy EDS and leave it as a publicly traded company at the same time? The Salomon bankers came up with an ingenious solution. GM would create a new class of GM common stock to trade on the earnings of EDS rather than GM. Perot could use these GM Class E (GME) shares as "carrot and handcuffs."

Even better, GME shares made the acquisition virtually free for GM. EDS would grow by a factor of four, once it took over GM's data processing business. This certain growth meant certain appreciation for the 85 percent of GME owned by GM. Granted, GM was merely moving its $3 billion data processing budget from one pocket to the other. But in the stock market, it was shifting profits from GM common stock, trading at a multiple of six times its earnings, to a stock that trades at 16 times earnings.

No one searched for operating flaws once the numbers fell into place. EDS senior vice president Fernandes recalls a surreal meeting of an EDS study group with Roger Smith and his CFO, F. Alan Smith. They met before the deal was finalized to discuss possible projects for EDS inside GM and to estimate the ensuing cost savings, in effect, to flesh out an operations argument for the deal. "It was like one of those meetings where no one is sure who the buyer is and who the seller is," Fernandes says.[1]

There were flaws, and *big* ones. The Smiths were lonely fans of EDS in Detroit. The eight members of that EDS study group were greeted coldly when they spread out to talk to other top GM executives. Fernandes called on GMAC Corporation, the car-loan and home-mortgage arm of GM. GMAC chief Bob Murphy came straight to the point. "I don't know why you are here," Fernandes recalls Murphy telling him. "I don't need you here. Do whatever you have to do, but don't bother me. . . . No one other than Roger shared the vision."[2]

The hostile reception made the merger with GM a profoundly new kind of transition for EDS. In normal takeovers, the customer's computer shop would be failing, and the angst and the recriminations would already be out in the open before EDS salesmen turned up. When the takeover was consummated as much as 18 months later, the internal DP managers would have fought the good fight and lost. Surrender to EDS is easier under such circumstances. Moreover, the boss is standing by to deal with rebellions. He's paying good money to EDS. He wants results.

None of that happened at GM. The computer jocks in Detroit weren't failing at their tasks. GM data processing was fragmented, but its workers were just as competent as their EDS counterparts and often more so. Worse, EDS was presented to GM as a done deal. GM executives had no chance to discuss the consequences with Roger Smith or prepare themselves mentally. Smith warned them that the deal was coming several days beforehand. "What we didn't realize was that EDS was taking over all the computers," says retired executive vice president Alex Mair. "It was a bold move. I wish he would have let us in on it, but it was a bold move."[3]

Nor was Smith standing by to put out fires. He had no real financial incentive. He had operating goals for EDS to consolidate GM computing and save money eventually, but that wasn't as compelling as fixing the disasters EDS found at its typical customer's computer shop. Smith apparently wanted collisions between EDS and his "frozen middle." He wanted EDS to chip away at it.

Clearly, Smith misjudged how bitter the clash would be. He ordered a meeting of GM computer managers on Monday, July 2, 1984. He sent Alan Smith to introduce Meyerson and Kenneth G. Riedlinger, the EDS senior vice president who would manage the GM account. Smith did the honors in a minute or two and excused himself. He was late for another meeting. The GM managers savaged Meyerson and Riedlinger for hours.

Roger Smith did have a good grasp of GM's problems. In early 1984, he implemented the most sweeping reorganization of GM since the 1920s. He realigned GM into a big car group, Buick-Oldsmobile-Cadillac (BOC), and a small car group, Chevrolet-Pontiac-Canada (CPC), and wiped out the Fisher Body and GM Assembly Division. The reorganization was intended to break down the rivalries between the car divisions. Fisher and GM Assembly were broken up so that the car divisions were masters of their own fate and not obliged to beg for support from central organizations. Smith also wanted middle managers to quit. He publicly wished that 25 percent would go away.

The plan worked better on paper than in reality. When EDS turned up on the scene, GM managers of any consequence were still spending most of their time in meetings on the reorganization. GM white-collar workers were not quitting. Wags classified themselves as BOC, CPC, and wait-and-see. EDS wandered in as an unwelcome stranger at a family donnybrook. EDS vice president Jim Buchanan was among the first on the ground in Detroit. "I'm not sure GM understood the consequences [of an EDS transition]," he says "In many cases I am not sure they were organized themselves well enough to go do anything about it."[4]

No one wasted a minute planning for the alliance. Mair wanted desperately for Smith to call a meeting and announce " 'Here's the plan. We'll acquire EDS. . . . Here's what they do extremely well. We realize they can't do it at GM in a week, but they'll start here and work out.' "[5] Mair's pleas fell on deaf ears. Smith was impatient for results.

EDS managers also wish they had paid more attention to politics and moved slower at GM. More and more, EDS is relying on former GM executives to manage its GM business. They would have been invaluable guides in the first, tense days of the alliance. But Perot already had his formula: an ounce of planning and an ocean of execution. GM was far bigger than anything his Eagles had tackled, but then so were the potential rewards. Perot grumbled when GM hired McKinsey & Company in 1985 to help sort out GM's computer strategy. He had no time to dither with consultants.

The alliance bogged down instantly. GM's sheer size was the toughest problem for EDS. The First Wave numbered about 100 people, or roughly one for every 8,000 GM employees. The odds improved by comparing EDSers to just GM's subset of data processing workers—one to 100—but there still weren't enough EDS employees to go around. EDS had only two emissaries for every three data processing sites at GM. Months later EDS still hadn't found all of the satellite installations.

What's more, their GM counterparts, after decades of experience as bureaucrats, were masters of the art of passive resistance. The automaker's executives didn't show up for meetings and dragged their feet in producing the information that EDS requested. Heller found himself answering the same question over and over: "Explain this. We're buying 100 percent of you and you're taking over us?"[6] The rebels turned to their old GM bosses for protection and found it.

EDS was perplexed by this effective resistance. They didn't understand why Smith could not place the call, as Perot always could, to shatter the opposition. But then, the role of bureaucracies is to diffuse power through a system of checks and balances and prevent grievous errors. The system also can be used to thwart change of any kind. Mair kept EDS out of the GM research center for two years.

Mair had a strong argument. GM was sophisticated in the ways of the Cray computers inside the research center. EDS knew little about these exotic computers. GM was working on computer problems that would make rocket scientists blanch. It is relatively easy to predict what happens during a 30-second engine burn in deep space. By contrast, the problem of automotive emissions is almost hopelessly conditional. Is the car traveling uphill? Which gear? What RPM? What are the weather conditions? How well is the engine tuned?

Where does engineering end at GM and data processing begin? Mair raised this knotty question after the fact. Five years later, EDS and GM still didn't have a comprehensive answer. The architects of the alliance never thought to raise it. It probably wasn't an issue to Perot. An EDSer could go anywhere and do anything. Perot wanted it all.

Few of EDS's conventional arguments worked on the GM computer specialists. In a Medicare shop, EDS could tell absorbed workers that they now worked for a company that lived and breathed data processing. The former Medicare workers no longer had to labor in obscurity or work with inadequate equipment. But GM engineers already had state-of-the-art computers and they were working on the frontiers of knowledge in their fields.

The EDS swagger also chafed in Detroit as it never had before. The EDS First Wave turned as always to bravado as a way to cope. Only the Few and the Proud could work 15-hour days, live in hotels for months at a time, and deal with hostile locals day after day. The First Wave developed a game-face to show the locals and indulged in foxhole camaraderie among themselves.

They caught the locals glaring at them and muttering about elitism, as locals always did during transitions, but they missed the larger picture at first. GM workers also considered themselves an elite. "I don't think we clearly perceived the nature of the GM culture," says Gary Fernandes. "Some of their people are second-generation GM. They wear GM underwear."[7]

The alliance was spinning out of control. Technically, EDS could act only as an adviser from July 2 until October 18, when the merger was finalized. But GM workers knew the basics of the takeover and suspected worse. "The word got out every way possible and in many cases the wrong way," says Jim Buchanan. "The news media got out ahead of us and started printing stories about EDS, our culture, our management style, that were in many cases gross exaggerations. . . ." EDS could do little. The situation was still fluid. Says Buchanan: "GM managers didn't know who was going to come to EDS and who was not, or which functions would be transferred. . . ."[8] EDS turned to Paul Sims, its industrial relations manager, to win over the sullen GM computer technicians.

Sims breaks every stereotype in the book at EDS. He sports a full beard, for example. A Detroit native, he served in the merchant marine and then worked for the Seafarers International Union as an organizer. EDS found him in Madison, Wisconsin, where he had just hung out his shingle as a lobbyist. After Sims helped EDS solve its political fights, he took over as account manager for the Medicaid project in Milwaukee, and then as EDS's industrial relations specialist.

The fastest way to find the fire in Paul Sims is to call him a union buster. In Sims's view of the world, management and labor are locked in an intricate, formal dance. Management leads. If the bosses are light on their feet and attentive, then everyone smiles and has fun, and unions remain wallflowers. That was a tough sell in Perot's EDS, where unions were the devil, pure and simple. Sims asked for as many transition veterans as other EDS units could spare for his "Operation Hearts and Minds," an effort to show the human face of EDS.

Among the 30 was Pat McAleer, who learned labor law the hard way in California 15 years earlier.

EDS was still fighting a forest fire with a garden hose. Sims would collar Perot, Meyerson, Heller, and Riedlinger for a day at a time and send them out on a tour of three or four GM job sites. Perot was combative. You want a union? he snapped, Fine, send me $3 a month and I'll represent you. It was hard to doubt his resolve or his ability when he promised to make Walter Reuther and John L. Lewis look like choir boys.

Sims cleared a room in the Troy Hilton and moved in PCs and printers. The EDS newsletter, "In Sync," was aimed to spread what news there was about the coming alliance. The black humor specialists at GM renamed it "In Toilet." GM was putting together an 'A' list of people who had to transfer to EDS and a 'B' list of computer/engineers who could transfer if they desired. Furious jockeying went on behind the scenes.

EDS-GM was not just a clash of elitist cultures. It was also a classic confrontation of staff and line employees. EDS's line personnel were paid for the results they produced. GM data processing staff members were paid for the knowledge in their heads. Staff often pursued esoteric objectives, knowledge for the sake of knowledge. Line learned not to waste any motion. Staff believed in seniority; line favored Young Turks. Staff wanted elaborate rules and procedures as an objective measure of performance. Line spurned rules; only results mattered.

It's obvious in that quick comparison why Roger Smith wanted GM to embrace and emulate EDS. Thousands of GM programmers pushed back the frontiers of knowledge, but many others marked time until retirement. Wrapped in the protective cocoon of GM's procedures, and automatically inheriting the fruits of UAW collective bargaining, the "frozen middle" at GM was quite cozy. A high school graduate at GM could earn $45,000 in his prime as a computer operator, work an uneventful 30 years, and retire on a full pension at age 48.

The reorganization had cut loose rafts of staff people with marginal assignments. They wouldn't quit, and it was not the GM way to fire them. They could kill any of Smith's ideas by retreating from them like the Russians from Napoleon until his plans died in an icy indifference. Roger Smith suffered no remorse when he cast 7,800 out of paradise—from 30-and-out to modest pensions, from cost-of-living adjustments to merit raises, period, from GM to EDS. Smith didn't know that EDS's style of nonstop action was the opposite extreme, but he would learn.

GM was not reacting well to the intensity of Ken Riedlinger. He wasn't military like the rest of Perot's Eagles, and he was a relative latecomer, but he was a master of gung ho. A graduate of St. Mary's of the Plains in Kansas, he was a Catholic missionary in South America. He found it hard to sit quietly. He had no time for small talk. Meetings with him never lasted longer than it took to ask the salient questions. He often pushed himself to the point of collapse. Twice, EDS packed him off to the Pritikin Institute in California to recuperate.

Riedlinger won the largest plum account in EDS history because he would move heaven and earth to reach his objective. Results rather than seniority counted at EDS. He prided himself on big thinking and unconventional answers. He could rip through a hundred answers in his head, trying out and discarding most of them. He might try a dozen of them in practice. If all 12 failed, an unfazed Riedlinger would conjure more and renew the attack.

Shotgun problem solving was bizarre enough in Detroit, but some of Riedlinger's answers raised eyebrows simply because of their scale. EDS needs training facilities? Why don't we buy and refit a college? A company-wide celebration? How about a private performance of the circus? Not even Henry Kissinger could have turned around the disgruntled GM workers in months, rather than years; but Riedlinger's flamboyance and direct style became part of the EDS problem.

Open warfare broke out that fall as GM finally put out its list of 'A' personnel and EDS disclosed its plan for shuttering and consolidating computer facilities. In November and December, 14 groups of GM white-collar workers filed union organizing petitions with the National Labor Relations Board.

The petitions asked the NLRB to schedule and supervise an election at the worksite. The petitions couldn't be taken lightly. Unions don't spend money on elections and attorneys unless their straw polls show a majority of the workers in favor of organizing. For the first time, GM faced a real threat of white-collar unionization. In November, 350 white-collar employees filed into the UAW Local 160 hall in Warren, Michigan. In December, 900 workers filled the hall to capacity and spilled out into the parking lot.

Money issues dominated the debate, as they always did in EDS transitions. GM anticipated that the angriest employees would be those who were reassigned to EDS just months shy of retiring under GM's generous pension. EDS benefits would not measure up. GM offered these workers financial incentives to retire early. Naturally, the golden handshake infuriated the next most senior group, the folks who just missed qualifying for it. Two GM veterans who missed the cut sued, alleging that their pensions had been changed arbitrarily in violation of the federal Employees Retirement Income Security Act.

The EDS consolidation created more heat. "We had guys who had worked at the Fisher computer center for years," Sims says. "We pulled the plug on it. We moved half of their functions to Dallas and the other half to Auburn Hills [Michigan] when it was up and running. . . . We said 'All you guys who were here, we have work for you but it's in Auburn Hills or Dallas.'"[9] Fisher, which disappeared in the reorganization in early 1984, had been a particularly prideful corner of GM. There were people at Fisher who had hoped that the GM acquisition in the 1920s would turn out to be temporary. Now the Fisher computer jocks weren't even GM employees. If the UAW had been able to force an election at the Fisher computer center while it still existed, the union would have won hands down.

In theory, petitions to the NLRB freeze conditions at the job site. Management cannot suddenly decide to make the changes workers want. However, if the employer has a business plan underway, he is allowed to proceed. Thus, the petitions could not halt EDS's existing plan to consolidate most of GM's data processing work at two huge information processing centers. The Fisher center closed, along with dozens of others. Riedlinger was the lightning rod. Disgruntled employees slashed his tires, mailed threatening letters, and placed hostile phone calls. EDS assigned guards to his home in Detroit.

Riedlinger fought back. He hired a Cleveland law firm with a reputation for playing hardball with unions. Riedlinger wrote a combative letter on December 10, co-authored by the Cleveland attorneys, promising GM workers that EDS would fight unionization "until total victory is ours." Riedlinger blamed the organizing petitions on "a small number of people [who] are disgruntled or motivated by an intention to get even with GM."

Riedlinger made several bad assumptions. Most of the GM workers were angry, and EDS was very much the target of their wrath. In a second letter in January 1985, Riedlinger asked for a fresh start. He apologized for appearing to be "arrogant or overbearing or uncaring."

The EDS executives who worked with Riedlinger defend him. Riedlinger was not allowed to "do what makes sense" because Perot and Meyerson were second-guessing him constantly. Unions were anathema to Perot; strikes at EDS would be bad for business. The McKinsey consultant working on GM's computer strategy observed, as Heller recalls it, "you know people who come to manage things as controversial like this are riding on the cowcatcher of the train. They are likely to get bumped off and run over."[10]

Riedlinger survived the union crisis. Sims found an attorney who used the time-honored tradition of dragging out the proceedings to the point that most of the petitions were moot when they came to trial. Half were dismissed. The union withdrew the rest. "The union guys would say EDS put their heels in the sand . . . that we elongated the process," says Sims. "I consider that my job. Management needs time. The union wants to do it as quickly as possible because they had to deal with the heat of the moment. I don't even consider it an adversarial process. It's a tactical process."[11]

Riedlinger did get bumped off the cowcatcher. EDS began hiring thousands of trainees and assigning them to GM data processing sites. EDS argued that the process of integration required more manpower, but GM had specific evidence to the contrary. The Fisher design automation computer system cost GM $2 million to operate. Under EDS, it cost $3 million. Albert Lee quoted a disgruntled GM employee at a different job site in his book, *Call Me Roger.* "We used to have 36 people doing this job. Now EDS has 86 and it still can't get the work done." GM wags cracked that EDS stood for "Ever Diminishing Service."

EDS introduced a new euphemism to the alliance to describe EDS expenses in excess of GM budgets: the *cost bubble.* EDS built its own training facilities in a 24-hour, seven-day-per-week forced march. EDS called in the reservists to staff the first 10-week phase of system engineer training. The results were impressive and expensive. By the end of 1985, EDS's 240 recruiters had hired 16,700 employees, most of them college graduates. EDS had added 103 classrooms totaling 282,000 square feet, 85 instructors, 14 computers, and 3,000 sets of a 17-volume videotape library on leadership. EDS also sent out traveling teams of instructors. When recent college graduates filtered out into GM, replacing 25-year veterans, they inspired more black humor. Q: how many EDSers does it take to change a light bulb? A: Don't know; They aren't finishing hiring yet.

Riedlinger lobbied Meyerson for more office space in Detroit. The request seemed well within the range of "whatever it takes." From the Troy Hilton, the First Wave moved to offices at the GM technology center in Warren, and then to the old Bendix headquarters in Southfield. They suffered plenty of hardships. For their first few days in the Bendix building, Riedlinger, Heller, Buchanan, Meler, and the rest of the top brass had a single phone. Riedlinger claimed first priority. Riedlinger's real estate demands set off new alarms nonetheless. Was Riedlinger using his blank check from GM to build an empire?

The basic flaw in the merger's financial structure was out in the open. Roger Smith was perfectly willing to shift his $3 billion data processing budget to EDS and its popular GME stock. He was delighted to substitute relatively low-paid EDS technicians for his own "frozen middle." He wasn't happy at all about the bills EDS was sending him, bills he had no way of controlling.

Unhappier still were the GM managers who lost bonus money because of the EDS shopping spree. For example, when EDS installed phone systems and computers in a GM plant, the expense came out of the plant manager's budget—and his bonus. Often it was doing roughly the same job and billing GM more money than the original internal budget.

The overcharges were simple mathematics. Until GM and EDS could agree on long-term contracts, EDS was to bill GM for its costs plus nine percent. Sometimes EDS was nine percent more efficient than the GM computer staff it replaced, and sometimes it wasn't. When it was less efficient, EDS prospered at the expense of the GM manager's budget and bonus.

GM managers were very sensitive to internal (or transfer) pricing issues. Officially, Fisher Body was scrapped in the reorganization because it held a tacit veto power over the car divisions. By dragging their feet on car designs they didn't like, Fisher executives effectively killed the projects. What rankled the car executives most about Fisher, however, were Fisher bonuses. Fisher's internal charges to the car divisions always seemed to ensure Fisher execs' bonuses. The cheers over Fisher's demise barely had died when a new, arrogant crew turned up with still more transfer pricing.

Long-term, fixed-price contracts were the answer, but they proved to be just a new chapter in the pricing dispute. Once EDS and GM agreed on an annual budget for EDS, GM could tear up its blank check. For its part, EDS could put its cost savings in its own pocket. But no one knew what the costs should be. GM managers also dragged their feet because they did not want to be the first to sign a bad deal with the garrulous Texans.

The contract issue eventually wound up in the lap of GM director, James Evans, chairman of the audit committee. As

Evans pointed out, "GM managers had no place to go except to EDS for these specific services. . . . There was a special need that everyone be protected . . . that they weren't being taken to the cleaners."[12]

Riedlinger was replaced as GM account manager after an EDS board of directors debate on the contract issue in April 1985. Both sides wanted the contracts badly. Smith wanted EDS to bear the expense of all of those thousands of people joining EDS. Perot wanted fixed prices so he could begin to improve EDS profit margins. Finally Smith observed, politely enough, that he hoped Riedlinger wouldn't wind up firing all those people. Riedlinger snapped back at him. His frustration was obvious to everyone. Meyerson called him on the carpet after the meeting. Riedlinger ultimately resigned.

EDS's situation in Detroit deteriorated. When Heller moved his entire technical services operation to Detroit, he stepped right into the middle of a chaotic effort to build a private GM telephone system. After the breakup of AT&T, no single company in the United States had the manpower to pull off such a huge, complex job. The GM operations in Flint were the first to switch over to the new phone system. As the April 1985 deadline neared, AT&T was flying in crews from Florida to work weekends in Flint.

Heller's staff was by no means responsible for the bugs in the Flint phone system, but EDS was blamed. "EDS shouldn't have pulled the switch," says a GM computer engineer reassigned to EDS. Perhaps 30 percent of the phones worked in the AC Delco plant. The Flint engine plant couldn't place a call to its sister facility in Tonawanda, New York. Heller learned the difference between computer problems and phone problems. Five percent down-time in the computer room is acceptable. Even two minutes of telephone outage is a visible and ugly gaffe.

The Flint debacle strengthened the hand of disgruntled GM executives. "I had lots of explaining to do for a good while," says Heller. "It still comes up every now and then. The people who don't like the idea of us don't forget those things."[13] In

May 1985, Heller was hospitalized for a seven-way, coronary artery bypass operation. He was back in Detroit in June, but he paced himself carefully.

Disaster struck next at the GM assembly plant in Hamtramck, Michigan. It was to be a model of factory automation. GM's staff specialists queued up to add their pet projects to the factory plan. The word *kludge* was invented by computer jocks to describe a mismatched system that is considerably less effective than the sum of its parts. GM invented a factory kludge. The paint robots were spraying each other; other robots didn't work at all, and neither did the electronic testing system. Poletown, as Hamtramck is called, was another fine mess EDS strolled into. Mair absolves Perot's troops. "EDS didn't hurt Poletown. If anything, they helped. There were so many new things I don't think there's anyone who would have tried that could have done any better."[14] EDS was abused anyway by GM soreheads looking for an excuse.

Jim Meler, EDS's designated transition man, was on the first plane to Detroit in the summer of 1984. He says, "There were times I would say 'Boy, let me out of here.' I'd leave the building and go for a long walk. I would come home every two weeks or so." Meler's family stayed in Dallas. There was no time for sightseeing. When Meler returned home, "It took me several months for my personality and dealings with my family to be back where it was."[15]

It's not possible to sum up the human costs of the alliance: the shattered retirement plans, the disillusionment of the GM faithful, the strain on the health and marriages of EDS workers. Riedlinger went to work for Ford. Riedlinger's replacement, Kennard Hill, was reduced to a gaunt shadow of himself by a reaggravated Vietnam war injury. Mair and his technical group reluctantly agreed to cooperate with EDS. "It was like directing someone to do something they didn't think they wanted to do," he says.[16]

Heller recovered his strength and his equanimity. Smith made the right decision, Heller says. GM insiders could not have bucked the bureaucracy as EDS did in consolidating GM computers. "If you grew up with it, you know it's impossible to do," he says. "It wasn't until we had been there a year that we had any reasonable appreciation for the magnitude of the task. By then we already had a fairly reasonable approach and were tackling it."[17]

It's easier to quantify the actual costs. EDS billings to GM bulged to $3.2 billion in 1986 before settling back to a steady $2.8 billion. Perot pronounced his Eagles unqualified successes. Smith was more cautious. "I would be willing to say that certainly they did achieve some of their goals. Achieved and surpassed every single objective we have set for them? . . .I would guess that's not quite true."[18] The clash of the titans was about to begin.

CHAPTER TEN

BENCHING THE IMPORT FIGHTER

Outspoken Ross Perot blew into Detroit in 1984 like a cool breeze in a long, hot summer. At auto conventions and banquets, Perot worked the crowds like a politician. Reporters loved his straight answers and country wit. Auto executives and union men admired his unassuming ways. On board at GM, Perot became the house evangelist of cooperation. In a stem-winding speech at a banquet of GM and United Auto Workers (UAW) officials in early 1985, he reminded both groups who their real enemy was. "The biggest thrill in my career will be the day we put cars on a ship and begin selling them in Japan," he says.[1]

As usual, skeptics searched his words for a hidden agenda. Reporters began asking him point blank: Did he want Roger Smith's job? The question hung in the air so pregnantly that Perot finally asked Smith's counsel. Smith told him to ignore it. He knew that Perot simply wanted to see the United States and GM on top again. Smith wanted the same thing. They were partners.

They could not be partners, of course. Both men were focused so narrowly on the task that they missed the larger truth. Perot still had little understanding and zero tolerance of bureaucracies. To him, mid-level resistance was deviant behavior. He couldn't imagine why Smith put up with it. He decided that Smith was ineffectual. For his part, Smith did not understand the consequences of turning loose a natural force like Perot inside GM. GM's bureaucracy would press him to isolate the irritant.

Neither man saw what retired UAW vice president Donald Ephlin did the night of the GM-UAW banquet. "I was struck by the fact that he and Roger were very much alike," Ephlin says. "They were both strong, take-charge kinds of people. The thought occurred to me. Is there room for two?"[2] There was not. Perot would symbolically divorce himself from Smith during a General Motors board meeting on November 4, 1985. Smith hung on for another year, mediating disputes between Perot and GM functionaries, but he paid dearly for it.

The GM bureaucracy was appalled by Perot. He argued correctly that GM was neglecting its obligations to its dealers, customers, and shareholders; the bureaucrats were running the company for themselves. Perot waded into one dispute after another as the advocate of dealers, auto workers, car owners, and shareholders, treading on hundreds of official toes. This wasn't a new Perot. As EDS's spiritual leader, Perot was hardly a passive figurehead. He policed his own company for lapses of faith and punished the guilty.

The aggrieved GM officials had no way of knowing that Perot was just being Perot. In their minds, he was singling them out for high-handedness while ignoring the arrogance of his troops at EDS. They did not appreciate his comments on unreliable GM transmissions and their other shortcomings. They wondered why he did not concentrate instead on getting the phones to work in Flint. (Perot complains that only two people at GM had the gumption to call him about EDS failures. Directness is not a virtue of bureaucracies.)

Perot was certain to raise hackles in the specialized, compartmentalized world of GM. Vice president Alex Mair was ultimately responsible for transmissions. Mair set up a display of disassembled transmissions and prepared a presentation to Perot. Specifically he wanted to ask, "What can electronic data processing do to help this problem?" Perot supposedly was in charge of computers. The battle lines already were drawn before Mair finished so he never invited Perot. Mair does admit, "He was complaining about things that were true."[3]

Again GM misread the EDS founder. Leadership was what Perot had to offer. He volunteered to fight in the new economic war against Japan. He had been mulling over the task back in 1983, when he told the Southern Governors Association, "We must learn to compete and win in international business competition. At this point we are losing . . . while management and labor bicker. We absolutely must form a team between management and labor."[4] He had sold EDS, his creation, to gain this opportunity.

It is understandable why GM middle managers did not recognize Perot as a team builder. Aloud, Perot said that foreign competitors were the enemy, but all of his actions pointed to another villain—GM middle managers. In Perot's monochrome world, the ordinary American individual was the equal of anyone so long as bureaucrats weren't sitting on him. Every time GM executives saw Perot coming, he was carrying his whip and leading an angry group of GM constituents.

The GM groups needed some help. The 20 largest U.S. Cadillac dealers held an angry meeting in Dallas in the summer of 1985. At that point, all of GM's chickens were coming home to roost in their showrooms. GM had dominated the luxury market until the 1980s. Now, just as competition stiffened, GM gave its dealers smaller Cadillacs that looked too much like their Buick and Oldsmobile cousins. Worse, they were often poorly built. It was these dealers who sent Perot out checking under GM cars for puddles of transmission fluid.

The Cadillac dealers invited GM top executive Robert Stempel and director Ross Perot to that meeting. Perot wanted to hear more about their problems. At one point, Perot asked them whether GM's surveys of all Cadillac dealers backed up their complaints. He was horrified to learn that GM didn't poll its dealers regularly; in fact, it never polled them at all. A red-faced Stempel learned how painful it was to be the goat at a Perot barbeque. Smith himself would learn later that summer.

Perot also rode to the defense of the United Auto Workers at the Arlington, Texas, assembly plant. GM wanted to close the facility in a retrenchment. One day, the union squired Perot around the facility and treated him to a dinner of red beans and rice. Perot came away with another piece of the puzzle. GM plant management was mistreating its workers to the point that product quality suffered.

Quibblers could note that several decades of union intransigence contributed to the hostile working environment, but they would miss the point. The unions saw the danger of foreign competition and wanted cooperation. GM's "frozen middle" did not. Perot urged the Arlington local to offer concessions to GM and lobbied GM to listen. Both sides profited from Perot's advice. The workers kept their jobs. GM got a better contract.

Car owners got satisfaction too. It's not unusual for GM directors to hear complaints about cars. Perot alone waded in to get to the bottom of them. He went so far as to rent a specially equipped car for a paraplegic in Massachusetts who couldn't keep his GM vehicle running. North American car chief Lloyd Reuss asked Perot to disconnect his one-man action line. He sent Perot a list of the telephone numbers and addresses of GM customer service representatives. Perot reluctantly agreed to refer the complaints. He warned Reuss that he didn't want to hear that GM was responding with form letters.

In retrospect, it was foolish for GM to rein in Perot over turf issues. His heart was in the right place. To have an ombudsman/director was great public relations and a good example for the ranks. But again GM employees were puzzled by the difference between what Perot said and what he did.

Perot made extraordinary territorial demands of his own. He wanted EDS left just as it was, period. Smith thought there was no danger in agreeing; he didn't want EDS to change. But the turf struggles started almost at once. Perot was angry when the New York Stock Exchange changed its stock symbol from EDS to GME. He complained again when GM preempted EDS and announced its subsidiary's earnings. Perot argued that EDS was a proven brand name and needed to be seen as independent. However, his demands could be interpreted as imperial.

Incentive stock, a holy doctrine at EDS, touched off the next confrontation. Perot wanted to grant 7 million shares of stock to the warriors leading the charge at GM, a potential $280 million to be split by about 1,000 EDS workers. From Perot's perspective, the awards made sense. His troops had never before tackled a transition as tough as this one. The situation called for heavy-duty gold handcuffs. The huge award was harder to justify on results because the EDS team was off to a shaky start.

Smith didn't argue about performance or results. He never really looked past the $280 million sum. It was more than EDS earned in 1985. "I told Ross I would need not to submit that to the General Motors incentive compensation committee. . . . I felt it would have been damaging to the relationship to propose something as ridiculous as that."[5] Smith vetoed the request by sticking it in his pocket.

Smith was venturing out onto thin ice in his relationship with Perot. The merger agreement said specifically, "All new EDS compensation decisions and employee benefits will continue to be made by the board of directors and management of new EDS." What that really meant, Smith was now saying, is that "matters of individual compensation are decided by [EDS] . . . except for maybe the very top two men." But the GM board decides how big the compensation pool will be.[6]

The GM chairman's reconstruction of the merger agreement was a nice bit of legal spin. He was welshing nonetheless. Perot made it perfectly clear to him why he wanted to keep control of compensation issues and how stock awards made EDS unique. The sole reason for creating GME shares was to preserve Perot's ability to reward performance at EDS in a way that put management and shareholders in the same boat. What Smith had not anticipated was how enthusiastically Perot would exert his rights.

Smith also missed the crime of omission in the merger. GM managers and their shareholders were not in the GME boat. The agreement gave EDS managers in Detroit the exclusive right to provide data processing services to GM. The profits those managers secured for EDS, without competition, held out the promise to them of a fortune in EDS stock. GM workers knew from reading the merger prospectus that many EDS executives were already millionaires. The $280 million award would send up howls of protest. "No one in GM could come close to having this kind of compensation," says former GM general counsel Elmer W. Johnson. "The EDS people. . . I think were perceived by GM people as pressing their right to autonomy to the point where it means nearly that they could dictate price terms."[7]

Perot knew that GM management would be envious of the stock bonuses. He also knew that GM would object to EDS pricing practices regardless of whether EDS was able to save GM money. Many EDS customers eventually complained. While he and Smith were negotiating the merger, Perot telecopied his reservations about the deal to Detroit. Smith collected them and responded in a memo:

PEROT:

> General Motors will own both EDS and GM. There is no conflict in allowing a fair profit to be earned by EDS for work done within GM.

SMITH:

> I agree and this is what we propose.

PEROT:

> . . . It is important to keep in mind that GM/EDS is so small compared to GM that the profit EDS is paid for its work to GM that allows GM/EDS to keep its high [price-earnings] multiple has an insignificant impact on GM profitability.

SMITH:

> I agree. . . . But a proper and reasonable EDS profit is important to all of us and is not "insignificant."

PEROT:

> The GM bonus and incentive plans for its divisions could create a negative attitude toward allowing GM/EDS to make a profit. This concern should be addressed.

SMITH:

> Not so. EDS profits will be included in overall GM bonus calculation. This is not a problem.

Perot also talked to Smith about the opposite reaction—the hostility that the EDS stock awards might create inside GM against the "rich Texans". Smith acknowledges, "I think we were concerned that the people . . . [with whom EDS] had to deal day to day might have that perception, yes."[8] Smith didn't think it would be a big problem.

Again, Smith failed to recognize that Perot came from a different world. If EDS was performing 1 percent of U.S. data processing, for example, it could afford to be extraordinarily generous to the people responsible for pushing its market share to 1.1 percent. GM in 1984 already owned over 40 percent of American car sales. Its primary focus was to ration the rewards and to keep greed in check. To Smith, compensation was a question of fairness. How well did the employee perform? Should he earn more or less than the going rate for his job? Smith didn't need handcuffs. GM employees seldom quit.

Perot didn't delve into his philosophy of compensation in the fax exchanges. He made a simple declaration:

PEROT:

> All EDS compensation decisions and employee benefits will continue to be made by Perot and Meyerson.

SMITH:

> I agree.

Unable to budge Smith during the spring and summer of 1985, Perot invited the GM chairman to come to Dallas. Smith could tell the Eagles himself why their incentive stock awards were too generous. "Town meetings," Perot called these sessions. The New Englanders who still tend their civic affairs in mass meetings would not have recognized Perot's variant. Perot wasn't searching for a consensus. He knew what he wanted done. The meetings were designed to demonstrate to holdouts how lonely their positions were. Each of the EDS officers was to make a presentation. EDS held a rehearsal the day before the meeting. Smith, a small man lugging an oversized briefcase, strolled into an ambush on September 3, 1985.

One by one, the EDS executives stood to make their case. Senior vice president William Gayden went straight to the heart of EDS's complaints. When Perot's attorneys questioned Smith under oath, the chairman described Gayden's comments this way:

SMITH:

> Mr Gayden did not talk about SIP shares. He said that we had been responsible for one of his best friend's divorce, for one of his best friends being discharged and for one of his best friends . . . having a heart attack.

ATTORNEY:

> We being . . .

SMITH:

> Me.

ATTORNEY:

> You personally?

SMITH:

> Yes, sir.

ATTORNEY:

> How had you done that?

SMITH:

> I had not done that, and I told him that.

Smith kept his composure until EDS chief financial officer Thomas Walter went to the board to try some new math on Smith. Senior vice president Gary Fernandes recalls, "You can't trick Roger with numbers. He nailed Tom right to the wall. He was right on. That was the end of the numbers."[9] Smith flew into one of his technicolor rages. For what seemed to be an eternity, Smith ranted about his treatment in the meeting. He had expected a dialogue, not an ambush.

The meeting resumed gingerly. Afterward, Perot drove Smith back to the airport. "I told Mr Perot I was very upset and disappointed that I would come all the way down to Dallas and have a personal attack [made on me] in a meeting . . . on an important subject. And Mr Perot apologized . . . and said, 'You know, I hope that the comments by Gayden, I would not take [them] too seriously.'"[10]

With lawyer Johnson's help, Smith wrote a letter to Perot the day after the meeting. He held out an offer of repeating 1984 EDS stock awards, which amounted to $34 million granted to 132 people. Smith wrote that he was bucking his finance staff who wanted to apply the five-year average of $14.5 million and 121 recipients. Smith wrote:

> I am disappointed that your people cannot understand that conditions can change . . . and that we must all change with [them]."

Perot and Smith compromised on that SIP crisis—Perot was allowed a last, large award—but the compensation issue never went away. In early 1986, GM balked at EDS cash bonuses totaling $18.5 million for approximately 1,200 employees. This time GM appeared on shaky ground. GM compensation chief Greg Lau compared the bonus sum to EDS's five previous programs ranging from $3 million to $6 million and involving 380 to 550 people. But the EDS workforce had tripled since the merger.

Johnson had been bothered from the start by the potential conflict between GME shareholders and GM common shareholders. He saw his own data processing budgets increase.

When he asked his subordinate department heads why, they told him they had no choice but to pay what EDS demanded. Could GM shareholders argue that management was allowing a transfer of wealth from GM to GME? GM first established an oversight committee of outside directors to review EDS business with GM. Along with the New York law firm of Weil Gotshal & Manges, Johnson began work on what was to be known as the "peace treaty."

It had four parts. The first was to give Perot a formal mandate as automaking troubleshooter. Perot and vice chairman Don Atwood were to study GM's operating problems and develop solutions and a timetable. The second part created a clear chain of command over EDS; Les Alberthal would answer to GM president Jim McDonald. Both men had reputations as low-key, fair-minded executives. McDonald was also the final authority on EDS disputes that did not require the attention of the oversight committee. Meyerson was to be his EDS contact. Finally, GM endorsed an eight-point action plan drafted by Meyerson and aimed at breaking the contract deadlocks.

Johnson presented the peace treaty to Perot on November 3, 1985, the day before the GM board meeting. Meyerson took charge of the meeting and moved through the eight points of his plan. Perot was not excited by it. He didn't want to waste time developing a computer strategy for GM or pricing protocols. Perot was interested in his new role as troubleshooter. He showed Johnson the speech he was going to make the following day, a broad attack on GM. Johnson notes, "I said 'I guess if I were you I might temper it a bit by saying something nice about somebody."[11] Perot penciled in comments praising McDonald, Atwood, and executive vice president Alex Cunningham as the finest car executives around. Smith was conspicuous by his absence.

Ostensibly Perot was urging the GM board to stop the Hughes acquisition. But the GM board had already approved it, so accomplishing his objective was difficult at best. The issue on the agenda that day was a housekeeping change in the GM charter necessary to finish the deal. Perot quickly came to his real point:

> Recently I visited with some of our Cadillac dealers. Please keep in mind that these dealers sell our top-of-the-line luxury cars. Here's what they had to say about our Cadillacs. The engine is underpowered. The transmission is unreliable and getting worse. The air conditioner compressor is defective. In the past 18 months they have gone to two shifts in the service department to keep up with the repair work. Because of the transmission problems, one dealer has gone from one repairman to five repairmen working two shifts.
>
> Finally I said, "Well if I could just do one thing for you fellows, what would you want me to do?"
>
> One dealer spoke up and said, "Get me a Honda dealership."
>
> Our core problem is that the GM system is too centralized. Very little responsibility and authority is given to experienced, talented executives and managers. GM is procedures-oriented rather than results-oriented. Too much time is spent in unproductive meetings. Matters that would take minutes or hours to resolve in a normal business environment take weeks, months, or may never reach decisions in GM. . . .
>
> The strongest indictment of our current methods is the Japanese. They come half way around the world with a completely different culture [but they] build factories in our country, hire UAW workers at union scale . . . build better, more reliable cars and get higher productivity. Toyota is generally considered to be the finest large volume car builder in the world. . . . One phrase best summarizes Toyota's success, the company slogan: "Every employee is a brother." Contrast this simple theme with words like "management," "labor" and "hourly worker" used so frequently in Detroit. . . .
>
> As stewards of one of the world's largest corporations, whose future success can dramatically impact the lives of several million people and the economy of the United States, I urge each of my fellow board members to think about the following ideas. We need to become more active in understanding what is really happening inside General Motors. If GM is to change it must change at the top, and we are the top. . . .

As board members, we must send a clear signal to the corporation that the shareholders are not simply a nuisance to be dealt with at annual meetings and avoided whenever possible. They own this company. We must make it clear that the management serves at the pleasure of the shareholders, and must not act as owners simply . . . because there is no concentration of ownership. Corporate America has a peculiar process that we must recognize. The managers of mature corporations . . . have gotten themselves into the position of effectively selecting the board members who will represent the shareholders. In this environment, the directors must be particularly sensitive to the stockholders, our owners.

Last Friday, I requested a meeting with the outside directors. This request was denied. I now make a request as a fellow director for a meeting with the outside directors at a time convenient to you. . . .

. . . Toyota . . . recovered from near bankruptcy. Fortunately, we are not in that position. I am concerned that our corporate wealth gives us a sense of false security. We must generate a sense of urgency while we are still strong. We can be the finest car company in the world. . . . The directors of GM must provide the vision and the leadership to move boldly toward that goal. Thank you. I request that the board vote on the issue outlined in my speech.[12]

Silence greeted him, silence and blank faces. The board did not schedule a meeting of outside directors. Smith thanked him for his remarks. Director Thomas Murphy, Smith's mentor and immediate predecessor, noted pointedly that the Hughes deal was not on the table. The board had already approved the acquisition, and Perot had supported it then. Smith moved on to new business.

Perot's call to arms on the Hughes transactions was a mistake, in 20/20 hindsight. Having failed to light a fire under GM management, he had hoped to enlist the board. The board could force Smith to begin addressing GM's problems with quality, leadership, and bureaucracy. Instead, he tossed another lighted bomb in the laps of his fellow directors. GM now had a Ross problem.

Time and again, Perot would fall into this trap. Nothing frustrated him more than inaction. He knew he was dead right in his analysis of GM, and so did everyone else in that teak-paneled boardroom. What he didn't understand was how difficult it was to effect a cure. As an outsider, Perot was not burdened by GM's history. When he took up the dealers' cause, for example, he didn't understand, or chose to ignore, that franchise relationships can resemble difficult marriages. Some of the directors in that room reacted to him as if had sat down at their dinner table as a guest and had sided with their wives in a long-running argument.

Perot touched unknowingly on the problem. GM was still rich. The crisis was not imminent. It was not imperative that the people in that board room confess their guilt, swear off their petty differences, and begin building bridges. Patience and tolerance are the peacetime tools needed to bury 50-year-old hatchets and build new relationships. Perot is not blessed with either of those qualities. That's what alarmed GM directors. After only a year on the GM board, Perot was presenting them with a black-and-white choice. Were they going to be management stooges or fellow revolutionaries?

There's more painful history here. Liability is not taken lightly in American board rooms. Even Perot walked around EDS muttering that his personal wealth made him the best target on the GM board. When Perot and GM finally broke out of each other's grasp a year later, shareholders would file no less than 15 suits. Perot's buyout agreement obliged GM to defend him and to pick up the tab for adverse judgments.

Perot's slap at professional managers didn't sit well either. The outside directors were professional managers and CEOs: John Smale of Procter and Gamble, James Robinson of American Express; Edmund Pratt of Pfizer; and James Evans, the retired chairman of Union Pacific. Tom Murphy was not only a retired GM chairman, but also an architect of the GM management system. Professional managers had been heroes back in the days when widows bought utility bonds for safety and the GM dividend was money in the bank. Those days are gone, this business aristocracy would have to admit, and the culprit is, pick one: OPEC, Japan, unions, stupid government policy. Not many of them can admit that the system is failing also. They are the system.

There wasn't a moment of doubt about where the board's sympathies lay, or more importantly, where its fingerprints could be found. Directors had elected Smith, afterall. If they had chosen to fire Smith for a botched acquisition of EDS, to name a strong case as of November 1985, shareholders' attorneys would find that the board had approved the deal unanimously. The board had welcomed a revolutionary into the royal chambers. They were learning how dangerous it was to have Ross Perot as an enemy.

CHAPTER ELEVEN

DOWN AND DIRTY

Ross Perot in the full flush of righteous anger looks like a bird of prey. He doesn't lose control as Roger Smith did in that September officers' meeting, but that fact makes his wrath more devastating. Smith's tantrums cause people to stare at the floor and wonder how to overcome this embarrassment. Perot's anger evokes fear. The thin lips, the unblinking eyes, the intervening beak, this is what a field mouse sees in its final moments.

EDS managers knew that Perot would not tolerate mistakes. He would lead them into an adjoining room before reprimanding them or call them into his office later, because a leader doesn't discipline his troops in public. The encounters were aversion therapy at its finest. Texas school teachers also saw this Perot. He asked for their thoughts during the investigative phase of his campaigns for school reform. After the solution was clear to him, he forced them to decide: friend or foe? All his fights polarize people. Writers call this the dark side of Perot, usually when they disagree with him. But there's nothing inherently good or evil in Perot's full-tilt prosecution. Perot is implacable, relentless Perot.

Perot is not unique among charismatics for this tendency to leap first. Sir Winston Churchill as home secretary once raced to the seedy side of London to take personal charge of a police siege of four desperadoes. Churchill's unrestrained zeal was the principal reason Britons retired him shortly after World War II. By definition, holy warriors are not reasonable people.

This chapter tells the stories of two men who faced the full fury of Perot, Texas bureaucrat Arnold Ashburn and law school student Jan C. Scruggs. The point of it is not to decide whether Ashburn was right or wrong when he tried to take the Texas Medicaid contract away from EDS in 1980, but rather if he should have been subjected to investigations by the press, his own department, the state's attorney general, and the FBI. He got a clean bill of health, but EDS got back its contract.

Scruggs, a cofounder of the Vietnam Veterans' Memorial Fund (VVMF), faced Perot when the Texan objected to the design of the memorial and questioned the fund's finances. Scruggs had solicited $170,000 from Perot. The General Accounting Office ultimately exonerated the fund of improprieties. Roger Smith had heard both of these tales by the end of 1985; they explain why the GM chairman proceeded as cautiously as he did.

The Texas Medicaid fight began in an emergency organizing session at EDS. Perot was vacationing in London when he learned that the state Health and Rehabilitative Services board had picked rival Bradford National Corporation to take over EDS's seminal account. This was the Medicaid system that Meyerson and his jumpsuit-clad programmers had put together over Christmas in 1967 and that EDS wrested away from Texas Blue Cross in 1974. Perot immediately boarded a jet and took charge by single-sideband radio. A small team of EDS executives waited for him in Dallas. They shed their other duties. They would focus on this problem until it was over—win or lose.

The question of right or wrong wasn't on the table. Perot assumed EDS would not lose a fair competition. EDS executives didn't dare raise the question. Eavesdroppers outside the third-floor conference room heard him shouting, I want to find the son of a bitch who let this happen and get him out of the company!

There were some reasons to be suspicious. Bradford National had bobbled New York state's Medicaid contract and had a lackluster reputation on Wall Street. Meyerson had investigated it as an acquisition target the year before and decided against it. The EDS team simply assumed that EDS would not legitimately lose a bid to Bradford.

Les Alberthal and the other executives working on the bid were elbowed aside. "We, quote, weren't doing what needed to be done to win the business," he says. Alberthal was happy to be out of it. "There's a procedure you use when you think you have been wronged in a contract," he adds. "That wasn't the means Perot used. He got into a holy war with Bradford, and basically out-muscled them."[1] The new team split up. One group began looking for skeletons in Bradford's closets. The second scoured Texas government for Bradford's unknown allies. Perot and Meyerson flew off to meet each of three board members personally. Rancher Hilmar Johnson, restaurateur Raul Jimenez, and attorney Terry Bray were no match for the persuasive Perot. They agreed to reconsider. Perot sued to stop the board's earlier award to Bradford.

The dispute centered on the complex question of which bid was lower. The EDS bid was higher than Bradford's for the data processing part of the contract, but lower for the first year's insurance premium. Since flu epidemics and recessions have a large bearing on the insurance risk, the state rebids that part of the contract in each of the four remaining years. The state assumed EDS was deliberately understating the first year's premium and hoping to make it up in the remaining years. The bid panel declared Bradford the low bidder and ruled that the companies were equally competent.

Indignities began raining immediately on Arnold Ashburn, the bid panel's chairman. Ashburn's boss, deputy commissioner Wesley Hjornevik stepped in to review the panel's work line by line. "It was clear the shit was going to hit the fan," says Hjornevik, a veteran NASA administrator. "It would have been a real blow for [EDS executives] to lose their home state."[2] Hjornevik agreed with the panel that Bradford was the low bidder.

However, he was troubled by the findings in the competence phase of the evaluation. "I found situations where both contractors had proposed acceptable ways of doing X, and Bradford was rated higher," he explains. Ashburn and many of the panel members dealt with the EDS people daily. When Hjornevik asked the panel members why they gave Bradford the benefit of the doubt, he says, "they would haul out the old contract and say. . . . 'We've been hassling these guys for four years to do this. We don't like to be dealt with this way.' EDS preaches an elitism. . . . Our people who were supervising the EDS contract found this superiority complex very grating."[3] Hjornevik decided that the bias didn't matter since Bradford had won on price. He reassigned Ashburn out of harm's way.

EDS also had noticed Ashburn's attitude. Deposing Ashburn some months later, EDS attorneys explored whether Ashburn wanted Bradford to fail so that the state could take over processing, or whether he felt he could justify hiring more staff to supervise Medicaid with Bradford as the contractor. The darker theories, that Bradford had influenced Ashburn illegally, were explored first by HRS investigators, normally the state's welfare fraud cops, and then by state and federal officials. They found nothing.

EDS operatives had better luck finding Bradford skeletons. Data processing contractors live in a small world. EDS knew that the navy was investigating Bradford for alleged billing irregularities and that the U.S. Attorney was looking into Bradford's business as well. These investigations were news, however, to the Texas newspapers and syndicated columnists, all of whom wrote of the widening Bradford mess.

The nadir of this campaign was a Fort Worth television station's investigative series. Kenneth Riedlinger had flushed out New York bureaucrat Michael Diem, who formerly supervised the Bradford National contract. Bradford had struck a $185,000 consulting deal with Management Circle, Inc., incorporated by D. E. Connors, then Diem's girlfriend, while

Diem was still employed by the state. Diem also declared that Bradford wanted him to spy on EDS.

The television station filmed meetings covertly so its five-part series had a gritty texture of authenticity. But the report was speculative at best when it wondered out loud what sins Bradford committed in Texas, and when it called Ashburn "a flunky." The television report hewed to Perot's side of the argument exactly. In other brawls, including the clash with GM, Perot would demonstrate his genius at making allies of reporters.

Mudslinging is a predictable feature of Perot missions. In mild form, Perot tweaks his enemies in the press with one of his patented jibes. Bradford National's chairman, Peter Del Col, ventured once or twice to cross swords with Perot in print. Perot snapped in response, "I wouldn't hire that guy to clean out the chicken house."[4] At this level, the clever insults can be explained away as tactics, and perhaps as a natural consequence of Perot's tendency toward overstatement.

But there's plenty of evidence that Perot takes his fights personally. Those who disagree with him are dismissed invariably as flawed witnesses. In the Bradford fight, EDS contended in press releases that one of Bradford's expert witnesses had a financial stake in Bradford, and that another worked for an Oklahoma public health official "who has spoken publicly on several occasions about her hatred for Ross Perot." Perhaps Perot is justified in dividing the world into people who love him and people who despise him. People react strongly to his personality.

The recurring conspiracy themes are harder to explain. Readers will recognize the charge that Ashburn wanted private contractors to fail so that he could expand his bureaucratic empire. Perot suspected the Social Security Administration of conspiring to the same end. Later Perot would accuse GM functionaries of a power grab, and he would suspect the Defense Department of covering up the existence of prisoners of war in Southeast Asia. Perot believes in conspiracies. Many people do in the antigovernment, antiestablishment piney woods in east Texas.

Nor would anyone inside that charismatic organization, EDS, find it odd that every situation is defined in terms of us and them. "This was almost a Ross Perot genetic disposition. If you are in a fight with someone . . . find the dirt," says EDS general counsel Richard Shlakman. Perot assumes that opposition to him is not only wrong, but corrupt. Shlakman concludes, "If you disagree with him on holy writ, then you're evil."[5]

Bradford was fading fast under Perot's attack. He was devastating in public forums. Acting HRS commissioner Marlin Johnston recalls a Perot appearance before the board, or to be precise, with the board behind him. He set up his lectern to face the audience and held forth for 20 minutes, his back to the board members. Perot also produced star witness Richard Schermerhorn, a New York state senator who claimed that Bradford could barely handle its New York contract and didn't need any more challenges.

The final day of the television exposé ended on an anticlimactic note. Consultants for the accounting firm Touche Ross told the HRS board that there was no evidence of wrongdoing in the bid evaluation. But Touche Ross also agreed with EDS that superior computer controls could lower the insurance cost and perhaps make Bradford's the higher bid after all. The consultants urged the state to change the way it handles Medicaid. The board threw out both bids and hired EDS to handle the program on an interim basis. The state paid Bradford $3.1 million to go away.

Hjornevik had resigned back when the controversy was just a month old. It was clear then what the board thought, and the board ran the department. Hjornevik says he finds nothing wrong in a Texans-first preference in state bidding, so long as the bid proposals spell it out beforehand. There's an unwritten preference today. "After what happened," says Hjornevik, "nobody's going to spend a half million [dollars] to participate in the bid competition."[6] And no one did until Perot Systems challenged EDS in 1988.

Ashburn salvaged his career in a different part of the agency, now called the Department of Human Services. It took me several weeks to reach him by phone. His words were rushed, and I could hear him inhale when he stopped for a breath. He rattled off the agencies that had investigated him in 1980. He wanted nothing like that experience again. He wanted nothing to do with me.

Not surprisingly, Scruggs also declined an interview request. Before the Vietnam Veterans Memorial controversy died out, Scruggs faced off against Perot, various attorneys, and a television investigative reporter. Because the fund was particularly vulnerable to public opinion, Perot scored points against Scruggs with two of his other favorite persuasive devices—the town hall meeting and the plebiscite. Scruggs is older and wiser. He isn't reopening old wars.

Scruggs hoped that the Vietnam memorial would heal old wounds. He ventured the idea for a Vietnam veterans' memorial during an organizing meeting for a Washington-area Vietnam veterans week. Scruggs was hooted down. The veterans at that meeting were more interested in self-help programs and government benefits. Attorney Robert W. Doubek sought out Scruggs afterward and offered to incorporate the fund for him.

As Scruggs envisioned the project, grassroots support for the memorial would finally recognize the sacrifice made by Vietnam veterans. One of the rules in the design competition would dictate that the memorial make no political statement about the war. Scruggs and Doubek hoped it would transcend the continuing division of hawks and doves. A third founder joined that summer, attorney and West Point graduate John P. Wheeler.

Doubek made the first contact with Perot. The fund was looking for prominent names for its national sponsoring committee. "He asked me, 'You're not those kooky Vietnam veterans, are you?'" Doubek recalls.[7] He answered no. Perot said that he had made a standing offer to President Jimmy Carter to fund a memorial, but he would not get involved until he knew what the memorial looked like. Nevertheless, when Scruggs called Perot a few weeks later asking for money to test a direct mail campaign, Perot contributed $10,000. Scruggs

called Perot regularly through 1980 and invited him to the
signing ceremony July 1 making the memorial law.

In March 1981 Scruggs asked Perot to underwrite the
design competition. Perot would say later that Scruggs called
him in desperation. Without $160,000 from him, in Perot's
version, the fund could not go forward. Doubek suspects that
Scruggs did plead with Perot. The fund was following a classic
fundraising strategy: land the big contributor by asking him
to support some vital part of the project and then use that big
gift as moral leverage on other potential donors. Actually, the
fund had $800,000 in the bank.

The fund sponsors and dignitaries gathered May 6, 1981,
in a hangar at Andrews Air Force Base to unveil the winning
design. "We all gulped and clapped our hands," says Doubek.[8]
The design was startlingly, starkly modern. The design winner, 21-year-old Yale student Maya Ying Lin, had succeeded
in making it a neutral memorial.

As modern as it is, its concept is as old as the Greeks who
gave us the word *cenotaph,* a monument to people whose remains are elsewhere. Two black granite walls start at ground
level and gradually sink 10 feet below grade before meeting
in a shallow vee. The names of all the war's casualties are
engraved on the wall in the order in which they died.

The fund claims Perot called Scruggs and divorced himself
from the project after he saw a rendition of the wall in *The
Navy Times* a week later. The memorial was not for the sur-
vivors of the Vietnam war, he said. (Perot denies he said this.)
Conservative veterans reached the same conclusion.

These men were the other half of the Vietnam war's bitter
harvest. Unlike Perot's "kooky" vets, who felt that they were
harmed mentally in an immoral war and shunned afterward,
these veterans were angry that they had not been allowed to
win. Later that May, a group of them gathered to discuss two
Public Broadcasting System documentaries which they believed portrayed Vietnam vets as deranged baby-killers. During that meeting, veteran Tom Carhart stood up and lamented
the Vietnam memorial.

The old wounds were ripped open again. The veterans thought the wall's vee shape was a mocking allusion to the hippies' two-fingered antiwar salute. To be below ground level was to bury war and its horrors. The granite was black because the war was a national disgrace. Carhart, a passionate, articulate West Pointer provided the rallying cry this time. The wall, he said, "was a black gash of shame and sorrow."

Carhart and Milton Copulos, a writer from the Heritage Foundation, a conservative think tank, fired the opening media salvos in a losing campaign to change the memorial design. Doubek, Scruggs, and Wheeler began receiving a daily ration of hate mail, but the memorial was moving ahead anyway. The Fine Arts Commission held hearings in November and December and approved the wall. A steady procession of veterans paraded through Perot's office in Dallas. By November, he could no longer remain on the sidelines. He called Scruggs and asked for Carhart's telephone number.

Public relations manager Bill Wright read Perot's reentry into the controversy as noblesse oblige. Carhart later referred to Perot as the "godfather of Vietnam veterans," a role that Perot himself clearly relishes. He adopted the 1,400 POWs who came home from Vietnam in 1973. He threw two parties for them that year and offered jobs to some. The POW group stayed close with periodic parties. Of the thousands of Christmas cards that flood the Perot household each year, the POW families send the majority. Perot feted POW Robinson Risner when he retired from the air force. During the ceremony, Perot arranged for a flyover of every combat craft that General Risner flew in his 30-year career.

Perot is not an ideologue about Vietnam. He agrees with the liberal vets: Returning servicemen were treated shabbily. He agrees with the hardliners also: The United States defeated itself in Southeast Asia. Perot learned his lesson. When conservative groups approach him about supporting the Contras in Nicaragua, he sends them packing. He tells them to come back when they can prove to him that America will fight to win in Central America.

Unknown to the fund, Perot had hired the Gallup organization to design an opinion poll about the memorial. Perot
had EDS mail the questionnaire to the POWs as a informal
test. The replies flooded in; Perot's POWs didn't like the wall
either. He called Scruggs on December 11 to issue his ultimatum: Change the design or face a public fight. On December
15, he threatened in an Associated Press article to proceed
with the Gallup poll and expose the memorial for the unpopular "trench" that it was.

Scruggs capitulated. Senator John Warner agreed to me-
diate a compromise. The fund and its critics were to meet in
a Senate hearing room on January 27. Secretary of the Interior
James Watt underscored the fund's precarious position. He
called Doubek in January to emphasize the importance of a
compromise. Doubek happened to be holding a request for a
building permit that needed Watt's signature. He asked Watt
about it. "Watt says, I think you can guess what would happen
to it today," Doubek says.[9] Copulos had enlisted Watt's support.

The fund met Perot and his contingent at the architect's
offices the day before the summit. The review of the memorial
model was as frosty as the Senate meeting was hot. Perot,
Risner, and Sybil Stockdale, wife of POW Admiral James
Stockdale, walked around it grim-faced. Says Doubek, "It was
like trying to talk to a bunch of posts."[10] Mrs. Stockdale was
interested in credentials. She wanted to know if the fund founders served in Vietnam. Well then, were they in combat?

The meeting the next day was grim. Every time the color
of the granite came up, a black army general shouted at the
critics that they were racists. The critics accused the fund of
imposing the memorial on veterans against their wishes. The
fund saw the critics as interlopers. Scruggs lost his composure,
much as Roger Smith did in 1985. "This is all rehearsed," he
shouted. "We could have brought hundreds of our veterans,
volunteers, and Gold Star mothers, . . . Where were you during the last three years? Why didn't you help?"[11] Perot, of
course, could answer that he did help. In fact, he saved the
design competition.

The group reached a compromise. A flag and statue would add a heroic counterpoint to the wall. At a second meeting in March, the critics, still outnumbering the fund, voted by show of hands to place the flag dead center above the juncture of the walls and the statue centered in the angle below. Perot brought up the last item on his agenda. The names should be arranged alphabetically rather than chronologically. Wheeler promised to prepare a presentation on the issue and closed the meeting. The fund did make the presentation, but not to Perot.

From this point, the fund and the Fine Arts Commission set about excluding Perot. They drew the line on artistic grounds. They didn't want the wall, as Doubek put it, to become a pedestal for the flag and a backdrop for the statue. They objected on principle. As Doubek wrote later, "we had no moral—and perhaps even legal right—to make such changes."[12] Indeed, a distraught Maya Lin already had hired an attorney. They feared for the project. If the memorial effort collapsed in a deadlock of doves and hawks, the memorial would be dead for years.

The fund pushed ahead on its own. It created an entrance to the wall to feature the flag and statue. Their opponents were furious that the fund broke ground in March before the placement issues had been settled. The opponents cried foul again when the wall was dedicated on Veteran's Day in 1982 without the statue. Conservative congressmen tried in the final days of Congress to relocate the flag and statue by law. But the critics had lost.

Conspiracy theories cropped up early. Within months of organized opposition, before Perot's reentry, reports circulated describing one of the design judges as a communist and a few of the others as antiwar advocates. It was easy to paint the memorial as a theft of the war by the effete Eastern establishment from the ordinary Americans who actually fought it. Copulos says today, "I have always thought the judging was rigged. That's my perception."[13]

Perot apparently had other suspicions. He began pressing the fund for the right to audit its books. After the fund rebuffed several verbal requests, Perot put his demands in writing in a May 7 letter to Jack Wheeler. His letter reminded the fund officers that they were fiduciaries of public money, and that he was a major patron of the memorial. Perot portrayed an audit as a routine demand he would make of EDS subsidiaries and charities that he supported. Other philanthropic groups had acquiesced, he wrote. However, when the fund pressed Perot emissary Richard Shlakman for names and dates, the EDS attorney was unable to provide any. Surely, Roger Smith and the Social Security Administration would have snorted at the righteous tone of Perot's letter.

Shlakman renewed Perot's request in a meeting with the fund on September 17 in Washington. Shlakman offered a compromise. Perot would settle for a copy of the fund's disbursement journal, which listed the checks the fund had written. Shlakman declined to divulge what misdeeds Perot suspected. Like an 800-pound gorilla, Shlakman told the fund representatives, Perot sleeps where he wants. In a letter to Shlakman that day, Williams & Connolly attorney Steven M. Umin rebuked the EDS attorney for failing to deliver the de-escalation that he had promised. Umin wrote that the fund would not respond to veiled accusations.

Shlakman called three days later with a second compromise. If the fund allowed Peat Marwick to audit receipts and disbursements, Perot would pay. A second Williams & Connolly attorney summarized the conversation in a memo to the fund dated September 21, 1982. Perot had authorized legal action if the fund did not acquiesce, Shlakman had said. While Shlakman couldn't say what form the suit would take, the attorney ventured that it might be filed by a group of veterans and that it could draw the attention of investigative reporters.

The fund declined again and braced for the storm. It set up a special independent audit committee made up of corporate heavyweights, including GM director Ed Pratt. The fund turned over the books, a history of the running feud, and Perot's audit demands. It was the committee's job to offset Perot influence in the business community if the storm struck. But the fund never heard from Perot again.

The fund did hear from attorney Roy Cohn. In a letter dated February 23, 1983, Cohn requested access to the fund's book on behalf of unnamed major contributors. Perot says he did not hire Cohn. Shlakman says he did.

An investigative reporter for television station WDVM requested access to the fund's books in the summer of 1983, and was refused. The reporter's five-part series on the fund's finances began November 7. The fund and congressmen petitioned the General Accounting Office (GAO) to conduct a study and clear the air.

The GAO report on May 24, 1984, and the television series at last revealed the suspicions about the fund. The kitchen-sink indictment leveled 32 charges, ranging from self-dealing and insider transactions to excessive costs. The GAO also looked into allegations that the fund contributed $2 million to the National Council of Churches—the NCC supposedly routed the funds to a left-wing Central American military group—and another $5,000 to a women's rights group.

The GAO found no improprieties. The report concludes: "[T]he fund has properly accounted for and adequately reported its receipts and disbursements. GAO also found that the prior audits of the fund operations were proper, and that the numerous allegations raised regarding the fund were not valid."

The GAO report has not laid the controversy to rest. "It's an antiwar monument," says F. Andrew Messing, president of the National Defense Council Foundation. "That's what ticked us off. Walk down there any given day at 3 P.M., and I'll give you ten bucks if you can show me anyone with dry eyes. Every-time you go down there you see people weeping. It's a sublim-inal message to the United States never to be involved in defending freedom."[14] Sandinista leader Daniel Ortega once tried to stage a press event there.

For years afterward, Doubek couldn't talk about the memorial without brooding for weeks. Today he compares it to *The Wizard of Oz.* "I was the tinman because I was looking for a heart. Maya Lin was Dorothy. [Fine Arts Commission chairman] J. Carter Brown was the good witch of the East," he says. "I did find a heart. I met my wife at the fund, got married, had kids. Until that time I was dying of terminal cynicism, trying to be a lawyer. It gave me a sense of achievement."[15]

Perot has not forgotten or forgiven. Did the GAO conduct an *audit*? he snaps.

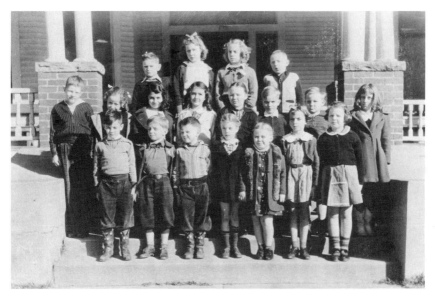
The Patty Hill School, circa 1936. Ross Perot is second from the left in the first row. Bette Perot is second from the right, first row. (Photo courtesy of James M. Tennison.)

Texarkana Junior College Student Council President Ross Perot. (Photo courtesy of Robert T. Coleman)

TJC Freshman Jane Maxwell drags 'Lil Abner Perot before 'Marrying Sam' (Frank Harland). (Photo courtesy of Robert T. Coleman)

The Perot home at 29th and Olive in Texarkana. (Photo courtesy of Robert T. Coleman)

EDS officers, circa 1970. Tom Marquez is at the extreme right. Tom Walter and Mort Meyerson bring up the rear. (Photo courtesy of EDS)

Early EDS employee Cecil Walter recreates the twilight rendezvous of computer operators. (Photo courtesy of EDS)

Perot working to improve POW treatment during the Vietnam War. (AP/Wide World Photos)

The Tehran heroes return: Perot, former captives Bill Gaylord and Paul Chiapparone, and rescuer Col. Arthur "Bull" Simons. (AP/Wide World Photos)

Author Ken Follett, foreground, and the Iran rescue team at a book signing party. (Photo courtesy of EDS)

Perot and actor Richard Crenna on the miniseries set. (Photo courtesy of EDS)

First Lady Nancy Reagan brings her "Just Say
No" campaign to Dallas. (Photo © Bob East III/
Picture Group)

Prince Charles shares a joke with the Churchill Award honoree in the EDS
lobby. (Photo courtesy of EDS)

Investment banker Ken Langone dressed Perot
in "California casual" during a 1987 Dallas
Press Club roast. (Photo © 1987 Jim Knowles)

GM Chairman Roger Smith can still laugh about it a week after his flawed
deal to buy back Perot's stock. (Photo © Peter Yates/Picture Group)

Morton H. Meyerson (Photo courtesy of EDS)

Jeffrey A. Heller (Photo courtesy of EDS)

Gary J. Fernandes (Photo courtesy of EDS)

Lester M. Alberthal, Jr. (Photo courtesy of EDS)

CHAPTER TWELVE

THE POLITICS OF APPEASEMENT

Roger Smith faced a dilemma as 1986 began. No one doubted his commitment to making the EDS acquisition work. That was an act of enlightened self interest for him, because an abject failure would forever color his years at General Motors. A charismatic Perot on board was the happier choice, but Smith knew now that compromise wasn't one of Perot's strong suits. GM director Ed Pratt, chairman of Pfizer Corporation, knew about the Vietnam Veteran Memorial Fund wrangle. Director Tom Murphy had heard duPont stories from a fellow trustee at the University of Illinois Foundation. Everyone in GM management had a full repertoire of EDS zealot stories as a result of the 18-month-old alliance. But if GM couldn't cope with Perot, could EDS survive without him?

Smith wasn't willing to risk the collapse of the EDS merger in a ugly public fight. Early in 1986, the nominating committee of the board came to Smith with a plan to kick Perot off the board. Smith asked the committee not to. "I believed that we could make the system work," he says. "It was working with GMAC. It was working with Hughes. I had every reason to believe we could make it work with EDS."[1]

GM managers had a surprising amount of autonomy, given the company's reputation for bureaucracy. When the reorganization three years earlier divided GM into Chevrolet-Pontiac-Canada (CPC), and Buick-Oldsmobile-Cadillac (BOC), Smith left the rest of the reorganization to the two group executives. CPC recreated GM's central staff tradition. Chevrolet, for example, drew on a CPC pool of engineers or designers as it needed those talents. BOC reorganized along product lines. Cadillac had its own exclusive engineering and design staffs. GM's brand of autonomy was just as much a tradition as EDS's individualism. Fisher Body, after all, operated for 60 years under the premise that its GM ties were temporary. Autonomy wasn't the issue.

Management style was. Of all of the thousands of cultural chasms EDS stumbled into across the GM empire, none was wider or deeper than the one on GM's executive floor. While Perot knew every last trick of leadership, Smith didn't have a clue. The GM chairman's specialty was symbolic pratfalls. Consider the difficult reelection UAW official Don Ephlin faced in 1986. Hard-liners attacked Ephlin for his efforts to meet GM halfway and preserve jobs for his members. Just days before the election, Smith approved the announcement of a major new production contract for nonunion GM Mexico. That's your payoff, Ephlin's adversaries taunted him. The union makes concessions and GM still shifts jobs out of the country. Ephlin survived, no thanks to Smith.

Earlier, GM spat in the union's eye after winning $2.5 billion in concessions from the UAW. GM's annual meeting proxy disclosed fat new bonuses for GM executives, just as the assembly floor workers were agreeing to sacrifices. Smith shelved the bonus plan after vehement protests. Smith followed that gaffe with another. He cut his own salary that year by $135 per month to equal one of the new concessions by GM hourly workers. The relative sacrifice of CEO and assembly-line worker made the gesture laughable. GM workers passed around this doggerel:

> When things go wrong as they usually will
> and your daily road seems all uphill
> when funds are low and debts are high

when you try to smile but can only cry,
and you really feel you'd like to quit
Don't come to me, I don't give a shit.
                    —signed Roger Smith[2]

Perot lost confidence in Smith after his temper tantrum in Dallas in September. Perot was diplomatic that day, but he leveled with Smith in a letter dated October 23, 1985: "You need to understand that your style intimidates people. Losing your temper hurts GM. . . . You need to be aware that people are afraid of you. This stifles candid, upward communication in GM." (Yes, Perot also cut off debate with his 'doncha see.' The difference is a question of style. Perot didn't bully EDS workers into performing heroics. It can't be done.)

Cultural differences also explain Perot's contempt for the GM bureaucracy. Perot cracks that GM's motto is Ready, aim, aim, aim, aim, while EDS gunners are firing all day long. Of course, EDS can fire all day and never run out of targets. By the 1970s GM had as much of the U.S. car business as the Justice Department was going to allow it to keep. The game had changed at GM. The new goal was profits. How much money could GM keep?

It is no accident that accountants ran General Motors in its heyday. GM managed both marketing and manufacturing by the numbers. Pricing was a ritual in those days. Hours after GM posted its new car prices, Chrysler and Ford fell into line, literally, positioning their models a few hundred dollars more or less than the comparable GM model. Accountants also ruled the factories, because economies of scale mattered more than quality. In 1963, GM kept 15 cents of every sales dollar it took in. High-tech EDS hasn't done that well since 1971.

Greed was the immediate threat to this money machine— and another justification for finance department primacy. The accountants rationed investment capital inside GM's far-flung empire. GM effectively made its plants bid against each other and against outside suppliers for new car or component projects. The accountants acted as police. GM had audit squads in the field making sure that plant managers weren't cooking the books in order to land a new project or a more attractive bonus; the bonus plan tied incentive pay to production.

GM could not have held dominion for all those decades if its employees didn't believe the system was fair. GM's management scientists were just as proud in their understated way as EDS's garrulous Marines. GM accountants boasted that they could find every last dollar of the $100 billion GM would handle in 1986. Now there was a GM subsidiary that wouldn't let them in the door. Worse, this group scoffed at their art. The lines were drawn.

The year 1986 began with mixed developments. In the plus column, Alberthal and McDonald had hammered together a master agreement covering EDS's work at GM. At long last, EDS's role inside GM was spelled out on paper. The frustrated EDS account managers now had a means of compelling the holdouts among GM management to honor the letter of the merger, if not the spirit. The master agreement also carved out some protections for General Motors. By the end of the year, paragraph 3.6 of the master agreement would be a pivotal clause:

> With respect to any services for which EDS is to be compensated on a cost plus management fee basis. . . . the GM central office may, at its expense, audit the books and records of EDS to the extent necessary to verify the applicability and accuracy of EDS charges for such services. Any such audit may be conducted at any time during normal business hours, upon reasonable notice to EDS, with or without a dispute as to such charges.

The bad news was the year-end closing of the books. Both sides agreed that EDS botched the job. EDS always treated the accounting function as a necessary evil. For example, the company forbade its outside auditors, Peat Marwick, from going directly to EDS operating groups for additional information. Instead, they were required to ask the EDS financial staff to get information for them. To Perot, making money was more important than counting it. EDS had to satisfy Securities and Exchange Commission and Internal Revenue Service regulations. That done, the bean counters were supposed to stay out of the way.

These weren't normal times. EDS had tripled in size when it took control of GM's data processing January 1, 1985. EDS's unloved and overworked accountants also found themselves in a fishbowl. GM accountants were now peering over the shoulders of their EDS counterparts. To consolidate the books of parent and subsidiary, the GM staff had to offset EDS fees with GM expenses in order to balance the company books. The exercise was a disaster.

EDS Europe closed its books December 13 to beat the year-end rush. When their GM Europe customers closed their books on December 31, nothing jibed. EDS turned in its final accounting to GM on January 21, a week late, and even then Peat Marwick suggested 21 corrections that EDS refused to make. GM's auditors, comparing their books to EDS's, found an additional 62 mistakes after January 21. The final discrepancy was not significant because of offsetting errors. EDS books understated revenues by $6.4 million, or a error of two tenths of a percent. Some of the errors were troublesome. Simple clerical errors erased $4 million in income. A bad formula for currency translation cost EDS another $1 million.

GM and EDS came to different conclusions. On March 13, when Perot heard of the difficult closing from GM's CFO, Alan Smith, he wrote: "Frankly I believe that most of the problems are the result of growing overnight. . . to an organization of nearly 40,000 people and revenues of roughly $3.4 billion." But accountants don't like excuses. They look upon year-end closes in the same way that the Nuclear Regulatory Commission regards safety drills at nuclear power plants. The GM staff had asked their EDS counterparts to run the rods back into the reactor core. In their view, the EDS performance was a chilling experience.

The GM auditors had a second reason to ask for the EDS books. GM managers thought that they were being overcharged for computing services. EDS answered that its charges were not out of line, but rather that GM had never seen its computer expenditures in one place before. Like good cops, the audit department shrugged off the alibis and asked for a search warrant. GM's chief auditor, G. R. Troost, served notice on January 22. GM would conduct a general audit of EDS as soon as the companies agreed on the details. Troost couldn't be specific about the time or money involved, but he could venture a guess on the former. The audit would take 17 weeks.

Perot was livid. Once again, Smith was breaking his word. Perot had explained to him the long-standing prejudice at EDS against central staff, people who produced work and expenses but no revenues. Compared to the operating and marketing problems on EDS's plate, bookkeeping was only a crumb. (Then again, if GM trusted EDS's numbers, the problem over the fixed-price contracts would not loom as large.) Perot saw the audit request as retribution. He had challenged Smith on the Hughes acquisition. Now the finance department enforcers wanted to pay him a visit.

Casting the auditors as gorillas was a common practice at GM. When auditors descended on wobbling GM operations, they usually found a crime and a culprit. Aggressive auditing was good management science in the 1960s when the usual problems were low car production and high factory costs. The auditors could solve either crime by running the numbers. Now the auditors were part of the problem at GM.

Consider the question of why doors don't fit. The Japanese don't use fancy management techniques to fix that problem; they use common sense. Honda makes one person responsible for all of the steps involving the doors. If they don't fit, management knows exactly who to call. At GM in the 1970s, Chevy stamped doors and tried to bolt them to Fisher bodies. When those parts didn't fit, not even King Solomon could fix the blame let alone the problem. That's why Fisher Body became history.

But GM still clung to centralization. GM cut costs at its ultramodern Buick City plant in Flint by shipping in doors from a Buick plant outside Detroit. Among the many problems with the first LeSabres to roll off that line were doors that didn't fit. When GM's bookkeeping cops arrived at the scene, they didn't like the tone of these interrogations. Q: Why can't you produce cars with doors that fit? A: Because you'd rather squeeze pennies than give me the tools I need to do the job. (GM eventually sorted out the Buick City plant. The 1989 LeSabre ranked number two in surveys of owner satisfaction.)

The finance department had an impressive reach in GM. Back in 1977, the finance department had taken on the obligation of supplying executive aides to the operating managers. These young people were fast-trackers. The overt reasoning was to help these executive aides understand the company; handling details for the operating bosses would give them a broader view. They also acted as the eyes and ears of finance. Former GM speechwriter and Smith biographer Albert Lee was to turn over his speech drafts to these aides rather than to the executive intended to deliver it.

Lee writes: "When my executive wanted to make a point that didn't sit well with them, the [aide] would politely steer me to his actual boss, assistant comptroller John Mischi. . . . Even when he was attempting civility. Mischi would call in a finance guy or two and chew them out in front of me, just to stay in practice."[3] Mischi was perfectly willing to substitute his wisdom for the operating executive's, Lee reports. There was general disdain on the finance side of GM for bodies of knowledge other than accounting. For example, Smith promoted an accountant to vice president of marketing even though the man had no experience in that area.

Perot had specific reasons to suspect the GM central staff of revenge. The finance department gave up more data processing people and responsibilities to EDS than any other group at GM. Turf struggles were still a daily fact of life for EDS. Once, when GM auditors walked down the hall to ask their programmers for a clever financial analysis, the answer was Yes, sir. Now the EDS account managers were presenting their customers with a bill. Ross Perot had hung a take-a-number machine at the door to the crime lab.

Perot flew to New York a day before the February board meeting to challenge Smith and CFO Alan Smith over the audits. Roger Smith was ill-equipped for the confrontation. Under optimum circumstances, he is a poor communicator.

Debating Perot is not a normal experience on this earth. Perot at maximum intensity can roll over anyone. One of the first challenges facing EDS attorneys in court in Virginia was to stop Perot from turning yes or no answers into 15-minute soliloquies. Perot thought he had convinced the Smiths to drop the audit.

Unlike Perot at EDS, however, the Smiths had to explain themselves to the finance staff. Accountants had run GM since 1958, and they ran it well for a majority of that time. Roger Smith wasn't exactly defending a birthright, but he was upholding a way of life. Vice president Jack Edman recited the catechism for EDS's CFO, Tom Walter, several days after the summit. "Fairness to all classes of GM shareholders," he wrote in a February 28, 1986 letter, "is a responsibility that we, as the management of General Motors, can neither delegate nor ignore." Edman thought the EDS's poor showing at the close of its books in 1985 raised doubts about its commitment to a professional job. Finally, he complained that EDS had turned the GM Finance's computer staff into merchants, instead of their proper role as key links in the GM "management control system."

Perot's efforts came to naught. EDS executives overheard Edman and Alan Smith in heated debate after the board meeting. Later, Perot and Smith walked out together to their cars. "Alan had a completely different attitude," Perot wrote to Roger Smith on February 25. He no longer agreed that EDS's accounting flaws were minor. Perot suspected that the GM finance staff wanted to subject EDS to GM policies, procedures—and audits. Perot concluded, "I agree with you that this is a serious mistake."

Smith says Perot made the mistake. He had not waived GM's rights under paragraph 3.6 of the master agreement during that February meeting. He would not knowingly give up GM's right to verify the costs in an EDS cost-plus project.

Far from the storm, Alberthal and McDonald were building a solid foundation for the alliance. In April, McDonald sent out a memo to GM staff describing a pricing scheme for EDS work. The first choice was a catalog of routine services compiled by GM and issued as the Uniform Published Rates

(UPR) book. The second preference was for long-term, fixed-rate contracts that reconciled EDS profit requirements with GM's goal to cut costs. McDonald urged his managers to write contracts in which EDS charges were to sink steadily over the years or contracts that allowed EDS and GM to share the cost savings. McDonald asked his executives to play ball. A few days later, GM's auditing management met in Warren, Michigan, with their EDS counterparts. It wasn't a lovefest, but everyone left encouraged.

McDonald, GM's most effective mediator, was stumped on Meyerson's salary. Perot wouldn't bend; he had promised a salary equal to one percent of profits to Meyerson, or $1.9 million in 1985 based on EDS profits of $190 million. Perot wrote to McDonald, "Mort is very sensitive about the months of controversy over his compensation. It has affected both his attitude and his performance."

GM was equally resolute about Meyerson's salary. GM lawyers had been told during their due-diligence work in 1984 that there were no salary covenants. But again, it was the amount that stopped Smith cold. Meyerson's putative salary surpassed every GM executive's with the possible exception of Smith. To pay a subsidiary chief more than the parent's officers was tinkering with the fundamentals of the universe in professionally managed corporate America. It did no good for Perot to argue that Meyerson was delivering on a fat new contract that was making GME shareholders rich. Those were sore points also in Detroit.

Meyerson and Perot tried to find a way for everyone to save face. Pay me one half of one percent of EDS earnings and turn over the other half percent as a bonus pool for the other EDS executives. McDonald was not moved. Well then, Perot countered, pay me the half percent—Perot had frozen his salary at $68,000 when EDS went public—and I'll turn over the money to Meyerson and his bonus pool. Nothing. Meyerson had had enough. He flew back to Dallas and told Perot he would not set foot in Detroit again.

It was at that point that Perot reached the end of his rope. To him, the controversy was never more complicated than whether Smith would keep his word. He had carefully explained to Smith what made EDS special and what would happen if GM began tampering with it. He needed no better proof that he was right than the dejected Meyerson. Perot ordered EDS to cut a check in excess of $1 million to Meyerson. Perot insists he had GM's blessing to make the settlement. Meyerson became vice chairman in charge of acquisitions.

EDS's annual analysts' meeting two weeks later was a marvel of airbrushed reality. President Meyerson and CFO Walter were stepping aside, Perot explained, because it was time to send their capable backups into the game. Perot praised Alberthal as "the right man at the right time" for EDS. Ross Reeves, who would resign two years later to join Perot Systems, described how EDS had brought order to GM's disjointed computer operation. Kennard Hill, Riedlinger's replacement, sounded the proper note of optimism at the conclusion. "The restructuring of GM is no longer a dream but something that is being implemented," he said. "In short we are creating the future." Hill, tortured by a back injury he first suffered in Vietnam and looking gaunt as death, would resign from EDS the following year.

Smith blinked again. GM thought it had legal standing to countermand Perot's settlement with Meyerson. The company bylaws vest an independent committee of the board with the authority to make the final decision on salaries and bonuses. That was the whole point of the yearlong battle. Yes, GM told Perot, you can determine who gets what, and then the board must bless your plan as reasonable. Smith was furious about the payment to Meyerson. "One," says Smith, "we had no knowledge of, and as a matter of fact, had been told that there was no contract with Mort. Second, the payment had been made without any communications to us, and third, the payment, even if you accepted the contract, was improperly calculated."[4] Nonetheless, Smith decided that the stakes were too high to force the issue.

His hunch was confirmed during a stormy confrontation with Perot on May 3. Perot's parting shot was a declaration of war. Smith recalls, "The words I remember that he used there—He said, 'You can try and terminate me but I will start

World War III. Those are the words I remember him using. My response . . . was 'Ross, let's try to make this thing work. There are lots of people involved in this thing and the best for all of us would be to go back and try to achieve the original purposes of the acquisition.' "[5]

The two weren't on the same wavelength. Smith went back to Detroit to set down his thoughts on new president Alberthal's salary in a lengthy letter. The letter probably was Smith's ham-handed way of nudging Perot toward the right decision on an issue that was sure to be examined closely by the GM staff.

For his part, Perot was incredulous that Smith still hadn't gotten the message. He had skipped the pleasantries in his summation—the letters crossed in the mail—and went straight to a 20-point memo of understanding that laid out his exclusive purview over EDS compensation. He left a line for Smith to countersign the document. "Basically," Perot summed up its contents, "this means I will run EDS just as I ran it before GM acquired EDS."

Just the tone of the memo clenched jaws in Detroit, but the fireworks were buried deep in his 20 points. Perot tossed out a brand-new, unilaterally determined figure of $60 million for the 1986 stock bonus program. Smith thought that he had solved the stock problem the year before. The offhand stock figure forced the inevitable conclusion in a way that rhetoric couldn't. Perot had usurped the powers of the salary and bonus committee of the GM board of directors and he was entirely unrepentant. Smith put off answering.

For all of Smith's bluster and imperiousness, he was a shy man. He is one of those people who are so smart that they are always a few cycles out of phase with the rest of humanity. He relied on hard work and keen analysis to rise to the top of GM, and did it literally a step at a time. He knew that GM needed leadership and tried to provide it. It was as if Smith wanted to break into a Broadway show tune, but he didn't trust his voice or his feet. He admired Perot's virtuosity. Perot marveled at Smith's achievements at first. When Perot heard Smith's story, and how president McDonald had risen up from the factory floor, he exclaimed enthusiastically, "They're just like us."

Smith wasn't, of course. Smith could trace his father's ancestry to a signer of the Magna Charta and his mother's to the Mayflower. The son of an entrepreneur, Smith attended an exclusive high school in Grosse Pointe. His lessons continued at home. No wasted motion was the elder Smith's credo. It was a far cry from Sell it; you can't eat it. Smith says he learned to play golf under the pressure of the clock. His father would allot 10 minutes per hole; not even pleasure was exempt from the science of time and motion. Smith learned his accounting trade at the University of Michigan.

He was an apt student of the GM system. Biographer Lee's first meeting with Smith was mind boggling. Lee's boss came along, and warned Lee that Smith might ignore him. Sure enough, Smith launched into a tirade when Lee interjected a comment. Outburst over, eyes still fixed on Lee's boss, Smith resumed, Tell Albert Lee . . .

Perot raised the stakes. He instructed GM's compensation manager Greg Lau in a phone conversation "that EDS compensation people no longer would communicate or provide info to Mr. Lau from now on . . . and that Mr Perot would be the focal point of all compensation issues," as Lau recorded the conversation in a memo dated May 9.

Smith tried again in a letter to Perot on May 14. He began his letter by charting the progress that the companies had made in other areas and then turned his attention to the last open question, executive compensation. Smith wrote that he was working on a plan that would give Perot the greatest flexibility possible. He warned him again that his hands were tied by the GM bylaws which reserved major salary decisions to an independent committee of the GM board. "All of the restrictions also apply to GM subsidiaries . . . and of course apply to EDS," he wrote.

Perot would not yield. "The idea of having the GM compensation staff fiddle with Les' salary and bonus accrual," Perot wrote back, "or having a detailed budget review from GM is completely inconsistent with everything we agreed to at the time of the purchase." If Smith wouldn't cosign his May 7 memo, then they were back to the same four options that the pair went over in person on May 4. Perot repeated them in writing:

1. The only worthwhile option is to work together in good faith. All of our experience demonstrates that we must have a written agreement to do that. Any matters we cannot resolve will be taken to the board.

2. As I told you, I am no longer willing to bend and compromise from our original agreement because it is so damaging to EDS. Therefore in the absence of any clear understanding between us, I will run EDS and when we disagree we are going to have whatever size fight is necessary, between us, with the board, or in full public view to get the matter resolved.

3. Your other option is to try to terminate me, in order to get rid of a nuisance. I want to make sure that you and every member of the GM board understand the magnitude and the length of the fight that would result from such action. It would last for years and would be terribly disruptive to GM, EDS and all concerned. I don't want any one to question my resolve or willingness to do this if you force me to. I have too many years and too much invested in EDS to see it destroyed.

4. The final solution, if you want to get rid of me, is to handle the matter on a businesslike basis and buy me out. In my judgement that would be a serious mistake on the part of GM, but if that is what you want to do, it does reduce the issue to business terms.

Smith sent his chief counsel, Elmer Johnson, to Dallas to sound out Perot on point 4. But Perot wouldn't sell the GM notes that promised to make up the difference between GME's market value by 1991 and $62.50 per share. The notes amounted to a bet that GME would not reach the target price, since they increased a dollar in value for each dollar that GME fell short of the target. Johnson recalls:

He thought it might be a very interesting holding to maintain, and I think he said some words to that effect, that these notes could have a life of their own. . . . I did not believe that it was at all a healthy state of affairs for a person to hold a very substantial amount of a security whose value depended on how low the GME stock sunk.[6]

On Johnson's counsel, GM dropped the issue.

Smith tried another accommodation. GM would turn over full control of EDS books to Perot and capitalize the subsidiary independently. If Perot was willing to verify and warrant to the GM board that EDS's reports to the SEC and the IRS were right, then GM audits were not necessary. The companies worked out that arrangement.

However, Jack Edman and Alan Smith had one more audit demand to make under paragraph 3.6 of the master agreement. CFO Alan Smith, in a letter dated June 11, addressed the one area remaining open, "that of reporting to the General Motors board of directors through the audit committee." It's not clear where this letter came from or why, and GM refuses to talk about it. Perot heard about it before he received it and hit the ceiling.

He called GM to ask for a copy. GM vice president J. E. Rhames was on the receiving end of Perot's pyrotechnics. Perot dropped another bomb. Henceforth, Perot was assuming the job of chief financial officer, Rhames wrote in his memo of the phone call. If GM wanted financial details, they could come to him and ask. (Perot says he never became CFO; there was never an official change of office.)

Perot was already talking to Doron Levin, then of *The Wall Street Journal*. Perot had props to illustrate his resolve to keep the GM central staff at bay. He slipped on a bright red cap normally worn by Orkin pest exterminators. "I've got Orkin stationery too," he told Levin.[7]

CHAPTER THIRTEEN

SPIN CONTROL

If GM's public relations staff had caught Perot's performance in New York and Los Angeles in the spring of 1986, they would have surrendered on the spot. It was a tough room, to borrow the language of the actors salted among the banquet tables at the preview of the miniseries "On Wings of Eagles." Entertainment reporters are courted week in and week out by producers and TV stars. They rub shoulders so regularly with the glitterati that neither Burt Lancaster nor Richard Crenna impress. Yet there was a stir of anticipation when National Broadcasting Company executives turned over the microphone to Henry Ross Perot.

Already disarmed to be meeting a real-life hero, the reporters were completely unprepared for the Perot Treatment. He opened with quips. His EDS colleagues didn't approve of Crenna, Perot reported. "They said, 'If the actor who plays you is tall and not short, and if he's good looking and not ugly, and if he doesn't have a really bad Texas accent this whole thing is going to be pure fiction.' "[1] Perot takes his banquets seriously. He scouts the room first. If the dais is raised, he'll ask the sponsors to return it to floor level. Don't want them to see me spill gravy on my tie, he quips. Actually, it spoils his just-folks approach.

Perot tells the entertainment writers that he is not the hero of "On Wings." Simons is. He begins telling Simons-stories in the Los Angeles preview. The Colonel was hospitalized in Dallas for heart problems shortly after the raid. Simons prevailed on Perot's aide, Merv Stauffer, to bring him his pistol.

> Now if I had asked Merv to bring me a pistol in the Intensive Care Unit he would have ignored me. . . . Now, Okay, you say, Merv's the exception. But when I got down there late that afternoon, there were nine doctors and the administrator standing outside of intensive care. They said, "Ross you going in to see Col. Simons?" I said yes. They said, "While you're there get him to give up the pistol." I says, "Look, folks, this is your hospital. If you don't want him to have a pistol, you tell him."[2]

Most of the writers were convulsed in laughter, pens forgotten. The rest were staring in disbelief. The last part of the Perot Treatment is the personal touch. He made a circuit of the dinner tables to shake hands and thank the reporters for coming. They left captivated completely. NBC was charmed also, needless to say. When Perot sat down to tape an introduction to the series installments, he waved off the network's cue cards. "Just cue me at 10 seconds," Perot instructed the crew. "Come on. Let's not kill my career in show business before it starts."[3]

Few contemporary Americans have shaped their own public image more successfully than Perot. Certainly no one has worked at it harder. Horse trading had brought Perot to the previews. NBC repaid Perot for his promotional genius by effectively turning over casting approval to him. Burt Lancaster, rather than Robert Preston, played Simons in the TV drama because Perot thought too many people remembered the latter as the "Music Man."

The rest of it is charisma. Ramrod, traditionalist Perot has a surprising affinity for the rumpled, skeptical representatives of the press. H. L. Mencken once wrote that a reporter comforts the afflicted and afflicts the comfortable. That job description fits the public Perot surprisingly well. He had approached the men and women of the Arlington Assembly Plant the summer before as fellow Texans, not as hourly workers as GM would classify them. He knew that bad decisions by Roger Smith could scatter their lives like so many billiard balls. Perot's fellow Texans were helpless, but he was not. He could hold Smith's feet to the fire. Reporters see themselves the same way. They were only too happy to help him toast Smith's toes.

Perot takes media interviews just as seriously as his banquets. The Treatment, focused on one person, is even more awesome. It follows the same pattern. He tells more jokes on himself. When Perot gets down to the business at hand, his answers crash through the reporter's questions as if they were a dam of twigs and leaves and sweep the unfortunate scribe away on a torrent of words. Ordinarily, this is a recipe for disaster in an interview. Reporters prefer to set the agenda. But Perot isn't ducking questions. He is racing ahead of them, providing details and insights the amazed scribe thought he would be digging for. His comments are bold, although not always on the record. His language is picturesque. Eventually, the reporter decides to hold on and enjoy the ride. It is difficult enough to interrupt him. It's nearly impossible to force him to acknowledge that he is not an auto worker. He is a billionaire with his own set of interests at GM.

Horse trading also works with journalists, so long as no one is crass enough to state the bargain out loud. The reporter cedes the agenda to Perot because the interviewee is delivering the goods. Both know that the writer needs a bold perspective and a wealth of details to make a story stand out in the 24-hour din of news coverage. Perot obliges, and then he stays in touch. It isn't unusual for a writer to hear from him several times a week while the story is in progress. Hi, this is Ross. Got everything you need?

When professionals do it for a living, it's called "spin control." It's an offshoot of television's emphasis on style over substance. Perceptions always count, but only the most startling of facts can break through the ennui. The news has to be packaged like boxes of detergent emblazoned "New and Improved." In politics, platoons of "spin doctors" stand by at news events to offer reporters packaging concepts.

Perot understands completely what "handlers" like Roger Ailes or Robert Teeter are doing to politics. He despises it. "Candidates don't talk about issues except at their peril," Perot complained shortly after the 1988 election.

> The media says "That's all we can get." Just shut these suck-ers off the news for three, four days until they start talking about something real. . . . As long as Ailes and Teeter can pre-dict with 100 percent certainty that we are dumb as they think we are, and . . . just like puppets we react like they predict we will, we are training our elected officials to trick us. We deserve what we get.[4]

Alas, NBC can't hang out an on-air "gone fishing" sign from 6 to 6:30 P.M. Vast swathes of the electorate don't care what NBC does. That's why we are willing to forgive Perot when he turns spin doctor. Perot usually comes at spin from the opposite direction. He's out to make waves, to raise issues, rather than to avoid them. Straight talk is so rare today that Perot comes across like a rain shower in the desert. "Step one in a free society is to raise the issue," he says. "Then with dead ringer certainty you're going to have a raging debate. . . . Then, out of that debate, with leadership, you'll have consensus."[5]

In practice, Perot means that he identifies his opponents, be they unqualified teachers in Texas, greedy investment bankers, or grasping GM functionaries. He fashions a banner for the antis to rally around, and sponsors polls to prove he is leading a silent majority. He surrounds himself with like-thinking people, and he fashions a call to arms: Companies will wear junk bonds around their necks like millstones. If debate springs up in this environment, it doesn't rise much above the "Tastes great; less filling" genre. Perot is looking for action, not dissent.

So isn't he just as manipulative as Ailes or Teeter? Yes, he is. What's more, he is better at spin. The Dallas Press Club saw him in all his ambivalent glory in 1987 as he jabbed both Smith and Gershon Kekst, a top PR practitioner on Wall Street. GM hired Kekst to batten down the hatches in Detroit for

Hurricane Ross. On Kekst's advice, Smith began comparing himself to a pro quarterback. He got too much of the credit for wins and too much blame for losses. "Well, Roger, as usual," Perot cracked, looking over his shoulder at a slide of the GM chairman, "you're half right."[6] The audience laughed and raced off to repeat what was, on its face, a much more clever bit of spin than Kekst's.

A *Texas Monthly* reporter in 1988 found Perot stalking the U.S. Department of the Interior. Perot was dismayed that a forest fire was burning out of control at Yellowstone National Park. Perot pounded his desk in frustration, and exclaimed "I'm better than that." He had been tipped that the Interior Department's policy was wrongheaded, but he had made only preliminary calls and then stopped. "I could have raised enough hell that they would have had to put the fire out. I know how media sensitive they are."[7] Even Yellowstone was Perot's burden, the magazine remarked. And the press was his weapon.

What saves Perot in the end is his amateur status. Even when he is being as nakedly manipulative as the spin doctors he despises, we forgive him because he isn't cynical about it. At least he isn't a hired gun, and he doesn't duck when his principles force him to take an unpopular stand. Twice Perot tangled with "60 Minutes," the biggest dog in the media yard, and both times he appeared on the wrong side of the program's premise.

The CBS news program first included him in a segment on tax avoidance. It's not hard to figure out where "60 Minutes" was going with that segment, but Perot held his own. Well, now that's the difference, he told "60 Minutes." You're trying to kill the goose and cook it for dinner. I'm trying to get it to lay another golden egg. Gems like that one are his trump card. Perot can deliver such a clever "sound bite" that the producer is compelled to air it even when it doesn't fit the program's point of view.

Bill Wright, EDS's PR manager, tried to talk him out of participating in the second "60 Minutes" segment covering the Vietnam veterans' memorial controversy. "I told him 'This is a classic for "60 Minutes," where the admirals, generals, and multi-millionaires are pitted against the handicapped and minorities.' "[8] Perot plunged ahead, but Wright had it figured correctly. The segment opened with Maya Lin describing her encounters with bigotry and it got worse from there. Perot shrugged it off. He was obligated, as the godfather of the Vietnam vets, to do his part.

Perot could not let go so easily early in his career. Most news figures can't get over the finality of black print on white pages. Perot sulked through several periods of self-imposed exile in his 20 years in public view. He learned through experience that news coverage, far from being absolute, follows a sine wave: sometimes positive, sometimes negative, always changing. Perot's mother kept a scrapbook. The rest of us have to make up our minds all over again when we begin reading the latest story about Perot.

The *Ramparts* piece, the coverage of the Congressional hearings, and the growing duPont mess marked Perot's first disaffection with the press. Surely only the most confident of billionaires would sit down with the left-wing *Ramparts* in 1971 and expect to prevail. Perot didn't win that one and he couldn't laugh it off back then. Newsweek listed Perot's trials and noted, "He has already grown uncharacteristically defensive."[9] Brooding might be a better description. He told a *Forbes* reporter at roughly the same time, "From my point of view the less publicity the better. No publicity at all is the ideal."[10]

In 1970, he found himself in a shooting war with the Dallas newspapers. EDS wanted a zoning change to build its new headquarters in the middle of a golf course on Forest Lane. EDS's prospective neighbors were adamantly opposed. Perot thought that the *Dallas Morning News* was covering the neighborhood spat with inappropriate glee. EDS security officers barred reporters from a two-hour showdown with the neighborhood group. He asked the *Morning News* to print a 1,000-word EDS statement unedited. The newspaper declined, offering instead a more conventional letter to the editor or a question-and-answer format as means of putting his message across without editorial filtering. He declined, later complaining, "The newspapers denied us an opportunity to have the same rights anyone else would have. I think it's unfortunate that because of my personal visibility, my company was unable to get fair treatment."[11] At one point, Perot threatened to move EDS out of Dallas.

He sulked again in 1981 after he failed to win city approval to install a helipad on his 22-acre estate. His war on drugs had exposed him to threats by organized crime, he argued. The opposition this time was his neighbor, J. Fred Bucy, then president of Texas Instruments. Bucy pointed out, correctly, that cars were less conspicuous than helicopters in their comings and goings and much harder to shoot down. Perot lost. He later complained to the *Morning News*, "This dispute appeared in over 200 newspapers across the country, which is the worst kind of thing that can happen to me. You see, that excites the nuts."[12] Apparently he forgot that he began the debate.

The crowning incident in this episode of thin skin was a *Texas Business* cover story in 1981 on the Bradford flap. The magazine's editors were thunderstruck when Tom Luce called. Perot had read an advance copy supplied by the magazine. Not only didn't he like it, he wanted it rewritten. The editors answered that the magazine was already off the press. Perot offered to pay for a second press run. The editors declined.

Coverage of the Iran rescue also lodged in Perot's craw. The *New York Times* wrote skeptically of his claim that EDS orchestrated the jailbreak. The *Times* piece still irked him years later when an interviewer asked him to write his own epitaph. "Made more money faster. Lost more money in one day. Led the biggest jailbreak in history. He died. Footnote, the *New York Times* questioned whether he did the jailbreak or not."[13] Reporters and historians have the last word. Perot is not the sort of person who could let them shoulder that responsibility without his help.

Perot still retreats from the spotlight periodically, but his absences now are tactical. He recognizes another penchant of the press. When the story has dragged on to the point that there are no fresh perspectives or new new details, the press has a proclivity to turn it upside down. For example, it was

inevitable that the press would write the story that Vice President Dan Quayle wasn't so inept after all. That's why Perot
in modern times told his PR people, I'm getting overexposed.
I'm going underground for a while.

Perot tried to squelch the Iran rescue story, but it was too
good not to be told. So many writers had called asking to
chronicle the escape that Perot determined to beat them to
the punch. Perot's concern, he told Wright, was that some
author would paint Bull Simons as a baby-killer. Wright was
given the task of finding an author subject to two conditions:
The author had to accept Perot's editorial control, and the book
had to be written in conversational English. Perot first signed
Nathan Adams, a senior editor at *Reader's Digest.* Adams quit
after a few weeks. "I thought critical access was being with-
held," he says.[14] Wright returned to his much-reduced list of
best-selling nonfiction authors.

Margot Perot nominated Ken Follett. She was reading the
spy novelist's *The Eye of the Needle* at the time. Follett's agent
threw up road blocks at first. Finally, Wright convinced him
to forward a package of material to Follett. The author was
thrilled; he welcomed a chance to return to his roots as a
reporter.

Perot gave Follett the maximum Treatment. He sent a
Cadillac convertible complete with longhorn hood ornament
to meet Follett at the airport. This "cowboy taxi" delivered
Follett and his family to a waiting helicopter across the airport. Follett was whisked, not to Perot's estate, but to an EDS
ranch just outside Dallas. Even when the ranch was gone,
replaced by a high-tech industrial park, herds of buffalo and
longhorn still roamed its acres. Follett was delighted. The
close-cropped billionaire and the British dandy began a joshing relationship that survived two years of collaboration and
four drafts of *On Wings of Eagles.*

The two started off on the wrong foot. After a short spate
of interviewing, Follett got a chilly phone call from Perot. The
author had mentioned offhand to a Perot acquaintance that
the billionaire liked to embroider his adventures. Follett got
the message, even though he was right about Perot's tendency
to put too fine a point on his stories.

Follett won some and lost some editorially. Perot wanted the U.S. State Department painted in the blackest black on Follett's pallette. Follett managed to tell the story in grays. Perot was dead set against the word *bribery* appearing in the book. EDS didn't believe in bribery, and Perot wanted no possibility of confusion on the subject. Follett raised it elliptically. Perot had the upper hand. He could call off the project at any time; Perot did promise in that event to reimburse William Morrow and Co. for Follett's $1 million advance. (Follett's perseverance was rewarded. *On Wings* sold 300,000 copies.)

Perot kept the relationship light. Humor always helps. He told Follett at one point that the book was a lost cause because it didn't have any steamy passages. Follett tossed some gratuitous romance into the third draft starring the writer, himself. Perot rewrote it with himself as the male lead. After the book came out, he zapped Follett again. He had kidded Follett about being a lady's man. Some time after the book was published, Perot was in London on business. He arranged for a female EDS manager to call Follett. She was to ask Follett if she could drop by to make a "delivery." She rang his doorbell and stood at his door—with a suitcase in her hand and a pillow under her dress.

Perot was repaid for his two years working over the book with a No. 2 pencil. *On Wings* is the one of the most effective shapers of corporate image ever. Follett's taut, absorbing exposition of the Iran rescue sells EDS more effectively than any literature put together by a corporate public relations department. (Perot was not a literary influence, he complains in jest. Not one of the thousands of editorial improvements offered up by him or the EDS executives found its way into the book.)

On Wings did wonders for Perot personally. How many executives are featured in television miniseries? The same sort of horsetrading scenario unfolded. Edgar Sherick was the producer of the NBC miniseries. Sherick marvels, "I have never in my life had that kind of input. I don't think I've ever had a situation where a living, vital person was so closely involved in the story we were going to tell."[15] Perot had script approval as well as casting approval. Again, he understood the rules. In the miniseries, antagonist Dadgar chased the men to the frontier to stand shaking his fist impotently across the border at Perot. Neither man was there in real life. But television requires that sort of visual denouement, and Perot delivered.

The Iran rescue team wasn't impressed by the miniseries. Keane Taylor says he couldn't recognize much reality in the television drama. He was impressed with Follett. The author double- and triple-checked facts. "I don't know how you could write it more accurately," Taylor says.[16]

Perot delivered the goods for Doron Levin's page-one story in *The Wall Street Journal* on July 22, 1986. Perot had told the *Journal* about his 18-month fight with GM but he had kept most of it off the record. Nonetheless, he tossed Levin a dandy quote. The answer at GM, he cracked, was to nuke the system and start over. Perot knew that GM management wouldn't miss his point, particularly the folks at ground zero, the finance staff. The metaphors would grow more strident. Perot would be forced to recycle them.

Perot twice compared the chore of revitalizing General Motors to teaching an elephant to tap dance: You find the sensitive spots and start poking. The first time he used the analogy he was explaining to a *New York Times Magazine* reporter why Roger Smith could hope to reform GM's bureaucracy. That Smith's tactics of fear and pain were already backfiring didn't faze Perot; he is no lover of elephants.

The second time he trotted out his pachyderm, Perot not only was right metaphorically, he also was wickedly effective. There was no mistaking the message on the October 6 *Business Week* cover, combining the elephant quote and a stern portrait of Perot. Perot was GM's new trainer. The prod was the press. The sore spot was the company's public dignity.

And GM was very much the dumb beast of Perot's analogy. GM executives couldn't strike back at Perot without admitting that problems existed. They couldn't acknowledge the problems without accepting the judgment of history. The GM board was trying to be discreet. The professional managers/directors there politely fixed their gaze on their shoes while thousands of jobs and millions of dollars in stock value were vaporized. In the brave new world of takeovers, however, critics like Perot and Boone Pickens were able to turn the daily stock tables into plebiscites. Critical press was the hardest adjustment facing professional managers like Smith.

GM wasn't eager to grant interviews to *Business Week*. Presumably, Smith had stalked down the hall to flay his unfortunate manager of public relations after the Levin article. The latter was hired in the first place to keep reporters at bay. Now he had very personal and painful reasons to maintain several miles distance between his boss and the worthies from *Business Week*. Of course, GM was adding to its media problems. Objectivity doesn't flourish on a steady diet of unanswered calls and no comments. Smith agreed to interviews under duress. He turned the encounter into a verbal fencing match by refusing to acknowledge the reporters' premise, the existence of problems or critics.

Perot was delighted to see me, *Business Week's* reporter in Dallas. GM finance staff hadn't picked up on the World War III allusions in the Levin article; GM was still pressing him for audits. GM had completed the 1985 model year books on May 29, 1986, and the news was still grim. EDS billings were 13 percent above GM's budget. By then, GM had appointed an account manager to ride herd over EDS business. He was John E. Mischi, the nemesis of speech writer Albert Lee. Mischi wrote a memo to Perot's nemesis, Jack Edman, restating the need for an audit. In the model-year accounting, Mischi wrote that GM found more evidence of slipshod accounting by EDS—billing delays, improper approvals of work, and insufficient detail to figure out what was done.

Smith's communiques began sounding like legal briefs. The GM chairman expressed approval of Perot's new role as CFO and EDS's status as a completely separate financial entity, in a letter on June 24. However, he stipulated that Perot:

> will personally certify and warrant to General Motors officers, to the board of directors, to the stockholders and to all government authorities to which EDS financial data is submitted that. . . the financial data, audit and transactions procedures at EDS are in accordance with applicable standards and gen-

erally accepted accounting and auditing standards and practices and that General Motors and its officers are entitled to
rely on your certification and warranty.

In a more ominous development, outside counsel Ira Millstein
prepared a black book for GM director Evans, chairman of the
oversight committee, documenting the audit squabble to date.

In September, chief auditor Troost resubmitted his request for an audit to Perot, citing paragraph 3.6 of the master
agreement, the right to audit EDS cost-plus contracts. Perot
called Troost directly to decline. As Troost recalled the conversation, "I explained that this may create a problem with
the board oversight committee. He said he would prefer to
deal directly with the oversight committee and give them all
the assurance they would require without involvement of the
General Motors audit staff. . . . I said I would report his position to General Motors management."[17]

Perot was very frustrated when he sat down to talk to me.
He discussed his meetings with the UAW and the Cadillac
dealers and the anguish those groups felt at GM's continued
drift. Elephants weren't the only creatures in his metaphorical
zoo. Snakes are dealt with summarily at EDS, he said. At GM,
"first thing you do is organize a committee on snakes. Then
you bring in a consultant who knows a lot about snakes. Third
thing you do is talk about it for a year."[18]

He was angriest—off the record—about Smith's bad faith.
He lifted a corner of the veil covering GM board room delib-
erations. I saw the details that proved his point. One was the
aborted attempt by the nominating committee to throw him
off the board. He said he went to those responsible and told
them not to consider it unless they loved pain forever. It was
my job to deliver the message again, not with a severed horse's
head à la Mario Puzo's *Godfather*, but rather with something
just as horrifying to the professional management aristocracy:
a critical story.

Maybe in a leisurely, thoughtful world, I would have pon-
dered my role as coconspirator and declined. I don't live in
that world. I was fighting an impossible deadline and I was

grateful for help. I may have joked even about my temporary duty as elephant prod. The mission seemed worth it. I hastily typed up my account of the interview and shipped it off to my colleagues in Detroit. I asked them to consider everything off the record until I could sit down and separate the public Perot in my notes from the behind-the-scenes Perot. They were flailing. GM's PR department was acting true to form. My Detroit colleagues' entreaties for interviews fell on deaf ears inside GM. It was an enlightened deafness, at least. Lee writes in *Call Me Roger*:

> In the public relations department there were discussions about what we should do about Ross Perot. . . . Public debate was out of the question considering Ross's skills and Roger's lack thereof. And someone, not knowing about the [May 7] ultimatum letter, even suggested a buyout. I said that would be a bad idea. President Johnson, Jack McNulty's former boss, had a similar problem with J. Edgar Hoover. When someone asked Johnson why he didn't fire Hoover, he said: "I would rather have him on the inside of the tent pissing out than on the outside of the tent pissing in."[19]

Bless them, they knew what was coming. When Smith finally agreed to meet with my colleagues he was busy applying happy faces:

> If someone calls [Perot] up he's not going to slam down the phone and say "I'm an outside director. I'm not going to talk to you." I would be disappointed in him if he did that. . . . He doesn't come to the meetings with purple suits on or anything. He's a good solid American businessman. . . . He's poking the organization. He wants the best for us, and he wants the best for his own company. I have no complaints.[20]

Roger Smith's faith was about to be shaken. What about the efforts on the board to remove him as a director? my colleagues asked. Smith turned bright red and shouted, spittle flying, Who told you that? Mr. Perot, they answered. No one said the press was a perfect weapon. I called Perot to confess that my colleagues accidentally had blown his cover. After a sharp exhalation and 20 seconds of silence on the other end of the line, Perot recovered. Well, he said, I'm unsaying that part of the story then. The strings were showing but he had gotten his message across.

The figurative severed horse head worked too. Richard C. Gerstenberg, Murphy's mentor and predecessor as chairman, invited Murphy to lunch at the Bloomfield Hills Country Club to find out what the hell was happening on the GM board. His advice to Murphy echoed Murphy's to Smith a year earlier—take care of the problem before morale registered in negative numbers.

Morale on the EDS side of the house also was nearing zero. EDS had not won many hearts and minds in Detroit, even though both sides were becoming too weary to fight. Perot rekindled it as a shooting war. Says Fernandes, "Even the GMers who liked us had a visceral, negative reaction. It's all right for you to be critical of your institution, but for someone else to do it publicly. . . ."[21]

Perot wasn't consulting Alberthal or even warning him for that matter. On one of Bill Wright's treks down the seventh-floor corridor to read the prevailing winds for Alberthal, EDS's PR manager spied a company PC in the conference room adjoining EDS and a strange man working at it. It was the *Journal*'s Doron Levin. "We had a rather bizarre situation," says Wright. "A sitting chairman of a corporation had mounted an all-out offensive in the media against the parent company. Big time, as only a few people I know can do it big time. Down the hall was Les Alberthal trying to keep the company together."[22]

Says Alberthal, "He was saying what the press wanted to hear. He was saying what the union wanted to hear. All he was doing was fanning the fire. To be constructive, to help the situation, you wouldn't go out to the press and do the things he was doing." Alberthal's is revisionist history. At the time, EDSers sided with Perot.[23]

Perot had the beast dancing frantically. He observed in the November 1986 *Ward's Auto World*:

In my opinion, we need to do a number of symbolic things to signal a new day at GM. For example, I would get rid of the [executive] 14th floor. I would get rid of the executive dining rooms. I would urge the senior executives to locate their offices where real people are doing real work—live with them, listen to them, spend time with them, find out straight up what it takes to win, and do it. Today our top people are isolated.

Negotiations on the long-term fixed-price contracts that Jim Buchanan and the rest of EDS's Detroit contigent had fought for were dead in the water. EDS account manager Kenn Hill was caught in the crossfire between Perot and GM. When Perot had learned of the audit that summer, he had picked up the phone to call Hill first. An anguished Hill called Mischi, his counterpart. The two had met that morning, and Mischi had not said a word about audits. Mischi supplied the letter to Hill after the fact.

Smith took a few feeble swats back at Perot. "Ross has an office that makes mine look like shanty town," Smith said near the end. But Smith was hogtied. He realized everything he said also fanned the flames. "The EDS employees at General Motors were loyal to EDS and at the time felt very loyal to Mr Perot," he says. "[Similarly] the General Motors employees didn't like to see their company besmirched in the news media for whatever reason."[24]

Perot was not so much fanning the flames as lighting backfires. The oversight committee was bearing down on him in all of its august majesty. He could not refuse audits under paragraph 3.6 of the January 1986 master agreement. To do so would require EDS to break its word. He offered a compromise. He would pay out of his pocket for Peat Marwick, rather than GM's staff, to perform the audit. Smith agreed.

Perot called Evans on November 1, 1986, to say he would agree to an audit by Peat Marwick. He invited Evans, as chairman of the audit committee, to come to him directly. Evans declined, asking Perot instead to go through channels. "But I said I welcomed the spirit which prompted him to call me and I was pleased beyond measure . . . to hear him say what I thought he said."[25]

Perot replied that there was no SEC requirement mandating the audit. Evans conceded the point. However, Evans maintained, the board faced "responsibilities and due diligence under recent case law . . . that gave us great pause. I felt specifically as chairman of the committee that he would not want to put us in any untenable position."[26]

Perot tried one last time, according to Evans:

> He said he would never want to place us in any untenable position and he thus hoped the matter could be worked out. But he would do it largely because I as one gentleman, requested him as another gentleman to do it.
>
> And I said "Ross, I'm really coming to you obviously as a friend and a man who has great respect for you, but I also earnestly believe that good corporate governance requires that the books and accounts and internal procedures and systems of a wholly owned subsidiary be verified by the parent audit staff."[27]

Evans would not let Perot off the hook. The purpose of the exercise was to make him recognize the system.

Evans reported the auditing compromise and his telephone conversation during the board meeting on the following Monday, November 4. Perot acknowledged the phone call unenthusiastically. He said the details were not worked out and complained once again that the SEC had no specific requirements for what GM asked of him. The audits began that month nonetheless and uncovered 327 deficiencies at the EDS sites reviewed. Evans was unwilling to characterize the findings as "mismanagement." Meanwhile, attorneys Luce and Johnson met to reopen the question of a buyout. GM thought the game was over. Actually Perot had one last bit of spin up his sleeve.

CHAPTER FOURTEEN

THE NUCLEAR OPTION

The buyout began pleasantly enough. Perot attorney Tom Luce and GM counsel Elmer Johnson met for a lunch at New York's Plaza Hotel on November 5, two days after the boardroom showdown. The tall, owlish men, who resemble each other vaguely, had been professional fixers too long to get caught up personally. Luce explained that Perot was frustrated, plain and simple, and dallying past January 1 would cost him $50 million under the Tax Reform Act of 1986. "I recall a little kidding," Johnson says, "[that the tax act] couldn't make that much difference. What's $50 million to Ross Perot? He said Ross Perot watches the little dollar amounts as well as the big dollar amounts, and don't ever think that he's not conscious of even a small tax advantage like that."[1]

Luce borrowed the language of a less genteel law specialty. Johnson says, "I remember him using a phrase that both of us had used a number of times, *irreconcilable differences*."[2] The two lawyers set about their work, scripting a tidy, quiet dissolution of the Perot/Smith marriage.

Instead, the buyout turned out to be one of the loudest divorces in the history of American business. How did that happen? A furious Johnson wanted to know, himself, on the morning of December 1, after Perot called a press conference to offer to give the money back. Perot had specifically agreed in paragraph 8 of the buyout agreement to stop criticizing GM, subject to a $7.5 million penalty. Johnson and Ira Millstein phoned Luce and demanded an explanation. Luce didn't have one.

Luce could only say lamely that he was as surprised as Johnson and Millstein were by the escrow offer. "I didn't know there was going to be a press conference," Luce says, "and therefore I couldn't answer any of the questions he was asking."[3] From the start, Luce had insisted that the negotiations were his idea and that he couldn't predict how Perot would react. But was it possible that Perot would defer to Luce on a $700 million deal? Even so, how could Luce completely misread his client of 12 years?

EDS officers understood what Luce was doing. For years they had marveled at Perot's intuitive genius, at how many facets there were to his thinking. In a sense, the entrepreneur convened a committee in his head to weigh decisions and formulate answers. They were good answers by the time the ideologue, leader, pragmatist, patriot and populist in Perot had signed off on them. EDS officers also knew what happened on those rare occasions when he failed to come up with a satisfactory answer. The buyout decision paralyzed Perot. Luce stepped in to save EDS.

There was no way for Perot's mental committee to agree on the buyout. Pragmatist Perot had decided that a deal, while "a serious mistake for GM ... does reduce the issue to business terms," as he put it in his May 19 letter to Smith. Ideologue Perot could not go along. A sharp deal was the best he could accomplish. The more one-sided he made it in his favor, the more this shifted the onus to GM's thin-skinned, rubber-stamp directors. In his mind, Perot wasn't selling out; he was acquiescing to a ridiculous and futile exercise. "My attitude all the way through," he says, "was that nobody would ever sign this agreement on the General Motors side .... But I guess I underestimated just how badly they wanted to buy me out."[4] Perot would not act until GM did. Luce had no way of knowing that Perot would fight on.

Perot manipulated EDS senior management also. The gulf was never wider between the group and its charismatic leader. Alberthal, Fernandes, and the others, men in their 40s who had never worked for another company—had no reason to be repulsed by GM's bureaucracy. (It must be said, they weren't thrilled by it either.) They had made their marks at EDS as engineers, salesmen, and administrators rather than charismatic leaders. They could compromise. Perot seldom gave them that option. Predictably he put the choice to them in stark terms; victory or defeat.

They turned to Meyerson to pull off another miracle. For a few months in late summer 1986, it looked as if he could. A Stanford University professor had tracked him down on his vacation in Switzerland. The professor was consulting AT&T on its difficult transition from regulated monopoly to free-market computer manufacturer, and wanted Meyerson's thoughts. Meyerson kept kicking the call around in his head until an old answer leaped up. What AT&T needed was EDS! If GM sold 25 percent of EDS to AT&T, sold another 50 percent to the public, and kept 25 percent, then EDS effectively would regain its independence. Meyerson raced back to Dallas.

Perot was enthusiastic, and Smith was encouraging also. (Separately, Smith sounded out IBM chairman, John Akers, about a similar joint venture.) He told Meyerson to proceed on his own; dragging GM's finance staff into the game would only slow him down. Meyerson, Stu Reeves, Alberthal, Walter, and Luce plunged into negotiations with AT&T executives. Fernandes came along at the start, but when he raised such skeptical questions as how AT&T would be any less bureaucratic and thus easier to deal with than GM, Meyerson stopped inviting him.

The tax code proved to be a tougher hurdle. Unless AT&T bought 80 percent or more of EDS, the phone giant would be denied attractive tax benefits. AT&T chairman, Jim Olson, flew to Detroit on a Saturday in October to try out a new concept on GM. Don Atwood met him at GM's hangar. Yes, GM was willing to sell all of EDS. Atwood stepped in and took over the negotiations for GM. Meyerson's miracle melted. Obviously substituting AT&T as a majority owner wasn't likely to restore EDS's independence.

Meyerson hung in there because of the unspoken agenda; an AT&T deal would provide a face-saving out for those who wanted it and a fresh start for those who wanted to stay. In Johnson's estimation, Perot would be out. AT&T could gauge the level of tensions inside the GM board room by walking past a newsstand. Johnson didn't think that Perot and AT&T would repeat that mistake. No one knew where Meyerson stood. While discussing what role he would play at AT&T, he was penciling into the deal a substantial finder's fee for himself. "The fee was off-putting to both AT&T and GM," Fernandes says.[5]

The deal collapsed because AT&T misread GM's eagerness to lose Perot. Atwood refused to commit GM to a long-term contract for EDS services. If GM was only a minority owner of EDS, he insisted, then GM should be able to bid its data processing competitively. That made the deal much less valuable to AT&T, since three fourths of EDS's business would be up for grabs periodically. Atwood shrugged: That would be true only if EDS proved uncompetitive. GM was asking $5 billion for EDS. AT&T was offering something closer to $3 billion. The deal died in a brief phone call between Olson and Smith on November 3, the same day Perot grudgingly agreed to GM audits.

The monthly officer meeting at EDS the following week was a grim affair. Meyerson's outlook had soured further after the AT&T deal slipped through his fingers. Worse, Atwood had dressed down Meyerson in public after Meyerson contradicted him during the negotiations by implying that it was not in GM's best interests to bid its data processing competitively. Perot certainly was no happier. Perot muttered that nothing got a response from GM except fresh insults. The group ran through the options once more. "The bulk of the options were ideas brought to the meeting by Ross and Mort," says Alberthal, "and they included such things as going out on strike and shutting down General Motors. There was a generalized term of nuking them, whatever that meant."[6]

Among the other thermonuclear options was a shareholder's lawsuit to force GM to live up to the merger agreement. A proxy fight was another possibility. Perot had been impressed by the remarks of former Treasury Secretary William Simon in a magazine article. Simon was nominated in casual discussion to replace Smith. Perot and Meyerson on one side, and Alberthal and Heller on the other, were talking at cross purposes. The first pair kept putting the choice on a personal level: "If you aren't brave enough . . ." Alberthal and Heller answered that bravery wasn't the question—responsibility was. Finally Alberthal and Heller stalked out of the room. Recalls Alberthal:

> "It . . . gave the impression to me from statements that Meyerson was making that if the senior officers wouldn't go to war . . . [then] we really didn't have the strength or stomach to be leaders, and generally . . . that if it wasn't to be war then the whole decision rested on everybody's shoulders. . . . I was tired of the implication that we weren't strong enough to do the right thing."

Alberthal found Meyerson later and told him that he wasn't listening to what the senior officers were saying. "There was no way I could support the kind of actions they were talking about."[7]

Other managers felt manipulated. Senior vice president Malcolm Gudis stands out among EDS officers as a copious taker of notes. He wrote in his notes of that meeting "This kangaroo court is presiding over EDS's burial." He explains, "I meant to infer that it was an activity where the decision had already been made."[8]

Perot left the room to allow the officers to discuss their options. They really had none. Nuking GM was out of the question regardless of whose welfare was foremost in their minds—their own or that of the other 40,000 EDS employees. They brought up AT&T again. Even if they were not independent under Ma Bell, they at least had no history either. Senior vice president Stuart Reeves expressed the fond hope that EDS would not bully its way into AT&T if they had a chance to start over.

They grasped at the one straw remaining. As Perot testified on the witness stand in Virginia, "I came back into the room and their counsel was that they wanted to get free of General Motors, and I think it was a unanimous feeling about that and a unanimous feeling that [Meyerson should] try to reopen the AT&T negotiations." Perot, Meyerson, Luce, and Walter voted no. The rest of the officers voted yes. Meyerson flew to New York to sound out AT&T, but the deal was dead.

Luce and Johnson were making swift progress on the buyout. Johnson's old Chicago law firm, Kirkland and Ellis, had a draft on Luce's desk within days of the Plaza lunch. In the first pass, Johnson wanted to keep Perot out of the computer-services business for five years. Perot wouldn't even read it. The first page had blanks where the prices would go. Perot told Luce, "I'm not going to agree to anything. I'm not going to discuss it further until Roger agrees to a price."[9]

Luce and Johnson met a second time on November 18 in Herndon, Virginia, where the EDS board was dedicating a new EDS information processing center and conducting its quarterly meeting. The lawyers found a small room to resume the negotiations. Luce told Johnson that Perot wouldn't budge until a price was on the table. Johnson nodded, and drew out Luce on other elements. The two began discussing how long Perot should be barred from hiring EDS people or competing against EDS. The first draft had a five-year noncompete period. Johnson briefed Smith as the two men flew back to Detroit on the corporate jet. Johnson called Luce that day. Smith had agreed on a price. "Mr Smith said that I should go ahead and proceed on the basis that that price, after all kinds of studies, would prove to be acceptable to GM," says Johnson.[10]

Perot asked for the $62.50 per share that GM had guaranteed by issuing notes to make up the difference between the market price and the target as of October 1991. Because GM was making good on the notes for Perot five years early, the shares were discounted somewhat. The final price was $60. GME shares were trading in the open market at $31. GM put Salomon Brothers bankers to work on the buyout to assess whether or not the deal was fair to GM's other shareholders.

Luce and Johnson settled in at the New York offices of Weil Gottschal & Manges for the final effort on November 21. Luce raised a problem. He told Johnson, "Ross might be asked to get involved in a reorganization of the Defense Department and similar projects, and, if he did, he would need to be able to supply data processing services to government bodies."[11] Johnson admired Perot's philanthropy and had no objections to waiving the nonhire and noncompete clauses for charitable work after 18 months. The pair also settled on a three-year computer-services industry exile for Perot instead of five.

The next day, Luce pointed out that the nonprofit hiring clause really meant nothing, since EDS routinely required all of its employees to sign their own noncompete agreements. Perot had the right to ask EDS people to join him, but the EDS employees had no right to agree. Again, Johnson had no problem with waiving the noncompete contracts of the 40,000 EDS employees so that they could join Perot in nonprofit work.

The two sides introduced other clauses. Perot wanted to make sure that his officers couldn't be lynched after his departure. The contract specifies that EDS executives could not be fired except for moral turpitude or reassigned against their will to any city except Dallas or Detroit. GM agreed to accelerate the vesting of senior EDS people's stock to January 1, 1988. Another clause required GM to honor the letter and the spirit of the 1984 merger agreement. For its part, GM added a gag clause that subjected either side to a $7.5 million penalty for criticizing the other.

Johnson checked in briefly with Smith and found that the draft was generally acceptable to GM. Luce warned Johnson again that Perot had not specifically sanctioned the negotiations and therefore might not agree. Luce called Perot that night to brief him. The two sat down in Perot's office on Saturday to go over the agreement line by line. Luce flew to Detroit on Sunday with specific instructions from Perot.

The two lawyers' stories diverge at this point. Luce insists that his dinner meeting with Johnson at the Bloomfield Hills Country Club had a specific purpose:

> I wanted him to know because I didn't want him hanging out . . . that I did not know if Mr. Perot would agree to the draft that I was coming to Detroit with. In particular I wanted to tell him that there were particular paragraphs that were very sensitive and that I would not have much flexibility. . . . I didn't want for him to be surprised . . . the next day [when] we were meeting in front of other people, as to the inflexibility of my position on certain things.[12]

Among the paragraphs were the ones that were litigated in Virginia. Luce says, "I told him that it was my judgment that Ross viewed himself in some ways as a general leaving the battlefield and that there was no way, based on my experience with Ross, that he would agree to do so without protecting the troops."[13] Johnson doesn't remember the warning or the "general" analogy. He didn't consider the meeting a negotiating session at all. After dinner, he took Luce to his home nearby and introduced him to his wife.

Luce and Johnson had a final session on Monday in an office building across Grand River Boulevard from GM headquarters. It lasted only a few hours. Luce told Johnson that if Smith approved it unofficially, he would present it to Perot. Johnson carried it across the street and returned shortly with Smith's approval. Luce flew back to Dallas.

Alberthal had left the Virginia board meeting for a week-long trip to London. He knew vaguely that Luce was exploring a buyout agreement; Perot buyout was one of the dozens of rumors he had heard floating around the company. When his corporate jet landed in Washington on November 25, he finally had confirmation. He had two urgent messages waiting for him: Call Meyerson and call Don Atwood. He called Meyerson first. Meyerson was curt. "Mort said I think we have come to an agreement whereby Ross, myself, Tom Walter and Bill Gayden are going to leave, and you need to call Don Atwood. . . . He's going to talk to you about stepping in and running EDS.' "[14]

Atwood asked him to fly immediately to Detroit. "What Don wanted to know from me was first would I take over and stay with EDS and run it, and secondly . . . what was I going to do to keep the company from falling apart?"[15] The meeting lasted only an hour. Alberthal told Atwood that EDS would survive. He flew home and warned his wife that he was going to be very busy for a long time.

Luce opened the officers' meeting the following day. The AT&T deal was dead. He then described the deal he had fashioned for Perot, Meyerson, Walter, Gayden, and three of the executives' senior aides. Perot took the floor. He said he was there to kick the agreement around with the senior managers. Luce remembers him asking directly if he should sign it. Perot thought he heard the answer "yes." "My sense is that all the officers were very pleased with the outcome," he says. "We hadn't gotten everything we wanted, but they felt it was a good outcome. . . . If they had given me any indication at all that they were concerned that would have stopped me in my tracks."[16]

Quite likely, Perot read his officers correctly. Even though this meeting was the controversial heart of EDS's case in Virginia—the proverbial "what EDSers knew and when they learned it"—it played out innocently for three reasons. For one, the officers knew the question was rhetorical. "I remember writing it off as being not that important because the agreement was being negotiated . . . without our involvement," says Alberthal.[17] Second, while the EDS officers had no idea what GM would do once Perot was no longer barring the door, they too realized that the status quo was untenable.

Last but not least, they were relieved to see that Perot had protected them as best he could. They couldn't be fired or transferred summarily. They had only to last 13 months until they owned all of their incentive stock outright. Perot had also given them a "get out of jail free" card. Meyerson jokingly called it the "free the slaves" clause. Admits Fernandes, "None of us really took strong exception to . . . the rights Perot was granted to hire EDS people, which was clearly an egregious thing for EDS. You have to ask yourself why. Deep down in my soul, I was not sure I would not want to use that as an escape hatch. . . . Human nature being what it is, I wouldn't be surprised that there was some of that at work."[18]

Fernandes also knew that Perot wanted the deal. He was stationed in London, so Luce had shipped him the consent forms to sign as an EDS director—but no agreement. Fernandes called Luce to tell him, "I was not inclined to sign the deal. I didn't ask to talk to Ross, but I got a call back from him very shortly. . . . It was basically a one-way conversation . . . for Ross to point out the positive things about the contract. . . . Sometimes with Ross you don't get much of an opportunity for response."[19] Fernandes signed his consent and sent it to Alberthal, in effect granting Alberthal his proxy.

There was still talk of other options. CFO Davis Hamlin cornered Perot after the meeting and asked him not to sign the buyout deal. "Ross was saying like 'well, you know, Davis, what do you think we ought to do?' " recalls Luce. "[Davis] said the option he preferred was for Ross and Mort and Bill and Tom to stay there and work out the disagreements with General Motors, and Ross kept saying 'Davis, we've tried. I don't know what else to do to try to work them out.' "[20] Hamlin was still in shock at end of a briefer meeting on Sunday, November 30. Hamlin left the meeting stunned, he says, thinking, "My gosh, this thing is done."[21] Alberthal, who had met with Tom Luce in his office on Saturday, went over to Luce's home on Sunday to sign a stack of documents three feet deep. Perot dropped by the Sunday meeting and commended his officers for getting on with the job at hand.

And what a job it was. Mergers are always stressful to employees, who can only react to what happens next. In that sense, EDSers had been listening for three years for the footsteps that would signal GM was taking over and turning their world upside down. Even though GM never did it, their working lives had been plunged into turmoil from the first day. There wasn't a corner of the company that hadn't been strained to the breaking point by the merger.

Once Perot was gone, all the original anxieties flooded back in. EDS employees stumbled through that Monday with a sense of foreboding. Had a way of life, a company culture, left with Perot? "GM is saying, 'Act like Perot and this is what we will do to you,'" a stunned EDS employee in Pennsylvania said at the time. GME stock was another blow. The stock fell from $31 to $26.88, a yearly low.

The EDS managers fanned out around the globe to put the happiest face on the news. The principal arguments made by Heller in Detroit or Gudis in London were sound ones. Relax, they said. Perot isn't gone—he stayed on with the title of "founder"—but the bad blood is. They did not use their most compelling evidence that GM must be more solicitous of EDS than ever: If the automaker did not win the hearts and minds of EDSers in the next three years—their old charismatic leader would be waiting across the street. Perot says he stopped Alberthal in the hall some weeks later to ask him why he had not explained the "free the slaves" clause to the company. Alberthal doesn't recall the encounter.

That Sunday evening in New York's Regency Hotel, GM directors traced through the web of loyalties binding EDS employees to their company, and ultimately to GM. The EDS acquisition never looked more in doubt. Atwood could offer limited assurances. He liked Alberthal, trusted him, and had formed a good working relationship with him since the previous April. Alberthal had told him that EDSers would stick. Atwood himself said the best solution was to turn Perot around and keep him on board, but both Atwood and Salomon Brothers chairman John Gutfreund thought it unlikely that Perot could relent.

They agreed that the present situation was intolerable. The compensation and audit issues had faded after Perot's attacks in the press. "There is a much larger issue," notes Johnson, "and that is the issue of the chairman of a subsidiary who is also a director of General Motors holding press conferences, talking to the press freely, using the press as an alternative to the forum of the board of directors. . . . I thought that was a governance issue in its largest sense."[22]

Director Marvin Goldberger wanted to know if Johnson had considered the option of firing Perot. Johnson had, and had dismissed it as too dangerous. After the news stories in

October, no one doubted his resolve to start World War III. Johnson wondered if the "alliance" could stand a protracted public battle.

Gutfreund warned the board that they were in for another spate of adverse criticism. In fact, it had already started. Reporter Levin of *The Wall Street Journal* had called that afternoon seeking confirmation of the buyout. The board meeting was moved up so that GM could get the deal done before the stock market opened. John Horan moved to bring the deal to the board. Goldberger seconded his motion. The committee approved it unanimously. The four-hour meeting broke up.

Johnson called Perot first thing Monday morning. He had some mechanics to discuss with Luce. He also wanted an assurance that Perot would sign the deal if the board did. Luce told Johnson that Perot was sitting nearby, and he turned over the phone. As it turned out, Perot wanted to wait several days before accepting the offer. "I think he felt his departure from the scene might be such a shock to the employees that it could go to the very wisdom of the transaction," says Johnson.[23]

Johnson was not willing to give Perot a last plebiscite. He insisted that Perot sign, and Perot promised that he would. Johnson called Luce back after the board action and Luce took the papers in for Perot to sign. Inexplicably, the money got lost in the wire transfer system for nearly an hour. When Luce had confirmed receipt he had the stock certificates delivered to GM. The deal was done.

Perot strode down the hall to EDS's ground floor cafeteria where the press was waiting. He got his spin in a bit of hallway repartee about management's willingness to pay premiums, "greenmail," to get rid of raiders. "All right Perot," he repeated the bit for the reporters, "What is this? Greenmail?" Another guy answered him, "No, it's hushmail.' "[24]

Perot began the press conference with a statement:

> At a time when GM is closing 11 plants, putting over 30,000 people out of work, cutting back on capital expenditures, losing market share and having problems with profitability, I have just received $700 million from GM in exchange for my Series E stock and notes. I cannot accept this money without giving

the GM directors another chance to consider this decision. This money will be held in escrow until December 15 in order to give the GM directors time to review this matter and the events that led to this decision."

If the GM directors conclude that this transaction of December 1 isn't in the best interests of GM and Series E shareholders, I will work with the GM directors to rescind this transaction.

Under questioning, he was magnificent as usual. GM had to listen to him as founder without portfolio, Perot said, because he was the best evidence GM had that the new EDS was stable and reliable. His role would be the same, he said. He would step in to help sell the big deals. "I don't need a big block of stock to remain concerned about what happens at EDS," he said. "Twenty years from now, if they need me, I'll be right here. . . . I'll be able to spend more time on my business interests away from EDS which are quite substantial. I intend to become very active investing in venture capital startups. . . . Don't worry about me. I am not going to show up tonight at a rescue mission."[25]

GM had the first evidence of how bad a deal it had struck. Perot made a joke during the press conference about the gag clause. Throwing open the floor to questions, he quipped, "Don't ask me any questions that will cost me money." Perot knew that Smith would not be able to enforce the gag clause without prolonging the story and deepening the public relations black eye.

GM's PR staff brought the first accounts to Smith. Smith summoned Johnson and demanded to know what was going on. "I expressed complete surprise and said I would call Mr. Luce and find out," says Johnson.[26] He and Millstein placed the call to Luce. "This is a flat violation of paragraph 8 [the gag rule.] How could Ross Perot do anything like this?" Millstein recalls saying.[27] Luce had no explanation. He told the lawyers he was ill and he was going home. Says Alberthal, "He was white. He was very, very upset because it made a blow to his integrity."[28]

Johnson, Millstein, GM's PR staff, and Wall Street spin artist Gershon Kekst held a brief summit. They recommended to the directors that they formally consider the escrow offer, decline it, and reconfirm the deal. That done, Johnson called Luce at home to read him the statement GM would issue and to find out what Luce had learned. Johnson reached his wife. He wasn't home yet.

EDS's attorneys learned in Virginia that Perot paid Luce $2 million after the buyout. As Perot explains it, "It was done for years of outstanding work in building the company I was now leaving. It was very much on my conscience that I had made everyone else extremely wealthy who has worked with me in building EDS except the one guy outside the company, who it was always inappropriate for me to give a stock award to."[29]

Johnson and Perot would spar repeatedly over the next two weeks as institutional investors called GM on the carpet to complain about the buyout and to urge GM to take the escrowed money back. The pair then traded barbs in the press for a year afterward. Johnson finally telephoned Perot after returning from a vacation in Arizona in January 1988. "I told him I had made a New Year's resolution that I wasn't going to say anything unkind about a man I admired as much as him, even though I had been severely disappointed in some of the things that had taken place." Johnson forgave Perot.[30]

Perot still had a couple of disappointments in store for Johnson. Baker & Botts attorney Phillip Smith pinned him down on the escrow account, Perot's final, devastating bit of spin:

SMITH:

Nothing prevented you from changing your mind, did it?

PEROT:

I would have given it back immediately to General Motors. . . .

SMITH:

I'm saying you were free to change your mind on that point if you wished. . . .

PEROT:

I didn't consider myself free to change my mind at all because I had made a public commitment I would do it.

SMITH:

There was no type of escrow agreement with anybody that would prevent you from changing your mind, was there?

PEROT:

I would have been glad to have entered into one with General Motors on the afternoon of the first, but I believe either by that afternoon or the second, [GM director] Evans for reasons best understood by General Motors made the statement that they didn't want to reconsider. But I left it in that status because the institutional investors and the stockholders asked me to until the end of the month.

SMITH:

But you never did enter into such an agreement, did you?

PEROT:

I saw no purpose in entering into it. It didn't happen. It was— it wasn't necessary.[31]

Perot knew GM would not recant. There never was an escrow account.

CHAPTER FIFTEEN

HIS MEAGER VISION

Perot won. Bodies were everywhere and his was one of them, but he prevailed once again. GM outside directors shouldered their responsibilities. The very next time the board's salary and bonus committee met, members took it upon themselves to cut the 1986 bonus plan for Smith and the other top GM executives. The temple pillars rocked again the following year when outside directors politely but firmly nixed Smith's plan to add three executive vice presidents to the board. The three were later accepted as nonvoting directors.

The board wasn't in full revolt. Its committees traditionally had the last word on management and board changes, salaries, and audits. But they didn't always make the effort to understand the changes being presented to them by the GM executives who served the committees as secretaries. Directors are paying more attention today. Lawsuits work wonderfully to focus one's concentration. Shareholders filed no less than 15 suits contesting the Perot buyout contract. Perot snorts that not one of the GM directors had bothered to read the 15-page agreement before accepting it.

GM's management was struggling to change also. Quietly the heated parking garages, the executive dining rooms, and the other trappings of privilege were disappearing at GM. GM hired corporate-culture expert William W. Scherkenbach away from Ford in the summer of 1987 to begin the task of substituting team-oriented management for GM's hoary system of institutionalized rivalry. Smith also hired "facilitator" Mark Sarkady to follow him around and save him from himself. Sarkady brought together the top 18 GM executives in 1988 for a rare informal meeting away from the office. When Smith fired a sharp question at a subordinate during this session, Sarkady interrupted the boss: "How would you feel, Roger, if somebody asked you a question like that?"[1] Smith apologized and started over.

GM even discovered symbolism. Smith declared in a speech in late 1988 that he was not letting up on reform even though he was approaching mandatory retirement age. GM had buttons ready that echoed his punch line: "I'm in!" Smith also came around in his view of the union. Donald Ephlin, GM's black-and-blue ally at the UAW, says, "I happen to like Roger. I think he's done some things poorly because he gets bad . . . input."[2] Smith in 1988 attended the UAW's General Motors Department retreat in northern Michigan, met his old adversaries in frank, friendly discussions, and stayed past his scheduled departure. The elephant was learning to tap dance.

Perot, meanwhile, barely changed his tune. Perot continues to swipe at Roger Smith from exile—and keep the pot stirred for the new management of EDS. Even so, GM and EDS have settled into a good relationship. GM did not trample on EDS culture as Perot predicted. EDS finally was able to get on with the job without Perot's seismic interruptions. Perot's influence still lingers. Hughes Aircraft Corporation people, for example, have not forgiven EDS for Perot's criticism of the Hughes deal. But EDS and GM can finally talk about the "alliance" without hearing snorts of derision from the ranks.

Perot relied on his stump speech in his first appearance after the buyout. Significantly the speech was a joint address by Smith and Perot before the Economic Club of Detroit on December 8, a week after the buyback. The joint speech was one of the loose ends of the hasty buyout deal. The divorcées kept the date and outdrew any speaker in the club's history, including former President Ronald Reagan.

Perot didn't disappoint the reporters and television crews crowded into Cobo Hall, although he had done a better job with the same speech in September at the North Dallas Chamber of Commerce. The antielite strains in his speech that day reach all the way back to Texarkana. "Whether we like to admit it or not today we are losing the world competitive battle. We are like the inheritors of great wealth. We are living the good life. We're taking out too much and we're putting back too little."[3]

In Perot's unchanging view of American big business, an isolated management aristocracy keeps failing the real Americans on the shop floor, who still possess uncommon competitive spirit and pioneer ingenuity. In subsequent speeches, Perot grew blunter in his criticism of bosses who make workers pay for management's mistakes. He takes the voice of a factory-floor worker to make his point. "If I'm the culprit let me ask you some questions while I have all you bigshots in the room. . . . Did I have anything to do with product design or engineering?. . . If you design it bad and engineer it bad I can't make it good on the factory floor. If you give me junk to put together it's going to be junk."[4]

Imagine this scene as a Norman-Rockwell painting. A man in coveralls, cap pushed back on his head, is holding a broken part in one hand, scratching his head with the other. Three co-workers are looking over his shoulder. The disgust evident on their faces tells the story. We'll have to paint a backdrop of partially assembled 1948 DeSotos for this tableau, because this isn't Detroit in the late 1980s.

The UAW was the first to realize how close to the precipice management and labor had rolled in 50 years of combat. But the guy on the floor taking home $60,000 a year and spending weekends at his lake home is a part of GM's problem also.

A *Fortune* cover story revealed the meagerness of Perot's vision. Perot wrote for a February, 1988 issue, "How I Would Turn Around GM." The article, unabridged Perot on GM, made the same points he had been making for two and a half years. Perot was still light on specifics and long on leadership generalizations. "Most committees will be scrapped. . . . All executives will move to car manufacturing plants and other production facilities. . . . GMers will fight in the marketplace, not with one another."[5]

Perot had not acknowledged that GM was taking those important, symbolic first steps, but that wasn't the most troublesome part of the article. The damning flaw in it was how absolutely devoid Perot was of either understanding or specifics. University of Michigan professor David Cole agreed with Perot two years earlier when Perot was urging Smith to acknowledge GM's problems. No more. "I was so upset when I read that article," says Cole, director of the UM Office for the Study of Automotive Transportation. "He was dealing with the obvious. He didn't have a grasp of the problems of implementing change in a massive organization. When someone like Perot comes along and trivializes the problem you don't do anyone any good."[6] Ephlin takes a blunter approach: "Doing it is a hell of lot different than saying it."[7]

Perot generalizes, "Management will no longer be used at GM. Leadership will be required to build the finest cars in the world, not management. Inventories can be managed. People will be led."[8] But led where? Global competition turned GM's world upside down. GM's edge in the 1960s, its size, is now the carmaker's obstacle. GM is no longer able to spread its tooling costs over a million Chevy Impalas, as it did in 1960s, and use those economies of scale to clobber Ford and Chrysler. There were 25 manufacturers in the late 1980s building 156 car lines and carving the global car market into smaller and smaller slices. The biggest production run in the 1988 model year was the Ford Escort at 388,000 vehicles.

Speed and fashion are the new virtues of a successful carmaker. Ford tapped a new taste for sleek, rounded cars. Chrysler found a market for minivans. Both companies capitalized on their head starts and carved out impressive gains on GM. Once GM was the cleverest company at reading the fashion winds. Perhaps its designers still are—under all those layers of control. In one of the definitive stories about Donald Petersen, the man responsible for Ford's renaissance, he shrugged when Ford's designers complained of their assignments. "Show us your own ideas," Petersen answered. The result: the Ford Taurus. Says GM retiree Alex Mair: "Time to market is everything. Now everyone else has styling savvy, and GM is not fast any more."[9] Perot is right about GM getting too many people involved.

In *Fortune,* Perot oversimplified the job of getting market savvy. "GM will listen to its customers, [and] listen to its dealers who sell cars to its customers. . . . Ideas fresh from the marketplace will make GM the best in the world.[10]

What happens when Olds dealers and Chevy dealers offer contradictory advice? GM needs twice the marketing flash and sizzle to make its Chevys and Pontiacs stand out from Fords— and from each other. Who buys Buicks, and what do they want that Oldsmobile owners don't?

Weeding out product lines and protecting sales are more difficult than finding another niche to exploit. GM has the most market share to give up, and therefore has the largest problem. GM began the decade of the 1980s with 46 percent of American auto sales and finished with 35 percent. GM's history has become its burden.

Perot's advice in *Fortune* was this: "GMers will no longer waste energy on divisive internal struggles for power and turf. This energy must be focused like a laser to make the finest cars in the world."[11] How does one rationalize product lines without internal struggle? Two years ago, GM began the process of shrinking its model offerings. Predictably, GM auto-workers, executives, and dealers want the ax to swing on other divisions. GM still loses ground occasionally. Oldsmobile horned in on Chevy's Lumina minivan project. The knock-off Olds Silhouette minivan helps Olds keep its sales up and its dealers happy. It does nothing to clarify how Chevy is different from Olds. Rationalization can't happen without compromise. That word never appears in Perot's *Fortune* essay.

No worries, wrote Perot: "All executives will move to car manufacturing plants and other production facilities. The leaders will be brushing up against real people building real cars, eating with them in the cafeteria and talking daily about what GM must do to build the finest cars in the world."[12] It's important advice, but it becomes less relevant by the day.

Every manufacturer is getting better. In the 1990s, "fit, finish, corrosion and reliability will go away as selectors," says UM's Cole. "No one without those factors will be in the game."[13]

Perot admonished: "All people who manage in an authoritarian way will be fired. GM cannot tap the full potential of the people with a manager whose philosophy is 'I had to eat dirt for 30 years; now it's my turn to make the other guys eat dirt.'"[14]

Everyone at GM faces a dinner of dirt. U.S. auto plants are unionized. Japanese car plants are not, even those in the United States. The UAW can't make the concessions that would bring GM to parity since its members are older and better paid than Nissan workers in Smyrna, Tennessee. Layoffs are a partial answer, but GM can't furlough its army of retirees. Nissan doesn't have pensioners here or in Japan.

Those handicaps define the limits of leadership in the U.S. car industry. Smith might well adopt the Toyota motto: "Every worker is a brother." GM would be the better company for it. It would lose ground more slowly, but it would still lose ground.

The Pontiac Fiero shows how uphill GM's struggle is. Pontiac did most of it right, and the sporty two-seater found a stable market of about 50,000 sales per year. Japanese companies produce cars in smaller numbers and still make money. GM could not. Some analysts estimate that GM must sell 250,000 cars to recoup its investment in a car model or a group of models sharing the underlying "platform." That's a hell of a niche in today's market.

Smith had the right answer, however imperfectly implemented: automation. With computers, GM can build several platforms in the same factories. A computer network could power a "pull" inventory system that orders up the parts and schedules the production of a replacement vehicle within hours of a car sale. GM is making progress on this plan. Plant managers once bragged about output. Now they boast about slim inventories.

EDS has not yet secured its place in this future. For its good showing at a GM Truck and Bus Division plant, EDS won the sponsorship of the GM automation system installed there. But GM engineers won the rest of the argument. EDS is only one of a handful of GM's authorized suppliers of factory automation. The car divisions are not required to use EDS exclusively. In a key loss, EDS was beaten out to supply GM's showcase small car factory under construction in Spring Hill, Tennessee.

EDS fell short in its first efforts to sell computer and communications links to GM dealers. The first version was too complicated and difficult to use. EDS withdrew it, losing sales momentum to rivals and handing another club to the diehard EDS haters inside GM.

Soreheads notwithstanding, Alberthal's job is much easier with Perot gone. EDS made its peace with the GM finance staff. The dread GM audits began in 1987. The first one was devastating. Reportedly GM found that it was paying for a Blue Cross computer in Iowa—the equivalent to the IBM "water heater" that EDS found on GM's books. EDS executives in Dallas took over accounting and beefed up the staff. The disputes about inventory lingered. "We finally agreed to disagree," says Alberthal.[15] In 1988, GM's auditors gave EDS an almost clean bill of health.

Today EDS is performing for GM. The company consolidated GM's 70 data processing sites into 17 and linked them by satellite and microwave into a single global computer network. GM needs substantially less computing horsepower because of the economies of scale. And EDS's buying power has extracted multi-million-dollar discounts from computer manufacturers. Savings on GM's private phone system, installed in 3 years instead of the 10 forecast, and on EDS-run health care plans add up to hundreds of millions of dollars each year.

And GM is giving EDS valuable experience in a $1.5 billion overhaul of its computer network. GM wants to move its actual data processing from EDS's large mainframe installations back into the factories where it can be done more effectively on powerful minicomputers and microcomputers. The plant computers will still be linked and coordinated by the EDS mainframe network. Yes, that's the distributed data processing that Perot fretted about in the late 1970s. After nearly three decades of consolidating data processing, EDS managers are thrilled to be managing a major dispersal project. "This is experience we would have killed for," crows Heller, the senior vice president responsible for it.[16]

EDS account managers have more red tape to deal with and less freedom. An account manager complains that incompetent people are now sometimes transferred rather than fired. GM insisted that EDS draft specific sick-leave policies and establish other procedures. Most EDSers accept the changes as inevitable. "With or without GM we still have to have more controls, more discipline to administer programs for a company of this size," says Jim Buchanan. EDS is not being made over into GM, he insists. "GM is very committee oriented," he says pointing to one difference. "In EDS we try to emphasize decision making by individuals."[17]

GM is forcing one welcome change at EDS. To deal with the automaker's middle management, EDS managers are learning how to sell. The classic EDS approach was to win over top management and bully everyone else. Roger Smith wasn't able to run interference for EDS in farflung GM. Every project manager has had to learn salesmanship.

"It's something I have to live with every day," says an EDS account manager who made the transition from GM. "Some people at GM will tell you, 'I want you to become my systems expert.' You sit with them in staff meetings. Others will tell you, 'I'll tell you what I want you to do. It won't be the development work because I want that for myself.' " The effort is making EDS account managers better business people.

While mellower, EDS is still groping for the proper degree of relaxation—a comfortable balance between Heller's jeans and boots and the FBI suits. General counsel Shlakman describes the cumbersome parts of EDS's culture as "the concrete boot." Says he, "We have not yet separated what is good and should be kept from the concrete boot."[18]

Perot was not seen enough in the final years to be missed in daily operations. He had not injected himself into company routine since 1979 except for projects that struck his fancy and chance encounters in free-fire zones like the halls, elevators, and lobby. Not even Meyerson was immune from the latter, when the president put up bluntly worded signs in the elevators urging employees to use the stairs for short hops. Perot ordered it rewritten with more pleases. EDS constantly was rapped for its militarist ways, he complained. Why offer proof on the elevator walls? In chance meetings, Perot banned balloon bouquets and singing telegrams as unbusinesslike.

One example of EDS's lingering identity crisis: Someone with no clue about the EDS culture, or perhaps someone with an evil mind, had arranged the delivery of a thank-you arrangement of jalapeño peppers and Corona beer. EDS management was paralyzed again. Should abstemious EDS allow beer on the premises?

In the end, EDS's biggest problem is its oldest problem. Turnover at EDS is still high—very high in Detroit. A GM accountant in the Pontiac division says the computer-room personnel are in a constant state of flux. "They either quit or they go off to systems engineering training and don't come back. They try really hard, but it takes three or four of them to come up with an answer for you."

The turnover problem is especially critical in the technical support division in Detroit, a central pool of 4,000 software developers. These people were among the army of college grads that EDS hired in 1985 and 1986. Complying with EDS standard procedure, they signed employee agreements promising to pay for the training if they didn't stay on the job for three years. The notes were up in 1988 and 1989, and the SEs quit in droves. "We brought them in from all parts of the country," explains an EDS account manager. "They want to get back to Minnesota or San Diego. If we don't have opportunities for them there, we've lost them."

Those decisions are a different kind of plebiscite on loyalty to leaders versus loyalty to institutions, the tug-of-war between charismatics and bureaucrats. The group with the lowest attrition rate at EDS is a surprising one. They're older and better established in their families and communities, and that

explains some of their sticking power. But they are unmis-
takably loyal. Yes, they'll agree, some diehard GM workers
will never accept the fact that they now work for EDS. But
those people weren't good GMers either, they explain. Yes,
that's right. The group with the least turnover at EDS is the
7,800 GM workers sent over by Roger Smith.

CHAPTER SIXTEEN

BACK OUTSIDE THE INNER CIRCLE

Perot's black-and-white analysis of GM didn't surprise his former colleagues at EDS. Perot wasn't interested in the nuances of the computer-services industry either. Meyerson was in charge of interpreting grays. Perot's passion was people. He had done as much as he could for the people at GM. He had underscored GM's deficiencies in a way that Smith and the board could not ignore. GM began talking and compromising with its workers. Perot's services as the "grain of sand" were no longer required. The point of the pearl, after all, is to neutralize the irritant. Perot was back on the street.

Perot was ejected from other inner circles as well. He clashed with the Reagan administration over POW and foreign-intelligence issues. *Newsweek* reported that an angry Perot withdrew a $2 million pledge for the Reagan library. Perot says he never promised the money. Even in his own hometown, his defense in 1988 of Dallas police officers led him into a racial confrontation. Attorney Luce had to extricate him again.

In public policy as well as business, Perot draws his strength from being an outsider. The Christmas flights in 1969 generated favorable publicity precisely because Perot was acting out of his own sense of moral outrage. He was not obliged to focus attention on the mistreatment of POWs. Similarly, when Perot pays ransoms, he is quite correctly seen as a humanitarian. If the government pays, it's bowing to terrorists. Perot doesn't need to worry about setting unfortunate precedents or justifying past decisions. Most of those virtues disappear the moment Perot comes inside.

Perot was ill-equipped to be an insider for other reasons. His delight in 1982 to be appointed to President Reagan's Foreign Intelligence Advisory Board had turned to disgust in 1985. He says he was frustrated that no one acted on his warnings about lax security at American embassies. He says he offered to pay out of his own pocket to replace with Americans the Russian civilian workers at the Moscow embassy. He resigned. Others believe Perot's frustration was more personal. We've seen Perot's low tolerance for talk. Once he charts the true course in his own mind, he can't dither in more meetings. He is constitutionally unable to continue talking.

That was the pattern for Perot's government assignments. The Carter administration asked him to sit in on planning sessions for the rescue of the 52 Americans taken hostage at the American embassy in Tehran. Perot proposed a sting operation. Under the pretext of delivering military spare parts to Iran, the military would first land trucks and commandos, and later, a rescue plane. The trucks would crash through the gates of the airport and drive into the cargo bay of the plane. Carter opted instead for a desert route and helicopters. After the hostages were released in January 1981, Perot complained, "They sat around wondering how many Iranians we could afford to kill. I said, 'What? Tell the men to shoot the first 50 and no more?' "[1]

Controls and limits. Perot had fought all of his life against the imperial "we" who dismissed his ideas out of hand. In business the problem was relatively easy to solve. Once he started EDS, he used his own rule, the all-purpose "Do what's right." Even at GM, Perot fought the bureaucrats to a draw and then left comforted by a $700 million bank wire and a public uprising against Smith.

Government is a much tougher adversary. The U.S. system was designed by men still smarting from the one-man rule of King George. Formally, it is an intricate web of checks and balances. Informal power is equally diffused. Career bureaucrats learn how to handle headstrong appointees and politicians. The latter come and go, while the civil service builds on its repertoire of parliamentary tricks.

The storm flags flew shortly after Perot joined the POW cause in 1969. Secretary of State Henry Kissinger was worried that as many as half of the POWs would die before he could extract the United States from Southeast Asia. Astronaut Frank Borman quietly enlisted support from foreign governments. Comedian Bob Hope added his public voice. Ross Perot chartered two Braniff Boeing 707s painted red and green. In the first, he flew 58 wives and 94 children of American POWs to Paris to confront North Vietnamese diplomats. He filled the second with food and medicine and reporters, and attempted to fly to Hanoi.

State department regulars were horrified, and with reason. As the POWs' advocate, he didn't concern himself with the American position in Paris on reparations and other terms of peace. In his four meetings with North Vietnamese diplomats in Laos and Cambodia, he cheerfully admitted that North Vietnamese children had suffered in American bombings. Perot was eager to establish linkage. The children of American POWs suffered also because their fathers were absent, he noted. Tell you what, I'll rebuild schools and clinics and you free the POWs. The North Vietnamese rejected it out of hand. Apparently his charms as an outsider were equally disconcerting to the Vietnamese. "They tended to blink a lot. They more or less fluttered their eyes when they heard it," a deadpan Perot told his flying squad of reporters.[2]

American diplomats had a more violent reaction. During his talks in Cambodia and Laos, Perot offered to inspect POW camps in South Vietnam and to arrange mail deliveries there. He sent Tom Marquez to Saigon to arrange it. The meetings in the embassy were fruitless. "Little satisfaction, obviously disinterested," an American Red Cross worker later wrote in his diary of the meetings. Marquez, a never-say-die EDS executive, next wangled a meeting with President Nguyen Thieu. The South Vietnamese government asked him to bring a letter of introduction from the American embassy. Back to the embassy they trooped. "Long and rough meeting at American Embassy," the same Red Cross officer wrote, "where the exchange was hardly friendly."

Roger Shields was then a deputy secretary of defense in charge of POW efforts. "It was a point of contention not only between Ross and State Department but with government in general," he says. "I think he thought in some cases that the government was an obstacle instead of helping him." His critics had persuasive arguments. For one, Perot was breaking the law. The Logan Act prohibits private citizens from negotiating for the United States. Furthermore, Perot was grandstanding. "It was only after it became clear that the government's formal efforts weren't accomplishing much that the government said to the private interests 'Well, go ahead. See what you can do,'" Shields says.[3]

Antiwar critics attacked Perot as a hawk posing as a humanitarian. In fact, Perot's compassion for hostages transcends politics. When the wife of Jeremy Levin, Beirut bureau chief for the Cable News Network, asked Perot for help, he sent her to the Reverend Jesse Jackson, who had dealt successfully with Lebanese Moslems for the release of navy flyer Robert Goodman. Levin escaped shortly thereafter. Jackson, says Perot, "went over and did it. Then he walked away. He didn't grandstand. . . . To Jackson's credit he's never taken credit for this."[4]

The grandstanding charge is tougher to dismiss. The facts are that Perot is eager to talk about his rescue and ransom attempts. Marine Corps Lieutenant Colonel Oliver North, the central figure in the Iran-Contra scandal, had approached Perot reluctantly to finance his covert ransom attempts. "As you know," North had written National Security Adviser Robert McFarlane in a memo, "I have never asked him for help in this regard believing that he would be inclined to talk about it. It may now be time to take that risk."

Perot supplied North with $500,000 to ransom General James Dozier from terrorists in Italy. The ransom failed, but the general was rescued by Italian police. At North's request, Perot funded several attempts to ransom American hostages in Beirut. In 1986, a middleman took $100,000 of Perot's money as a down payment for American University librarian Peter Kilburn—and disappeared. Kilburn was executed by his captors.

North was right about Perot's willingness to talk. Days after the Iran-Contra scandal surfaced, Perot was on ABC's "Nightline" describing his involvement and voicing his skepticism that North acted alone. "My sense has always been that the people who do these types of things are very meticulous about getting approval for their actions," he told Sam Donaldson.[5] Privately, Perot was incensed that North was being made the scapegoat. He thought it impossible that the colonel was acting on his own. Even so, Perot disagreed with the other half of North's mission. He had wanted nothing to do with North's support of the Contras in Nicaragua and told him so in certain terms. The ransom efforts were an easy decision. Perot is ready to come to the aid of any American being held hostage overseas.

Duty and honor best explain Perot's hostage involvements. When an American raid on a Son Tay, North Vietnam, prison camp failed in the early 1970s, Perot was appalled at the public's response. The raid failed because the North Vietnamese had moved the prisoners. The attempt, led by Colonel Bull Simons, was executed flawlessly. Perot flew to Fort Bragg, North Carolina, to meet the raiders. "I made it very clear to them what it meant to the POW families and what I was sure it meant to [the POWs]."[6]

After the United States won the release of the POWs at the Paris peace talks in 1973, Perot threw a party at the Fairmont Hotel in San Francisco to introduce the raiders to the 1,400 POWs. The idea came to Perot in a phone conversation with navy pilot Jerry Denton, later a U.S. senator. Says Perot, "He told me he had two calls. He called his wife and he called me. I told him he wasted his call because he should have called the raiders."[7] Among the memories of that party: John Wayne returning to the Fairmont after a night on the town with enlisted men and demanding that the hotel staff open a restaurant for them. Perot continued to host occasional reunions for them. He counts as his most valuable possession a picture signed by all of the POWs.

Perot's support was an indescribable tonic for the POWs and their families as well. Perot was the best evidence that the United States cared about the POWs. The Vietnamese read the American captives chapter and verse on the American antiwar movement. They also tortured the Americans. General Robinson Risner was kept 10 months in the dark in solitary confinement and subjected to "the ropes." His arms were bound so tightly behind him and his feet drawn up behind his head so that ribs popped loose from his sternum. His captors forced "confessions" from him. "What was especially difficult for us was that some outstanding Americans had begun to say the same things that we had been tortured into saying," Risner wrote later. "We were seeing Communism as it really was—harsh, repressive, and cruel."[8]

The news of Perot's Christmas flights and other exploits filtered into the camps as more airmen were shot down. Outside of the POWs' immediate families, few Americans tried harder to improve conditions for them or showed more gratitude for their sacrifices than Ross Perot. It's not wise to bring up the subject of grandstanding with Risner or the other POWs. They are fiercely loyal to him.

Private efforts on behalf of the POWs registered on the Vietnamese. Says Shields:

> I don't think there is any question but what his [and others] activities highlighted concerns . . . in a way that the government couldn't. You would expect the government to say "abide by the Geneva Conventions.". . . Tons and tons of mail were dumped at Paris peace talks. The North Vietnamese would refuse to accept these things, but the point was made clearly

when a mail truck comes up and a thousand bags of letters were dumped. We finally needed a warehouse.[9]

Perot sent Colonel Simons into Laos in 1974 to see if any Americans were still being held. Simons spent 3 months in the country, where he served 18 months of the war organizing guerrilla men. "He had tremendous intelligence contacts. He worked them all and produced nothing," Perot says.[10] Perot says he kept working for the 2,500 Americans missing in action in Vietnam. The National League of Families of Prisoners of War and Missing in Action says Perot dropped his support.

The MIA families needed help badly. Their league, among other groups, thought Americans were still being held. The Nixon administration in 1973 declared that all of the POWs still alive were now home. The Carter presidency downplayed the issue. The MIA section in the Defense Department had withered to nine people by 1980, and they were being warned about reassignment. Says Ann Mills Griffiths, executive director of the National League: "Unless you have seen elderly parents . . . in tears, appalled at themselves for walking up and down in front of the White House, you won't understand how difficult those years were."[11]

The POW issue struck a sympathetic chord in Reagan. He ordered the Defense Department to make it a priority when he took office. Refugees filtering out of Laos were telling stories about American POWs still being held in 1976 and 1977. In early 1989, the Defense Intelligence Agency was pursuing leads on 99 cases of eyewitness reports of Caucasian prisoners in Indochina.

The MIA reports tormented the Defense and State officials working on them. There wasn't conclusive evidence of who was being held and where. Without specific information, the United States was helpless to intervene. During the Carter presidency, moreover, the MIA question was assigned secondary priority. The government planned to negotiate normalized relations with Vietnam, which it thought would lead inevitably to a resolution of the MIA cases. Instead, the talks and the MIA effort died with Vietnam's invasion of Cambodia. The

National League and other critics began speaking of a "mind-set to debunk" POW evidence inside the government, much of it born of frustration.

Assistant Secretary of Defense Richard L. Armitage revived the MIA quest in 1981. The Reagan administration posture was to resist linking normalized relations and the MIA question. Instead, Armitage, Griffiths, and Colonel Richard T. Childress (the National Security Council's point man on MIAs) urged the Vietnamese to pave the way for broader talks by settling the humanitarian issues first. Armitage met secretly in New York with Vietnamese officials in 1983. The Vietnamese began doling out remains of American servicemen from what appears to government experts to be a store. The partial thaw was the first progress in a decade, but the slow pace was agony for the families of missing men. They began enlisting Perot's aid. He championed a direct approach: Trade for them.

There were several problems with Perot's answer. The first was a U.S. law forbidding normal relations with Vietnam. The second was a tricky obstacle to negotiations: how to get the communist regime, already isolated from the world politically and economically, to admit the damning existence of American prisoners.

Perot had that answer also. Appearing before the House Subcommittee on Asian Affairs on October 15, 1986, Perot offered his services. "I have a horse," he ventured in testimony. "You want to buy it, You say, 'Ross, do you want to sell your horse or not?' That's where we start. Nobody has ever come head to head with the Vietnamese in a trading situation."[12]

Chairman Stephen J. Solarz, (D-N.Y.) replied, "This is a little different, Mr. Perot. It is not like we have said 'We want to buy your horse. What do you want for it?' They say they don't have a horse to sell."[13] Solarz's subcommittee in a tie vote killed a proposal to create a special MIA commission under Perot's chairmanship.

Perot didn't give up. He was convinced that the government could prove the horse existed, that Americans were still held in Southeast Asia. A steady procession of adventurers and promoters had been parading through his office after Reagan made the MIAs a cause célèbre. Many of these men offered to sell Perot the proverbial smoking gun. Perot knew only too well that most MIA stories were no more substantial than smoke, but he reached for his checkbook anyway. He agreed to put up $4.2 million in an unsuccessful attempt to buy a videotape purporting to show Americans in captivity.

Perot also contributed money to more problematic missions. U.S. Army Lieutenant Colonel James "Bo" Gritz led an armed expedition into Laos from Thailand in 1983. Not only was it unsuccessful, it stymied official talks with the Laotians for a year. The Thai government expelled Gritz. When Gritz reentered Thailand on a false passport in 1986, the U.S. government arrested him. Gritz claimed Perot as a backer and produced photocopies of two checks to prove it. Perot says he gave Gritz money to placate him.

Gritz was just one player in a fund-raising industry that sprang up around the MIA issue. "Must raise $13,671.71 by [two weeks hence] or vital intelligence operations may have to be stopped," one fund-raiser pleaded in a 1986 mailing. An appeal by a different group declared: "According to a key source in the Defense Intelligence Agency approximately 100 POWs remain." Another solicitation described "stark brutality: starved and clad only in filthy rags, American soldiers and airmen are kept chained in tiny bamboo cages, ... made to work like animals pulling heavy plows." Rebuttals by the government and the National League's Misinformation Committee fed a Kafkaesque theory that the Defense Department was covering up evidence of POWs to justify its own inaction.

Perot subscribed to this theory. He told Solarz's subcommittee:

> "Let me give you one colorful conversation that will help put it in perspective about why the system is not working. I had a senior person in a sensitive position come to me and ask "Ross, don't you wonder how we can live with ourselves?"
> I said, "Yes, as a matter of fact, I do."
> "It is simple. We set the [information] screens so tight that nothing can get through."[14]

The Reagan administration appointed a POW review group under retired Army General Eugene Tighe. The Tighe group was to review the active MIA witness incidents and determine if the government was in fact covering up the existence of POWs. (The group found no evidence of a cover-up.) Perot declined an invitation to join the Tighe commission. He began a more sweeping investigation of his own. He zeroed in on Armitage.

He was developing a conspiracy theme advanced by such unlikely partners as Gritz and Daniel Sheehan, head of the Christic Institute, a public-interest law firm. Sheehan tried unsuccessfully to link Armitage with an outlaw element in the Central Intelligence Agency that sold arms and drugs. Sheehan in a lawsuit affidavit accused Armitage of setting up a front company for drug smugglers while attached to the U.S. Embassy in Bangkok. Armitage actually was working in Washington at the time as an aide to Senator Bob Dole. A Miami judge threw out Sheehan's suit, assessed him $1 million in court costs, and chided him for abusing the court system.

Perot did find instances of bad judgment by Armitage. Armitage had come to the aid of a Vietnamese woman convicted of operating a gambling house in Virginia. He had written a character reference for the woman on Pentagon stationery. Perot took his case to Vice President George Bush in October 1986. Bush told him to present his evidence to the proper authorities. Perot sat down with FBI director William Webster. He also confronted Armitage and urged him to resign.

The story broke in the *Boston Globe* the following January. Caspar Weinberger, then secretary of defense, backed Armitage. "These are old allegations which have been looked into and found to be completely groundless," Weinberger said in a statement. Perot complained to Washington muckraker Jack Anderson: "What does it take for a U.S. government official to lose his security clearance?"[15]

We know that it is a short leap for Perot to decide that his opponents are not only wrong but also evil. The context, however, is important here. Stranger things were happening in Washington than the unfounded charges against Armitage. The North story was unreeling. Improbably, an NSC aide was arranging arms sales to Iran and funneling the profits to Central American revolutionaries. At the same time, the U.S. Justice Department was closing in on a rogue element in the Central Intelligence Agency. Former CIA agent Edwin Wilson, convicted of illegal arms sales, was already in prison. Perot was profoundly suspicious of the U.S. intelligence community.

That much was vintage Perot. He expects bureaucracy to fail us. He stands ready to substitute his own judgment and skills. He fell into a debate with Congressman Solarz over his private investigation:

SOLARZ:

You have indicated that you knew some people who had information that would be helpful.

PEROT:

That is right.

SOLARZ:

Could you tell us who they are?

PEROT:

No, here we go again. These people came to me in confidence. They had waited for years. For some reason I showed up on the scene and their level of trust was such they said they would talk to me informally, but they would go public only under subpoena.

SOLARZ:

We are in a position to subpoena people.

PEROT:

I would have to ask them.

SOLARZ:

In other words, you know people who have information that could contribute to a solution to this problem. They have told you that they can only divulge that information if subpoenaed. Yet you won't give us their names so we can subpoena them?

PEROT:

Not without getting their approval.

SOLARZ:

In other words, even if they refuse to give you their approval and you believe that what they have to say would help contribute a solution of this problem, you would refuse to give us their names so we could subpoena them?

PEROT:

I would first go to them and ask for their approval and encourage them to talk to you. Aren't we playing a game? I will do everything I can to help you. I will talk to them and do my best to get them to come talk to you.

SOLARZ:

The thing you can do right now is give us their names. If you want to do it confidentially that is fine.

PEROT:

I would have to talk to them first.

SOLARZ:

What if they refuse?

PEROT:

I will decide what to do then based on my conversations with them one at a time.

Nothing came of Perot's sleuthing except hard feelings. "He accepted all of the false information from outside sources," Childress says, "and rejected all of the information from inside the government."[16] The White House sent former National Security Adviser Frank Carlucci to ask Perot to back down. Perot refused.

He would stand in for the government one more time before he threw up his hands in frustration. The Vietnamese, still religious readers of the American press, invited Perot to Hanoi. They had wanted higher contacts with the U.S. government. Armitage, Griffiths, and Childress had suggested that the White House appoint Army General George Vessey, retired chairman of the Joint Chiefs of Staff, as a special presidential emissary. Vessey's mission would carry the standard disclaimer: There could be no linkage of MIAs and trade, reparations, or other topics.

White House aides briefed Perot on the status of the MIA talks and caught their breath. What if Perot asked Foreign Minister Nguyen Co Thach point-blank if Vietnam was still holding Americans? An official denial would become yet another hurdle. Thach was fond of reminding Americans that their own government once said no one was left alive. Worse, what if he tried and failed to ransom POWs and concluded therefore that no Americans were left alive?

Perot did anger the administration's MIA team in his three-day visit in March. Perot told the Vietnamese of the Vessey mission and then urged the U.S. government to expand Vessey's role—in effect, to bargain with the Vietnamese. He accused the government of arrogance in its dealings with Vietnam. The Vietnamese had 100,000 MIAs, Thach told Perot. Villagers wanted to know why their government would look first for 2,500 Americans.

In fact, nothing prevented the villagers from looking for their own dead except the absence of dental records, X rays, or others means of positive identification. "Our Vietnamese friends appear to be very talented at making experts out of one-time visitors," Griffiths wrote in a National League statement. "What was reported in the press we have heard over and over."

Nor would the White House relent. The Vessey mission would not go forward until the Vietnamese agreed that its scope was humanitarian issues only. Perot was furious. Vessey made his trip in August of 1987. In modest linkage, American forensics teams are working routinely now in Vietnam after the U.S. offered humanitarian aid, beginning with artificial limbs for disabled Vietnamese.

Perot's image suffered in the startling spectacle of him elbowing aside Congress as a watchdog of government and the President as shaper of foreign policy. "Puzzling and nettlesome to the administration," wrote *Time*.[17] "Defeat may have at least helped Perot to recognize his limits," said *Newsweek*.[18]

Had Perot finally fallen under the sway of his own publicity? No, this was not a new Perot. The thought of men brutalized for 20 years tore at his leader's soul. He wanted action, and provided it, just as he had in 1969. This time, however, he had access to government at the highest level. As an insider, his difficulty with shades of gray was all the more apparent.

Perot would have one more painful lesson in the difference between governance and advocacy. When Dallas entered a bad recession in 1986, its minority neighborhoods fell into a depression. In short order, Dallas was the most crime-ridden city in the nation. The Dallas Police Department drew the unhappy chore of becoming an army of occupation. The city piled up more grim statistics: 29 citizens were shot by police in 1986. By 1987, race tensions were palpable. The city council began work on an ordinance creating a police review board. In January 1988, the number of policemen shot in the line of duty was a grim statistic: Three officers had fallen in a matter of weeks.

The Dallas Police Association asked Perot for help. He decided the question quickly and on leadership principles. The city was asking its police officers to patrol neighborhoods run by Jamaican druglords armed with Uzi machine pistols. Now the city wanted a review board to prosecute police for their mistakes. Perot berated city officials: "I told [them] 'I've been in outfits that have good morale. I've been in outfits that have bad morale, but I'm telling you you have got an outfit with no morale at all.' "[19]

Perot looked before he leaped, but with his leader's blinders on. He met with police officers in big groups and small, and he commissioned a survey of morale by the same employee consultants that EDS used to read the pulse of its workers. The police felt mistreated by the media, so Perot scheduled a series of off-the-record roundtable meetings between the press and the police. It was in these meetings that Perot espoused cordoning off minority neighborhoods and searching door-to-door for weapons and narcotics.

If Perot had sought out minority community leaders, perhaps he could have saved himself from what came next. The point of their efforts to establish a review board was their mistrust of the police. To suspend the Constitutional protection against illegal search and seizure was a poor answer to minority grievances. The idea of cordons was repulsive also. Minority leaders traced the economic deprivation in their neighborhoods to their exclusion from the Dallas mainstream. Black and Hispanic leaders confronted Perot in an angry meeting.

Perot's campaign sputtered and died after a news story broke describing his own confrontation with the Dallas police a year earlier. Officers had stopped his daughter-in-law for speeding. They noticed a pistol in her car. Although the officers could have cited her for a misdemeanor offense, they accepted her explanation that she needed it for security. Later the two officers were summoned to Perot's office. The officers assumed Perot wanted to thank them. Instead, wrote reporter Laura Miller in the *Dallas Times Herald*: "Perot screamed and yelled. He belittled them. He chewed them out. He made fun of the way they looked."[20]

Minority leaders quickly noted that minorities are arrested every day on weapons violations. Perot dropped out of the controversy after a final, angry session with the media:

> I have no ax to grind. All I want is a better city. . . . It bothers me a lot to have spent 20 years of my life and tens of millions of dollars trying to help the minorities in this state and get the kind of reaction I'm getting right now. I never expected anyone to thank me and nobody ever did. But I sure as hell didn't expect to get my teeth kicked in [and be called] a racist.[21]

Luce, Perot's attorney, helped the city rewrite the police review board ordinance to make it more palatable to police.

Perot's us-and-them style had failed him again. Perhaps he realized at this point that he could not stand at the center of any organization that he did not create himself. It's possible to read this interpretation in his fulminations against the press: "I'm about to decide that the perception around here is that if you are not an elected official, I ought to just sit out in the office and make money. Fine. Create jobs. Make money. That's your slot in life, Perot. Fine."[22] Perot was already putting together Perot Systems.

CHAPTER SEVENTEEN

BAD BLOOD AND BETRAYAL

Postmaster General Anthony M. Frank arrived early in Ross Perot's office on February 9, 1988, so they went to lunch. The two men had much in common. Frank, whose parents had fled Nazi Germany on the eve of World War II, built a giant savings and loan institution in San Francisco from scratch. He too had sold out to an automaker, Ford Motor Company. He stayed on as chairman of Ford's First Nationwide Savings and helped to drag the stuffy thrift industry into new technologies and interstate competition. He had taken over the job of U.S. Postmaster General the day before this lunch. He later cracked to reporters that he won the appointment for two reasons: He had accepted the job, and Ross Perot had declined it. Frank, a sardonic wit, is nearly Perot's equal with the press. Perot's *Fortune* cover, "How I Would Turn Around GM" was on the newsstands. They traded war stories. They got along famously.

As enjoyable as the lunch was, Frank was a man on a mission. After Perot had turned down the Postal Board of Governors, he called back the next day to offer his candidates. Offhand, he mentioned his interest in harnessing computer technology to tame the Postal Service's rising costs. This was Frank's first mission as postmaster general. Was Perot serious about his offer? Indeed he was. "He said he was extremely interested," Frank says, "that he wanted to undertake very large projects."[1]

Frank moved cautiously at first. He invited Perot to a board dinner in Washington on the night of March 7 to meet the governors informally and to begin the sale. Frank need not have worried. In restrospect, the postmaster could have short-circuited much of the controversy over the Perot contract if he had rented the Kennedy Center and invited all of Washington to hear Perot at his folksy finest. The next day, Frank dashed off a note to one of his deputies: "In anticipation of making money available for the company of last night's guest, could you ask someone to send me a memo on the A. D. Little [consulting] contract? . . . How much is it, what does it cover, how satisfied are we with it, and is the contract cancellable or transferable? Those are questions that come to mind."

Perot was back in business—and tracking a collision course with his old friends and colleagues at EDS. The postal service arguably fit the public-service exceptions to Perot's deal with GM. As usual, however, Perot was not thinking one dimensionally or small. He cut a two-part deal with the Postal Service. Perot Systems would identify automation prospects in an 18-month study to be billed at cost, as the GM buyout required. Then Perot Systems Corporation would implement the projects and split the savings with the USPS. Perot was asking for 50 cents of every dollar he saved.

Perot's horrified former employees didn't need a degree in rocket science to recognize the potential. How much could automation cut from the $38 billion USPS budget, 83 percent of which is labor costs? Perot set a goal for his fledgling company of $100 million in annual profits within 10 years. That would mean perhaps $1.5 billion in revenues and 10,000 employees.

The aftershocks kept coming for Alberthal and EDS senior management. Perot construed his agreement with GM to mean he could hire at will from EDS. Forever. EDS fought back, lobbying successfully to stop the USPS contract. Nine months later, EDS and its founder were waging all-out war. Finally, a frustrated but still supremely confident Perot was telling *Inc.* magazine for its January 1989 cover story, "I would like to send a message to everyone in that camp. You should do everything you can to beat Perot Systems, . . . But ignore those who tell you that if Perot Systems wins you'll be out of a job because I'll give you the first opportunity to join us."

There's no simple explanation of what led Perot down this road. Fate is the outer skin on this metaphysical onion. Perot was waiting for the phone to ring. He was looking for big data processing projects, jobs that would make a difference. If the IRS, or the Defense Department, had called on him as a businessman and a patriot, he would have sent for his luggage later. The Postal Service didn't quite have the sex appeal, but it made up for that shortcoming in raw commercial potential. But not even Perot could have predicted that the Postal Service would call or that Frank would be so simpatico.

Superlative horsetrader that he is, Perot got the rest of his objectives in negotiation. Of the hundreds of ways he could have helped the post office without personal gain, he structured a deal to catapult his new company into the computer-services big leagues inside 10 years. Clearly, he coveted the excitement, the acclaim, and the rewards of building another major corporation. Creating jobs, he liked to say, was what he did best.

The proof of this is Perot Systems' launch on June 1, 1988, the exact day his contract allowed him to begin a nonprofit company. Throughout his life, Perot superstitiously timed such major events as his marriage, the founding of EDS, and its sale to GM to occur on his birthday, June 27. This time around, Perot wasn't wasting 27 days. An EDS old-timer draws parallels between Perot's 18 months in limbo and Napoleon's exile on Alba or General George Patton's banishment to the dummy front on D-Day. There's no crueler treatment of leaders than to strip them of followers and purpose.

Perot's shrewd deal also maximized his opportunities to hire away the top guns at EDS. From the start, he assured the post office that he had top-flight EDS executives waiting in the wings. The USPS took his word for it in the end; normally the government demands names and curricula vitae.

Why would Perot raid EDS? Some former colleagues interpreted it as Perot's attempts to assuage his guilt. He had sold his company into bondage to bureaucrats. It was the biggest mistake of his life. His right to hire from EDS, the "free-the-slaves clause" in the buyout, helped to keep GM honest. Perot Systems was even stronger medicine against the dread automaker and outright salvation for some. Perot argues, "I thought the net effect would probably be to give EDS a new opportunity to operate the way General Motors guaranteed it could operate in 1984 . . . and would be a tremendous boost to morale inside EDS."[2]

It sounds preposterous to people who don't understand Ross Perot. It's his duty to start Perot Systems? He is obligated to compete against EDS? You and I couldn't say such things with straight faces. And no one would believe for a minute that it wasn't the $100 million annual profits that motivated us. Perot is different from us. Says Shlakman, "Once he has determined the rightness of his position, he is not a hypocrite when he espouses it. He believes. A part of his genius is that he can be self-delusional when most of us are only hypocritical."[3]

Perot Systems did not improve morale at EDS. The opposite was happening. The "slaves" realized intuitively that some of them were more worthy of freedom than others. All EDS employees would be considered at Perot Systems, but only the best would be hired. In practice, the buyout clause worked to "uncage the Eagles." Each one that flew lessened the value of EDS for those left behind.

Yes, unfettered competition for talent is the way of the world for most companies, but it is not for EDS. When the gold handcuffs lost their effectiveness in the early 1970s after EDS stock plunged, Perot had already fitted his employees with a pair of carbon-steel cuffs. Every EDS employee, right down to the janitors, was prohibited from competing against the company or recruiting colleagues for a period of three years after they quit. It was these contracts, Luce complained, that would foil Perot's nonprofit crusades if they were not waived also.

As a result, only Perot Systems, of all of the computer services companies of the world, could hire EDS workers with impunity. (Perot immediately clapped the cuffs back on his new PSC employees. PSC employees must wait seven years for all their new stock to vest and promise not compete with or recruit from the company for two years after separation.) EDS employees began speculating who among them would be Perot's new Eagles.

Finally, Perot Systems was born because Perot does not accept defeat. Roger Smith was now wrong and evil. Speechwriter Albert Lee in *Call Me Roger* had first raised the possibility that Perot would be back in business in 18 months and would be taking EDS back body by body. Perot would only laugh at the question. He'd lost a battle in the buyout, but not the war. The war between charismatic and bureaucrat will never be over. "I would allow anybody that General Motors wanted to have the benefits of this agreement . . . ," says Perot, "and I would go back and run EDS. . . . I would make EDS so interesting and so exciting that I didn't care what these guys had. . . . Nobody would want to leave."[4]

Perot Systems was another experiment in corporate effectiveness and responsibility. The first Perot Systems document was a company philosophy:

> Together we will build a team that will create and maintain an atmosphere of mutual trust and respect, listen to the people who do the work, hold team members accountable for results, with team members being given great flexibility in deciding how to achieve results, with the clear understanding that ETHICAL STANDARDS MUST NEVER BE COMPROMISED.

There was no discussion of the 1962 EDS manifesto or what went wrong. Perot knew one mistake he wouldn't repeat. Perot Systems would not be for sale.

Paul Chiapparone was the first to hear about Perot Systems over lunch in early spring of 1988. Chiapparone, one of the two men Perot rescued from Iran, declined to join. He had helped build EDS into a major corporation. He couldn't leave it behind. Chiapparone reported to Alberthal that Perot was starting a new company.

Perot did better with the remaining men on his list. Pat Horner, who had sold EDS's first contract to the post office, and DeSoto Jordan, EDS's top lobbyist, were critical new recruits for Perot Systems. They, as well as systems expert Ross Reeves, federal salesman Don Drobny, and GM business manager Bruce Heath had all dropped by Perot's office during 1987 to say, in effect, "call me if you start a new company." They had recognized Perot as a rainmaker. They were the type of people who would be frustrated in any organization.

It still wasn't an easy decision. DeSoto Jordan met Luce in a Dallas hotel to go over Perot's rights under the buyout. Says Luce, "He told me it was a difficult decision for him, that he had a lot of friends at EDS, that EDS had treated him very, very fairly over the years, that he enjoyed working with Les [Alberthal]. . . . [H]e thought the ground-floor opportunity at Perot Systems was a once-in-a-lifetime opportunity."[5]

Together with John King and chief financial officer Meryl Smith, the PSC Eight, as they came to be called in the Virginia lawsuit, met Perot in the L'Enfant Hotel in Washington in early spring. The purpose of the meeting was to kick around the goals and philosophies of a new company. They ran through the EDS roster to see who would be likely recruits. Fernandes? Nobody thought he would want to go back to work. Heller? The group shrugged. Chiapparone? He had declined.

The eight agreed that they didn't want to mess with a company that did not have the potential to earn $100 million in 10 years. The Perot family would own 40 percent of Perot Systems. Each of the eight would begin with 2 percent, to be vested over seven years. The rest of the stock would go into the company's treasury for future awards. The employees would decide when or if Perot Systems went public. They agreed on a likely market price for Perot Systems of 15 times earnings, or $1.5 billion. Surely each of the eight ran through the math in their heads. If they never got another share on PSC's journey to $100 million in profits, each of the eight would be worth $30 million.

Trust was the first casualty of Perot Systems. EDS top management had been nervous and watchful ever since Chiapparone's early alert. The company had picked up rumors about the Postal Service deal a month or so before it happened. Perot thought EDS had the L'Enfant staked out. EDS says it did not. "It was not exclusively recruiting headquarters," he answered an EDS attorney. "EDS had it under surveillance. You probably know more about it than I do."[6]

Heart in his throat, Alberthal phoned Meyerson to invite him to breakfast at a fancy coffee shop in Dallas. Meyerson's following at EDS was equal to, if not larger than Perot's. "I asked him in that discussion was he involved anywhere [with PSC]," Alberthal says.[7] No, Meyerson answered; he had declined also. As Perot explains, "I told Mort he would certainly be welcome to be a part of it and I personally would have been delighted to have had him as a part of it, because he's so talented. He had other interests and other commitments at the time."[8]

Alberthal forged ahead at a meeting of the top 150 managers at the Hyatt Regency Hotel in Scottsdale, Arizona later that spring. He warned the EDS officers beforehand that he was going to ask them to stand as a sign of their commitment to EDS. As he explains:

> The rumors were "Was Paul (Chiapparone) going to stay?" "Was Alberthal going to go with Perot?" What we needed to do was to look the people in the face and say "We are the senior managers of this company. We are loyal to the company and its people, period. I'm going to ask you to stand up. If you can't be honest with me and the people, tell me now." Nobody said a word.[9]

Alberthal carried through with his bit of theater. He vowed not to stand idly by while Perot stole EDS employees. He asked the officers to stand to signal their commitment to EDS. These people are your leaders and they are committed, Alberthal stated. Only Jordan of PSC Eight was asked to stand. He did.

Jordan wasn't the only Perot Systems recruit to violate the trust of EDS. Horner and Gary Wright were shopping for office space for Perot Systems in Northern Virginia while they were still employed at EDS. (On Saturday, on their own time, Horner insists.) Jordan was supplying Postmaster General Frank with Washington reactions to the upcoming deal.

The anxiety ended May 28. Perot called both Alberthal and GM attorney Elmer Johnson on the Friday of Memorial Day weekend. If Perot declared war in that conversation, Johnson missed it. The attorney called GM vice chairman Don Atwood on his car phone on the way to the airport and told him not to be concerned, that Perot was not targetting EDS. Alberthal was more cautious. He heard Perot promise him World War III if EDS opposed him. He asked Perot how many employees he was taking with him. Perot answered that he didn't know.

EDS found out first thing Tuesday morning, June 2. DeSoto Jordan and Bill Wright had a strategy session with Alberthal at 8 A.M. that day on how to handle the press inquiries about Perot Systems. Jordan was late. Wright was waiting for him at the elevator door. Wright recalls, "He said I'm leaving the company to join Perot, just stepped out of the elevator and said it." Jordan excused himself to confront Alberthal. Jordan rejoined Wright a minute later. Alberthal was tied up. "We went into my office," Wright says. "He says, 'Before you ask, it was a deal I couldn't turn down for my family. It was a deal of a lifetime.' "[10]

Jordan got straight to the point with Alberthal as well. The latter reacted badly. "Dee and I, his wife, my wife, we had been friends for years," Alberthal says. "I felt that it was violation of trust, not only to me personally, but to the company. At that point, I literally wrote him off. I had no use for [him]. . . . I said, 'Dee, if that's the way you feel, get out.' I haven't spoken to him since."[11]

Meanwhile, Drobny was telling his boss, Fernandes. Reeves was telling Heller. One by one, the senior executives went to Alberthal's office. They got copies of the buyout contract to search for the words they were hearing from the PSC Eight. Heller returned to his office and the waiting Reeves. Heller says:

There are a bunch of administrative things in these sorts of proceedings but I made it brief and easy. . . . Ross [Reeves] had a car that was owned by EDS. Ross had a personal computer owned by EDS in his home. He had keys and access to things. He had cards. He had stickers. Those sorts of things. I didn't condone it all personally, but he was old enough to figure out what he needed to do. Outside of working and helping an endeavor that I viewed as being dangerous and detrimental to EDS and its people, I wished them luck.[12]

EDS banishes its malcontents with much of the same ceremony as the army strips dishonorable soldiers of epaulets and insignias and breaks their swords in two. After EDS has collected all of its property from the quitter, the unfortunate is escorted down the long drive at EDS to the gate and its guard house, manned 24 hours a day. The guards scrape the EDS decal off the outcast's windshield. Without a specific invitation, he cannot return.

EDS doubled the guard. Perot's daughter Nancy wasn't permitted to enter the EDS compound to meet her friends. Nor were Perot's aides able to pick up his mail; EDS began returning it to the post office. (Alberthal answers that Nancy Perot was turned away by mistake and that Perot had dragged his feet changing his address.) EDS called Ross Reeves's mortgage. Reeves grumbled that it cost him thousands of dollars to replace it in a rush. EDS's managers shunned each new defector. Fernandes finally tried a new tack. "Seemed to me we weren't doing our job going to these guys [and] saying . . . we like you. Seemed like every time we heard about another one we'd think, 'Sorry son of a bitch.' "[13]

The Ross Perots, Junior and Senior, flew to Washington for the Postal Service press conference. Frank did most of the talking, but Perot spoke briefly. He said his men were "the fighting generals of the computer industry. They have blood on their boots and dirty uniforms."[14] Despite the bellicose imagery, Perot also said EDS had nothing to fear from its founder and eight other men.

He knew better. Perot refused to sign a contract that carried a routine clause allowing the Postal Service to break the contract unilaterally. That clause, Perot complained, would amount to an engraved invitation to critics inside and outside government. The parties resolved that problem with a side letter from Perot to Frank stating, "This letter confirms that I will agree to terminate the above-referenced contract during the initial ninety (90) day study period if you determine that the continuation of the contract is not in the best interest of the United States Postal Service and so request in writing."

The post office regulars saw a storm on the horizon. Research chief Kenneth J. Hunter warned Frank in a memo about creating an appearance of favoritism for Perot and urged him to drop the negotiations. Of the bureaucrats kicking around the idea, Hunter wrote, "Some felt the potential benefits of such a partnership warrant further exploration of the opportunities but most are concerned with the [political] risks involved." The Postal Service bureacracy finally signed off on a negotiated contract "based on the determination made of the unique capabilities and arrangements of R. Perot for this effort."

EDS opened several fronts in Washington. Alberthal met personally with Congressman Jack Brooks (D-Tex.) Brooks authored a law requiring competitive bids for government contracts. Typically, he cast a jaundiced eye on any negotiated awards like the USPS deal with Perot Systems. Brooks demanded that Frank rescind the deal and start over with competitive bidding. Frank asked the U.S. Court of Appeals to decide if the quasi-private Postal Service was covered under Brooks's law. Brooks promised to correct that oversight if it wasn't.

EDS and another computer-services rival, Planning Research Corporation, also brought a formal complaint before the General Services Administration (GSA) Contract Board of Appeals. EDS said it was not protesting the contract because of Perot; it would protest any government contract that it was shut out of arbitrarily. Bullroar, answered Perot.

EDS and Perot lobbyists begin to meet each other arriving and departing the offices of key lawmakers. Perot had recruited away Jordan, EDS's savvy and effective advocate, but the company still had powerful friends by marriage. Senators

Carl Levin (D-Mich.) and Paul Simon (D-Ill.) weighed in against the contract. Simon drafted a resolution on the back of an envelope on the Senate floor suspending the contract for 90 days and ordering a Government Accounting Office study.

Jordan was caught flatfooted. Simon had no obvious interest in the fight. He was recruited by a Kirkland & Ellis attorney, a law partner of former GM attorney Elmer Johnson. Simon made no apologies. "If you question whether or not he is a good businessman, you take a good look at this contract," he snapped to reporters.[15]

Postmaster General Frank was getting a painful lesson in the difference between government and business. He says, "I thought Mr. Perot and presumably the people that he would surround himself with were unique. The fact that we would be the only client of a firm with obvious motivation. . . . [I thought] would have considerable significance to the Postal Service."[16]

Frank blamed GM, and brought his considerable media skills to bear. He told *The Wall Street Journal*, "We've got a $500,000 contract here that's caught in a Roger Smith and Ross Perot crossfire, and if we back down the score is GM, one, American people, nothing."[17] He added in a San Francisco speech, "I consider their actions a display of pettiness unparalleled in my time."[18]

Finally, Frank picked up the phone and called Roger Smith:

> I told him how distressed I was that General Motors appeared to be trying to . . . negate an opportunity for the Postal Service to save some money. . . . Mr. Smith's reaction was . . . "Well, Tony, you worked for Ford Motor Co. and you know that subsidiaries of automobile companies are autonomous." . . . And then he indicated that he had read the contract between us and Perot Systems over the weekend . . . and that he considered it to be highly unusual. . . . I said "Well, we had a highly unusual contract given General Motors on our long-life vehicles," and he said "that was a contract arrived at by open bidding."[19]

Perot was outclassed. Officially GM had no role in the lobbying assault. Alberthal says he briefed his boss at GM,

Don Atwood, on EDS's GSA challenge. Atwood asked Alberthal to check in with GM's attorneys and to make sure that the carmaker would not be dragged into the battle. The last thing GM wanted was to perpetuate the Perot-Smith feud. But GM can steer public policy and leave nary a ripple on the surface. For example, GM quickly silenced the state pension funds screaming for Smith's scalp after the buyout. The revolt by institutional shareholders collapsed in part because GM could remind fund managers that they were partners by virtue of the carmaker's substantial investment and employment in their states. The purpose of bureaucracies is to compel obedience.

Spin control was failing Perot this time. The Postal Service deal was as sharp as any in Perot's long and moneyed history, but it was a bit too obvious. To average Americans, finding ways to make the post office more efficient was roughly as difficult as getting wet in the middle of the Pacific Ocean. Automating the mail isn't that easy really, but it didn't look right for Perot to stake out the entire pie for himself and demand half of the spoils. One newspaper cartoonist drew an "H. Ross Perot—Patriot" commemorative stamp with front and back views. The front showed him draped in a flag. The back showed him clutching bills and a moneybag behind his back.

Nor could he position himself as a tiny start-up beset by the largest corporation on earth, try as he might to put this spin on news coverage. He told the *Dallas Times Herald,* "I called these guys before it started and said we can't have a war because it won't hurt me . . . and it really will hurt EDS. They fired the first shot and hit themselves in the foot. . . . Gosh almighty, I can't believe these are my boys."[20]

Reporters were seeing through this one also. *Detroit News* reporter Helen Fogel traveled to Dallas to take the local pulse. Perot was no David slaying Goliaths on his own turf, she discovered. "Texans see it as a fair fight—with maybe a little edge to Perot."[21] The management newsletter *Gallagher Report* awarded Perot its "worst executive of the month" accolades. "Corporate monkey wrench goes to PSC chief Ross Perot for sweetheart no-bid contract with USPS," the newsletter telegraphed.[22]

Frank finally threw in the towel. The postmaster general telephoned Perot. The deal "couldn't fly in its present form," Frank said. "Our people would have to discuss modifying the contract. That's the only way that I could see it going ahead." Frank conceded the issue officially at an August 10 Senate hearing. Perot would no longer have exclusive rights to implement automation schemes. Whatever projects surfaced in the Perot Systems study would be bid competitively.

EDS had become the enemy. On the stand in Virginia, Perot pointed out how these were no longer his boys. He offered as evidence his phone call on May 28 to inform EDS and GM about Perot Systems:

> Tension started to build in me because in old EDS that would have been a five-alarm alert. I told them I was hiring people from EDS. I told them I was starting a new company. . . . I figured by Tuesday they would have them all turned around and back at EDS and I would be out scrambling again. I was just amazed that they all took off for a long weekend and nobody did anything.[23]

He crowed to the *Dallas Morning News,* "How would you like to be competing against a non-profit company? If you have the overhead that EDS has, it gets a little brutal to compete. It will be like turning a bunch of bulldogs loose on a bunch of poodles."[24]

Had Perot forgotten that he described Alberthal only two years earlier as "the right man at the right time" for EDS? And what of his promise 18 months earlier? "20 years from now, if they need me, I'll be right here." His former colleagues fashioned several explanations. In the first, they reasoned that Perot saw himself as interchangeable with EDS. Therefore, the company could not survive him. Of course, this theme reaches back to social theorist Weber and the first writings about charismatic leadership.

If Perot had lost the distinction between his company and himself, it was a common mistake. Writers, and even Roger Smith, relegated EDS to Perot's shadow. The truth is that Meyerson had added a more humanistic New Testament to the Perot gospel years before GM bought the company. And two of every three EDSers had joined the company in the two years of GM's ownership. Nevertheless, Perot told Alberthal a few weeks after the buyout that holding EDS together was an uphill struggle, and he should not blame himself if he failed. Perot wasn't clear whether he meant GM would trip up Alberthal, or that EDS would not survive his loss. Alberthal took it to mean the latter.

In the next extension of this argument, Perot would be frustrated mightily when EDS continued to win. PR manager Wright used this clever bit of "spin" to put the idea across. "He's like a captain abandoning ship. He is in his lifeboat and he is angry because the ship won't sink." The analogy infuriated Perot, but EDSers seized upon it to explain the wild swing in Perot's attitude toward them. For the relatively modest changes at EDS—higher-profile auditors and somewhat more constrained account managers—Perot's opinion of them had changed 180 degrees. They had become wrong and evil.

Child custody fights are a closer parallel. The spouse who packs up and leaves is frozen in that bitter instant. The former home echoes forever with the same ugly fights. The bitter spouse recruits the children as accomplices against the 'ex'. Perot did some of this recruiting. Meeting Fernandes at a social function, he wondered out loud why EDS managers were not using the weapon he handed them, exploiting GM's fear of mass defections. Perot made the point again in a telephone conversation with CFO Davis Hamlin. Perot Systems was the perfect opportunity for EDS to hit up GM for special stock awards.

(Hamlin had called Perot to ask him to remove his helicopter from the landing pad at EDS and his longhorns and buffalo from the Plano industrial park. Perot could not resist tweaking the courtly, drawling Hamlin, an employee since 1965. Perot's pilot and mechanic weren't allowed to enter the building to use the bathrooms, Perot noted. Hamlin exploded. Perot recalls, "I laughingly said 'no problem, I'll just put a port-a-can by the hangar,' and then he exploded again because he realized I could do that. And I said 'Davis, I understand that you are upset and I am sorry that you are upset' and he said that, you know they were under a lot of pressure.")[25]

General Motors and EDS were not frozen in time. After the buyout, GM was more motivated than ever to make the acquisition work. Smith had 18 months to win over EDS—or else. Moreover, the job of building a relationship was vastly simplified with Perot gone and the press quiet. January 1, 1988, was the first significant date in Perot's buyback contract. At Perot's urging, GM accelerated the vesting of the stock owned by the top 200 EDS managers so they could quit EDS-GM on that date without financial penalty. January 1 came and went; nothing happened.

Of course EDS was not free to choose which parent to support. Despite the popular view of the struggle as a divorce between Roger Smith and Ross Perot, neither executive owned EDS. The company belongs to its shareholders. EDS managers have a legal obligation to protect the shareholders. On September 27, 1988, EDS sued Perot, alleging that he broke his agreement with GM. And on October 22, Circuit Judge William Plummer entered a temporary restraining order against Perot.

Perot broke even putting the spin on this decision. Frank called Perot the next day, amused. "I recall telling him . . . I had 10 [news] clips and five had the headline, 'Perot Wins,' and five had the headline, 'Perot Loses.' "[26] Naturally, Perot told Frank that he had won.

He had not. While Judge Plummer agreed with Perot that his new company was free to solicit business so long as it wasn't profitable for PSC, he warned Perot that he was not to write contracts in two parts—nonprofit pricing before December 1, 1989, and profitable terms afterward. Not only was the USPS contract dead, but Perot Systems was sentenced to spin its wheels for the next 14 months.

Perot also lost in a much larger sense. Unlike bureaucrats, who can order us around, charismatic leaders can only inspire us to follow their example. The relationship between leader and follower is built on trust. Often, a single word or deed can transform a charismatic leader into a charlatan. For many EDSers, Perot Systems was that deed. "He told us he would be there for us 20 years later," says McAleer, one of the Wild Bunch, now a manager running a major account. "And he wasn't."[27]

CHAPTER EIGHTEEN

CUSTODY FIGHT

Elmer W. Johnson was the reluctant star of *EDS* v. *Henry Ross Perot and Perot Systems Corp.* when it went to trial in April of 1989. It was painfully obvious to everyone that GM got the short end of its deal with Perot. Attorney Johnson was an author of the agreement along with Perot's attorney Tom Luce. So the objective of Perot's attorneys when Johnson took the stand was to tug his professional competence down around his knees. It wasn't even his fight any more. Johnson had given up on hidebound General Motors himself in the summer of 1988, resigned his position as vice chairman, and returned to his old law firm, Kirkland & Ellis. He sat on the stand red-faced and uncharacteristically abrupt under questioning by Perot attorney Thomas Barr:

BARR:

> Did you interpret this agreement for yourself based on your knowledge and experience as a lawyer or did you interpret this agreement based upon what Mr. Luce told you?

JOHNSON:

> I based it on . . . my own understanding as a lawyer of the overarching purpose of this agreement. . . .

BARR:

Now, you are a reasonably experienced lawyer, I suppose. Are you not?

JOHNSON:

Yes, sir.

BARR:

And you knew that Mr. Luce was your adversary in this negotiation, did you not?

JOHNSON:

Yes, sir, I understood that.

BARR:

You knew he was there to get the best deal that he possibly could for his client?

JOHNSON:

I understood that, and I understood he is also a man of integrity.[1]

Johnson bore up well, considering the wide gulf between the deal he thought he had secured and the words Perot was now interpreting literally. Back on the stand the next day, an indignant Johnson snapped back at his tormentor: "We certainly didn't have time in two weeks to write a thousand-page agreement. . . based on the assumption that the people I was dealing with had the ultimate, extreme Machiavellian deviousness that you think I should have assumed. . . ."[2]

Johnson did make bad assumptions. It's very easy to misread Perot. He is so good at making virtues of his goals that even his adversaries begin believing that he doesn't have a self-serving bone in his body. Of course, he does. There aren't many accidental billionaires in the world. It is not even deviousness on his part in most instances. Perot, the Norman Rockwell patriot, is genuine. So is Perot the east Texas horse-trader. In any one of his deals an astute observer can see both personifications, like one of those CrackerJack prize pic-

tures with the plastic, prismatic lens that flip back and forth
between two images.

His colleagues at EDS can't say to this day whether the
sale of EDS to General Motors in 1984 was a master stroke
of estate planning by Perot or, as he argued, a chance to enlist
in the war against Japan, Inc. Clearly, it was both. Nor can
they say with certainty that he was not out to protect their
interests in the buyback in 1986—as he said, even after he
walked away with a $700 million bank wire. Says EDS general
counsel Richard Shlakman: "Saving all those EDSers from
GM and Roger Smith is a load of crock and a holy grail at the
same time. He genuinely believes it."[3]

His deal with GM is the one-dimensional exception. There
is no happy face to put on it; he tricked the automaker. He
was not giving up gracefully as Johnson was allowed to believe. Instead, he was going to use the letter of GM's ill-starred
deal to stomp all over the spirit of it.

Consider the minor issue of Perot approaching the PSC
Eight before June 1. Says a smug Perot, "Now a big, sophisticated organization like General Motors, if they didn't want
me to be able to talk to people about joining me, all their
lawyers had to do was stick in 'shall not seek to hire or hire' . . .
but they didn't . . . and that was no accident."[4] However, no
amount of Philadelphia lawyering can bring the office hunting
expedition by Horner and Gary Wright, undertaken before
their resignations from EDS, within most people's concept of
fair play.

Perot will argue that the original sin was GM's, that the
act of buying his silence was perverse. Says he, "In the spirit
of what was intended everybody at General Motors knew that
the price to get me to leave was to put these provisions in
there, and they knew the reason I wanted them was to be able
to form a company."[5] Johnson disagrees, but we don't need to
decide the facts to dispose of this argument. If buying silence
is perverse, so is selling it. Perot gave up the moral high
ground the minute he pocketed the money.

The trial hinged on two interpretations. In the first disputed passage of a slender 15-page agreement, Perot was pro-

hibited for three years from "providing for a profit" computer services in competition to EDS. Luce asked for the phrase in paragraph 10, Johnson testified, so that Perot could continue his charitable activities. Perot wanted the words applied literally. So long as he sold his services at break-even costs or less, he could compete with EDS anywhere, any time. In his temporary restraining order, Judge Plummer found the middle ground. He could perform commercial work so long as he never made a profit on it.

The second key paragraph was 13(b)—two sentences, 58 words, that comprise the "free-the-slaves" clause:

> In any case where the Stockholder may hire an employee of the Company without violating Paragraph 10(b) hereof, the employee may accept such position without any liability or forfeiture under any noncompetition or other restrictive agreements with the Company. The Company waives and cancels any prior restrictions on any employee to the extent such restrictions are inconsistent herewith.

Again, Perot pressed for the literal meaning. From June 1, 1988, until the end of time, Perot could hire anyone away from EDS without violating paragraph 10(b). Therefore the free-the-slaves clause ran forever. Johnson thought the paragraph simply completed the exemption for charitable crusades. Not only could Perot ask EDS workers to join him, but the employees also were free to go. EDS argued that it should expire with the contract on December 1, 1989. The paragraph amounted to a key to unlock the gold and steel handcuffs on EDS employees. Perot meant it to serve as an escape hatch for them. At least some of the EDS officers recognized this second benefit back in November 1986.

At the time, no one brought up the clause's third role— as a valuable asset. Only Perot, Meyerson, Gayden, and Walter—they had identical agreements—could hire at will from EDS. If rival Computer Sciences Corporation (CSC) wanted to make Heller an offer he couldn't refuse, EDS could make him sit on the sidelines for three years first. If, on the other hand, one of the buyback four joined CSC, took control of the company, or perhaps just sold his contract to the El Segundo, California firm, then CSC could hire employees away from EDS at will.

Gayden explained it this way in his deposition:

> Come next December I have the right to hire [an EDS employee] for anything I want to do and he's relieved of all restrictions. . . . And if I assign this to the ABC Co., all of that goes with it.
>
> EDS Attorney Smith: That's a damn valuable right, isn't it?
>
> Gayden: Damn right.
>
> Smith: What do you reckon it's worth?
>
> Gayden: Make me an offer.
>
> Perot counsel Barr, interjecting: He may have to do that before this is through.[6]

Perhaps Perot could still paint himself as a liberator if the only restrictions at stake here were noncompetition agreements. Americans hold it as a right of indignant employees to be able to walk across the street. The handcuffs were not the only restriction, however. In theory, 13(b) also waived the agreements that prohibit EDS workers from quitting and taking EDS trade secrets or customer data with them. It's true that some states prosecute employees for theft of intellectual property, but the criminal code is by no means perfect protection.

Alberthal raised the secrecy issue in a meeting with Perot in late October. Perot assured him that he had no interest in EDS computer programs or customer data. He drafted a definitive set of guidelines for his new hires that began, "You are being offered employment by Perot Systems because of your abilities not because of your knowledge of any trade secrets of EDS. You should not communicate to Perot Systems, and Perot Systems will neither solicit nor accept from you, any trade secrets of EDS." Says Perot, "I am as certain as we can be that nobody did."[7]

How do salesmen leave behind contacts and sources? For example, an acquaintance told PSC president Horner that McGraw-Hill, Inc., was sizing up an automation project that might interest PSC. Horner had once hired the acquaintance as an EDS consultant. Horner beat out EDS for McGraw-Hill's business. Similarly, a software company tipped Perot Systems that ICH, Inc., an insurance conglomerate, was negotiating with EDS. Perot won ICH also.

EDS sent its Learjet to New York to ferry the McGraw-Hill technocrat back to Dallas. EDS offered to undertake the contract for a fraction of Perot Systems' price. But Perot Systems employees were already at work at McGraw-Hill. In major concessions to his nervous customer, Perot had agreed to tackle the 18-month job under a series of one-day contracts and to release executives from their noncompete agreements with Perot Systems if EDS tied him up in court.

Perot strutted. "It's like watching my life repeated before my eyes. In 1962 when I started EDS IBM organized a five-man team to put me out of business. That was like being in all-out nuclear war. This is like a light, spring shower."[8]

More spin. Starting EDS was by far the easier task. Perot introduced IBM to guerrilla warfare, and he had a brand-new industry and an entire country in which to operate. EDS veteran Rusty Gunn recalls Perot's sublime delight when he landed PepsiCo, Inc., as an account, popping up in IBM's suburban New York backyard. On the few occasions when IBM caught Perot in the act, as it did when the Dallas office threatened to withhold its new life insurance software, 62-CFO, from Mercantile Security Life, its hands were tied by its antitrust consent order.

EDS is not hindered by government scrutiny and Perot Systems is not a better mousetrap. Perot had added few new wrinkles to Perot Systems. He promised to stay lean by subcontracting instead of hiring. He also wanted to share savings with clients instead of charging fixed prices. Neither idea made PSC a cash machine. Computer services was becoming a mature industry. Everyone knew what contracts were coming up for bid and who the contenders were. Profit margins were shrinking.

Perot Systems scrambled for business after it lost its key Postal Services deal. It drew up a hasty list of sales prospects.

These contracts were hardly what the founders had in mind at the L'Enfant Hotel planning meetings, but they had no choice. As they pointed out in sales presentations, "We're going to have to kiss some frogs before we kiss a prince."

(EDS was the butt of jokes in those slide presentations, just as IBM once was. Perot Systems customized a "Far Side" cartoon, featuring a castle bristling with soldiers and armament and with the legend "EDS" written on the wall. In front of the drawbridge, a small man was shouting, "You don't understand. I said I'm Al Tillis the Bum.")

What's more, the EDS slaves reacted cautiously to Perot Systems entreaties. Horner admits, "The lawsuit activity that EDS had undertaken had created a real fear in some of the prospects that we were talking to, and there were a lot who felt like for some reason, they couldn't come to work for Perot Systems." [9]

Perot plotted a preemptive strike. EDS's contract for Texas Medicaid processing, up for rebid in 1989, provided Perot a perfect opportunity to inflict insult as well as injury on EDS. This is the contract Perot went to war for in 1968 against the Social Security Administration, in 1975 against Blue Cross, and in 1980 against the hapless Bradford National. The state was negotiating a new term with EDS when Perot stepped into the fray.

It was Perot's best shot. He knew not only the business but also EDS's weaknesses. He also had enormous influence in Austin. He did have one problem; he didn't have the time or the staff to produce the stacks of documents the state required of bidders to qualify themselves and the data processing systems they intend to use. Nor did he have the time to estimate the insurance claims and establish a premium.

So he submitted a "me-too" bid. He proposed simply to step in and take over EDS's operation. In his November 4 bid letter, Perot observed in paragraphs 7 and 8: "Perot Systems will employ all qualified EDS personnel currently working on the Texas Medicaid Program. (The Virginia court ruling explicitly gives Perot Systems the right to hire any EDS employee, and to compete directly with EDS). . . . Using the EDS

Medicaid System and EDS Medicaid staff optimizes a smooth transition for the State of Texas."

Alas, EDS wouldn't hand over the technical specifications of its Medicaid system to Perot Systems. (Perot fought for four years to keep similar EDS Medicaid software out of the hands of the Social Security Administration.) Perot needed new rules. He hired top lobbyists Rusty Kelley and Buddy Jones, the men who helped him reform public education four years earlier. He went to war once more in Austin, this time against EDS.

The state had changed the rules after Perot mudwrestled Bradford National Corporation into submission. Before, the processor carried the full insurance risk and therefore was obliged to factor into the price such catastrophic events as influenza epidemics and recessions. After Bradford, the state built a safety net for the carrier. If payments exceeded estimates, the state would step in to pick up a part of the burden. If they fell below 90 percent, the carrier was obliged to share its savings.

Perot and his lobbyists pointed out to everyone in Austin that EDS's costs had yet to fall below 90 percent. As Ross Reeves explains it, "It was kind of like the Air Force budget where they try to fly out the gasoline at the end of the last quarter so they make sure they spend the dollars."[10] Perot was asking the state to assume all of the insurance risk. He would do the processing at cost, as his deal with GM required. He figured the state would save 40 cents on the dollar.

He succeeded in one of his objectives at least—scaring the hell out of EDS management. Top managers had faced down the first wave of anxiety. There were no mass defections. The golden handcuffs were holding. The Medicaid challenge, however, was an exponential escalation. Perot was trying to grab an entire operating unit, the contract that served EDS as sacred cow and cash cow.

Perot exploded another bombshell. He waved a purloined EDS memo at reporters. EDS was asking its Medicaid processing staff members to review their files and purge embarrassing documents. There were Perot loyalists in Austin! Perot compared the leak to one of the more titillating stories that summer, Colonel Oliver North's secretary, Fawn Hall, smuggling documents in her underclothes. "Fawn Hall lives in Dallas," he crowed. Actually the covert news was sent to Perot through the mail and signed "from the Dolphin." EDS was searching people as they left the locked room containing Medicaid bid materials.

Perot scored other hits in the press. That for EDS to earn 40 percent gross margins on Medicaid was obscene, he declared. He also railed against EDS for policing the copiers and searching employees. To make sure EDS didn't forget him, his company took out an advertisement in the *Austin American Statesman*: "Health care administration. Challenging career opportunity for health care and data processing professionals with previous experience."

Perot was striking out politically. The Bradford flap was still fresh in the minds of many politicians. He had been delighted with the new state plan in 1981 when the alternative was taking the contract away from EDS. Now he was telling them that EDS had a license to steal. Perot was six years late in raising this issue. J. Livingston Kosberg, then chairman of the Department of Human Services, notes, "The contract under which we were paying EDS was approved while Mr. Perot was chairman of the company."[11]

His cunning was showing again. On the face of it, Perot was offering "the option of having the Medicaid work done in a non-profit foundation funded by Ross Perot for the benefit of the needy in the State of Texas," as he said in his bid letter. Actually the politicos in Austin know a thing or two about betrayal and blood feuds. They saw he was dragging the state into a bizarre and bitter custody fight. They refused to pick a side. The state eventually threw out the Perot Systems bid.

Perot called Roger Smith to sue for peace. "I believe he said the suit was harmful to both parties and that we should attempt to settle," Smith recalls. "I told him it was an EDS matter that I would check and call him back."[12] In several meetings, EDS and Perot hammered out a basic structure.

Perot wanted EDS to ease off competition in Washington if Perot Systems would give up in Austin. EDS says the negotiations never rose above an impasse on paragraph 13(b), which Perot said allowed him to tap EDS for his manpower forever. EDS was just as sure that 13(b) died with the agreement in 1989. Says EDS senior vice president John Castle, "In hindsight I don't know that he was ever motivated to settle."[13] Virginia Circuit Court Judge William G. Plummer would decide.

One glance at the former Marine Corps officer, moonfaced, bespectacled and crew cut, conveys his low threshhold for nonsense. The judge kept both platoons of lawyers doublestepping through their cases, cutting off the unproductive thrusts and parries summarily. The surprise was how pleasantly he did it.

Even Judge Plummer seemed mesmerized when Perot took the stand October 19. His testimony raced past yes and no in a flash, flooding one issue and then the next, cascading through recreated dialogue, splashing into reflective pools, and racing on again. The Perot Treatment worked, even in court. Justice usually is administered by the eyedropper. Perot was making his own case and using a firehose to do it.

The observers were waiting for the collision when EDS attorney William Slusser stood up to cross examine Perot. Sure enough, Perot caught Slusser's fourth question in mid-stride and raced off. He snapped,

> That's incorrect. Now, that's part of this mythology that is floating through your whole case. Now—

SLUSSER:

> Excuse me a minute, Mr. Perot?

PEROT ATTORNEY DAVID BOIES:

> May he finish, Your Honor?

SLUSSER:

> Your Honor, he had an uninterrupted chance to spin his yarn on direct [examination]. I would like to have responsive questions on cross.

JUDGE PLUMMER:

> The objection is overruled. Just ask questions. Please, Mr.
> Perot, just answer them.[14]

Perot and Alberthal in testimony quickly established the
two interpretations of the 15-page agreement. Alberthal had
a tougher time convincing the court that no one at EDS had
realized the secondary benefits of paragraph 13(b) in November, 1986. Alberthal conceded that "free the slaves" was a loose
reference to 13(b). and that Perot intended to use paragraph
10 to start a new company. "Counselor," he replied finally,
"during that Thanksgiving period emotion was running quite
high. It was everyone's impression, mine included—mine was
specific knowledge—that the deal had been done. Ross had
sold out. . . . So there may have been a lot of those discussions
but I don't recall registering on any of those comments as
being pertinent."[15]

On the stand in April, Attorneys Johnson and Luce disagreed also about the genesis of 13(b). Luce said he used the
analogy of a general leaving the battlefield to demonstrate
the intent of the clause. Perot would not withdraw until his
troops were protected. Johnson didn't remember it. The witness was adamant about what he didn't hear:

EDS ATTORNEY DAVID FISKE:

> Did anyone ever express to you, from the Perot side of the
> table, that 13B was intended to give Mr. Perot a right to hire
> EDS employees in perpetuity?

JOHNSON:

> No, sir.

FISKE:

> If someone had expressed that to you, what would you have
> done?

JOHNSON:

> I would have called off negotiations immediately.

PEROT ATTORNEY BARR:

> Mr. Johnson, you mean if somebody would have said "I would like this to last in perpetuity" you would have jumped up and said "Negotiations are off," and you would have walked out of the room? Are you telling us that?

JOHNSON:

> I would say, "If you insist on that, negotiations are over."[16]

GM lacked other essential details. The corporation says it did not know that Perot had signed a standard EDS employment agreement on February 29, 1972, barring him from competition and recruitment. (Perot says GM did.) Assuming the contract was still binding, it was much more restrictive than GM's 1986 deal. Says Johnson, "I recall Luce saying. . . that this [noncompete stipulation] would be very difficult to get Mr. Perot to do because . . . he was philosophically, personally opposed to such things."[17]

However, EDS was suing Perot and not GM. As Barr noted during his summation: "[13(b)] works both ways. It's good for Perot Systems and it is good for the employees of EDS. It may not be great for General Motors. Indeed, I would say, as Mr. Perot said on the first of December, this is a stupid contract from General Motors' point of view."[18] Barr asked the judge to set 20 or 25 years as the life of 13(b). He compared Perot Systems to the valiant defenders of the Alamo, standing against GM's hordes.

Judge Plummer quipped that Perot perhaps hoped this fight would turn out differently. The judge promised to show the court a "Far Side" cartoon. This one showed a vendor selling tee-shirts at the Alamo emblazoned "I kicked Santa Anna's butt at the Alamo." The Mexican soldiers were on the wall above the vendor, who had crossed out his price and dropped it from $5 to $4 to $2.50 to 50 cents.

The cartoon was passed from hand to hand in a ripple of laughter as Plummer issued his decision. Perot wasn't smiling.

> In the court's opinion, no time limit was set out at all in 13 (b). . . . I then look to the intent of the parties. It is fairly obvious

Mr. Perot's intent was to have it limitless. It is not so clear that was the intent of the other side. I therefore find that there was no clear meeting of the minds upon that particular issue as to the time limits of 13(b). I believe under the law I am then required to a finding as to what would be reasonable under all of the circumstances. . . .

Certainly the primary purpose of 13(b) was to allow EDS employees to accept a job with Mr. Perot without violating their individual contractual restrictions with EDS. . . . If this time period was terminated at the end of the three-year period, that, in effect would eliminate the opportunity for the employees to become employed by a profit seeking company and to partici- pate in an ongoing business in this field. . . .

I find that a reasonable time for these employees to make up their minds as to whether or not they wish to leave and seek employment with Mr. Perot, and for Mr. Perot to offer them jobs, would be a period of five years from the date the contract was signed, that is, that it will run until December 1 of '91.[19]

Perot stalked out of the courtroom and out of the building. He strode up the slight grade toward downtown Fairfax trail- ing his retinue of attorneys in his wake. First EDS took away his homerun contract with the Postal Service. Now it was locking the doors. He had 30 months to free the slaves rather than a lifetime.

CHAPTER NINETEEN

NEVER GIVE IN

The view from the law firm conference room had changed since my last visit. The office building across the street had vanished in the three months since I sat in this room laboring through the depositions and exhibits of *EDS* v. *Perot*. The low-rise couldn't compete in the overbuilt downtown Dallas office market against the fancy new skyscrapers adorned in marble and black glass. It was cheaper to pave it as a parking lot and wait for better times. Real estate, like writing books, is a cyclical adventure. Some days, it's chicken; some days it's feathers.

The last time I was in this room I could barely contain my surprise and delight. Cheerful secretaries were delivering to me the depositions of all of the principals in this book. Some of them were three inches thick, minus exhibits. Here I learned the real story of Perot Systems, stripped of media spin. Here I became the first outsider to piece together GM's side of its showdown with Ross Perot. I saw the court fight in all of its ambiguities and contradictions.

I was back today for a helping of feathers. EDS's PR manager, Bill Wright, had arranged a meeting between Baker & Botts partner Phil Smith and me. The law firm had shown me some material I should not have seen, Wright explained. Smith was making his point by pulling the title pages of the depositions from a manila folder. The word *Confidential* at the top of each page had been highlighted in yellow. Of course, I had seen the headings before, but I assumed that restriction no longer applied now that the trial was over. Smith said his secretaries had made the same mistake. I should not have seen any of it.

His objective today was damage control. He was obliged to disclose his mistake to the other parties to the lawsuit. It would be an easier chore if he could also tell them he had contained the problem. He wanted the material back. He wanted my assurance that I wouldn't use it in this book. If I refused to give those assurances, he continued, he might be forced to sue me to demonstrate his good faith to the court. Even if he didn't sue, he continued, Perot would. And Perot would never believe that I saw the material by accident. He would add EDS and Baker & Botts to his action, claiming that the three of us conspired against him.

The thought had already flashed through my head. Was I being used? I searched Smith's face for clues. He seemed genuinely distressed, but then lawyers don't succeed in trial practice without a sense of theatrics. Wright confirmed Smith's story. The realization had dawned on Smith in September. He had just begun a contempt action against Perot. Plummer had agreed to hear evidence that he had violated the terms of the Virginia court injunction. At the end of the session, Plummer had warned both parties that confidentiality still applied. Wright said Smith turned white on the return flight and wondered out loud, What did we show that writer anyway?

I searched my memory for other clues and found none. Smith's staff had done nothing suspicious. They had not steered me to this document or that one. Nor had they refused to show me specific depositions. I had full access to both sides of the dispute. They made photocopies for me and presented me with a bill. I wrote a check in payment.

I couldn't rule out a deliberate leak. The fight between Perot and his old company had turned that bitter. Wright was furious about the book *Irreconcilable Differences*, which was published just as the trial got underway in Virginia. Author Doron Levin had disclosed the exchange of faxes between Smith and Perot and other documents that supported Perot's version of his fight with Roger Smith. Levin never told how he obtained them, but Wright thought he knew. If Wright did steer my book, he topped Perot as a spin doctor. There's not a single fingerprint; not even I can say if the leak was deliberate or inadvertent.

Smith continued to press his case. Even if I was not obliged by law to return the deposition material, he argued, it wasn't mine to keep, was it? If I found a bag of money in the road, I'd turn it in, right? Why couldn't I write a book without the confidential information? So what if it didn't have the impact without the material?

I knew my answer was going to be no. Smith was asking me to turn my face away from what I knew to be true, and I couldn't do it. I'm a reporter. It's who I am and how I define myself. I told him I'd consult an attorney and give him an answer as quickly as I could. When I did, my answer was a tidy legalistic evasion. The damage was done when the information entered my head. I couldn't give it back short of a lobotomy. Nothing I could promise, or he could do, would change that fact.

Smith joined the casualty list in this drama, along with Johnson, Alberthal, EDS's former GM account manager Ken Riedlinger, and a cast of thousands. Perot's attorneys went before Plummer to argue that the disclosure demonstrated bad faith on the part of EDS. They wanted the contempt action thrown out. Plummer agreed. There was no legal means to prevent me from using the deposition materials. Throwing out the contempt action was the only way for Plummer to even the score. Smith had lost his case.

Perot turned spin doctor again, apparently to try to get GM to come after me. When he called a *Wall Street Journal* reporter to announce the dismissal of EDS's case, of the 20-odd depositions I had read, he mentioned only Roger Smith's. This was no slip. Smith's name never came up in the hearing.

Perot Systems told Plummer that I intended to "fully expose" customer lists, company strategy, and other trade secrets that I had obtained from Perot's deposition and others.

Apparently, the *Journal* reporter thought to ask why EDS's attorneys would do something that stupid. "It's bizarre," Perot replied with all of the English he could put on his answer, "because they [EDS's attorneys] were most insistent that Roger's deposition be kept in confidence for reasons that would be obvious if you read it." Readers now know what was in Smith's deposition. The *Journal* reporter did not. He noted that lawyer Smith's mistake and my book "could mean more embarrassment for GM Chairman Roger B. Smith."[1]

I joined the list of people in this tale who found themselves facing repugnant choices. Luce joined this list on December 1, comprehending that Perot would fight on; and Roger Smith in the fall of 1985, realizing that he could not keep his word to Perot. Legalisms aside, Baker & Botts had helped me, and now I was refusing even to set the record straight. I couldn't appear to choose sides.

My answer led me to understand the real nature of America's competitiveness problem, that has preoccupied Perot throughout the 1980s. He points out that Japanese visitors once described EDS as a group of fanatics. "They meant that as a compliment," he says. "The Japanese meant we were driven by success, driven to win, and we worked as a unified team."[2] Perot assumed it was his leadership that made EDS a Japanese-like company, but his contribution is only half of the formula. Perot gave EDS its drive. It was the company that delivered the teamwork. Perot is not a team player. He is a product of a state built by people who relied on their own counsel and resources.

We've kept our frontier spirit. We're not only individualists in the late 20th century, we're also narrow specialists. Attorney Smith and I both believe in the Bill of Rights, but he serves the Sixth Amendment guaranteeing a fair trial, and I serve the First preserving freedom of the press. When the interests of justice and the press clash, so do we. Perhaps neither of us would have taken ourselves, or our jobs so seriously back in the 1940s.

Today's specialists run free. After GM struck a deal to buy EDS, for example, the Salomon Brothers bankers and their GM counterparts could congratulate each other and go home blissfully ignorant of the collision they had set in motion. Accountant Roger Smith could believe he was buying leadership and cultural change. Leader Perot could think he was reforming an institution he didn't understand or particularly like.

Perot is the most rigid and uncompromising specialist of the lot. He is a leader. That's how he defines himself. It's who he is. Once he reduces the mission to a simple set of marching orders the only result he'll accept is victory. Even when he sees a bloody collision ahead, he is incapable of turning the wheel to avoid it. Most of the bodies in the road between Dallas and Detroit are of his doing.

It's not power or money or glory that drives him, in my opinion. Rather, it's the siren song of challenge and the sweet taste of victory. He wants results. He trusts his own judgment completely and stands ready to inject it at the first moment of indecision. "I have a very high level of frustration with things that can be done so much better," Perot says, "money that is available for people who are truly needy that is handled so poorly, the State Department's inability to act in situations where they could do something . . ."[3]

He realizes that his low tolerance for frustration rules out politics. When a majority of Texas Republicans wrote in his name on a straw ballot in the 1970s as their choice to run for governor, he declined. He continues to decline invitations to run for president. He doesn't have the patience to deal with the inanities of public office. He can't compromise. He sees bureaucracy as maddeningly slow and ineffective at its best, and wrongheaded and corrupt at its worst. His defeats at its hands in New York, Detroit, Washington, and Dallas appear to have convinced him that he can't work inside the system. This bitter day was coming regardless of GM.

Perot in the late 1980s is brooding again. Friends note his strained relationship with Dallas and ask him why he keeps trying. He doesn't know why he stays, he replies. His snit is reminiscent of the zoning fight in 1970 when he held out the threat of moving EDS out of Dallas. He won't move now either, but he is building a high wall along the front of his 22-acre estate.

He bristles also when he takes calls from Washington. Congress wants him to testify, he believes, because his straight talk draws media coverage. He asks them point blank, Do you want to talk about it or do you want to do something about it? He knows the answer already. They won't listen to him or act on his advice. They just want to get the monkey up there to dance. This, too, harks back to his disgust with the Carter administration and the Iran hostages.

He has met modest resistance in his public appearances. A smattering of University of Texas students booed when he described investment bankers as the get-rich-quick equivalent of dope dealers. ("[Investment banking] is a crooked game. It makes Las Vegas look like an honest racket."[4]) And an interviewer on a Public Broadcasting Service television show found more truth than humor in his offhand jest, "The more I listen to you, the more I think the Ross Perot answer is 'shoot all the lawyers, shoot all the school administrators, shoot all the investment bankers and the ordinary people can take care of themselves.' "[5]

He has become more sensitive about his money and his image. He required a photo agency to send him for review the pictures shot of him playing with boats at his lake home in Texas. (Boats are his indulgence. He has three racing boats, one of them powered by twin jet engines, and a 45-foot cabin cruiser.) When the agency shipped him the slides, it tucked in the standard form requiring him to take financial responsibility for them. For 600 slides, however, the potential tab fell just short of $1 million. He was livid. He figured the photos would be lost simply because he was good for $1 million. He shipped the box back unopened.

The agency later added injury to insult. One of the slides was a particularly unflattering shot of him on his surfboard with his hair slicked down and a bulldog scowl on his face. He seethed when the photo turned up in *Business Week* and then *Newsweek*. Everybody was whacking away at him like a piece of meat, he complained. But then, he wanted to hide from the press in the early 1970s also.

What's new this time is his losses at GM. He paid the ultimate price for surrendering to his eagerness to fight the Japanese. He admits that selling EDS was his worst mistake. It cost him his followers. Unable to let Roger Smith win, Perot forced his old colleagues to choose sides. Starting over at age 58, Perot is taking on EDS; his old company has become "the system."

Even Perot will have trouble following in Perot's footsteps. Industry leader EDS has so much money and raw telecommunications and computer power, it may be impossible to catch. Perot described his struggle against IBM as climbing an icy cliff barehanded. He exaggerated then, but his metaphor fits his new challenge perfectly. And EDS sees him coming.

The computer-services business is much different today than it was in 1962. Industries in distress are still the best sales prospects, but the stakes are much higher. In the natural gas pipeline business, for example, hard times and deregulation have done away with fixed prices. Today, pipelines must haggle with consumers and producers. When industry leader Enron turned to EDS to help it manage this complex new business, EDS tackled a 10-year, $1 billion contract.

Similarly, EDS bought First City Bancorp's computer system and invested $20 million in preferred stock in the Houston bank. Both companies insist the transactions are unrelated, but the facts are that EDS landed a $550 million account, and the bank completed a badly needed recapitalization. Unnerved, EDS competitors lobbied Congress to outlaw reciprocal deals in the massive federal bailout of savings and loan associations.

Perot can afford to bid against EDS on big contracts like these. But he can't afford to lose customers that large. He can't spread the risk of a failure by a large, distressed customer— as EDS can—over $5 billion in other business. It's not his style to gamble. He never was a gunslinger.

The solidest launch would be a large government project. But Perot Systems is not likely to strike another deal like the Postal Service contract without competitive bidding. In open competitions, Perot suffers the same handicap he faced in Austin in the Medicaid fight. The government evaluates bids by comparing experience and equipment. Perot Systems has neither. When EDS first tackled the government market in 1977, it bought the necessary history by acquiring a small federal contractor.

Perot could take the same tack. Indeed, a large acquisition would not only give him a better shot at EDS, it would also maximize his ability to free the slaves. (Remember that Perot argues that his rights can be assigned or sold.)

Executed poorly, however, an acquisition has significant potential to become a second duPont. There would be inevitable frictions between the acquired executives and the new managers Perot recruited away from EDS. Nor could Perot turn an acquisition into an irresistible job offer. For its first years anyway, an acquired company would not have the rapid growth and the stock appreciation that made the gold handcuffs so attractive and effective at EDS.

Perot can't replace the followers he gave up at EDS. The company wouldn't have happened without Bill Starnes, Anne Ellis, and the other systems engineers who performed the night-roaming heroics of the early EDS. It couldn't have grown if Heller, Fernandes, and the other Vietnam vets had given up and fled the apartments on Jackson Street in San Francisco and Third Avenue in New York where they lived in groups of eight. They still owe a debt to Perot. They gained pride and confidence as a result of the opportunities that he gave them. But since June 1, 1988, they no longer believe that he walks on water.

Perot Systems is being staffed by proven managers in their 30s and 40s. They've had to scramble for opportunities since they lost the Postal Service account. They have won some innings, and they will win more. However, it's not likely that they can achieve the missionary zeal of EDS in the late 1960s, when Perot's Eagles were clouting every pitch out of the park. EDS then was the happy confluence of the right people in the right business at the right time. Perot Systems Corporation may never achieve that magic.

Pride and presumption finally caught up with Perot even though he had watched for hubris from the very start. He climbed all over Downtain, EDS employee No. 7, when one of Downtain's computer systems went awry. You're starting to believe your own press clippings, Perot chided him. He was policing himself in 1979 when he promoted Meyerson to president. "The company is evolving into an organization instead of a hot sandlot football team," he told analysts then. By turning over EDS to Meyerson, Perot ducked the bullet that kills most entrepreneurs. Perot realized that running a major corporation is different than leading a holy war. Perot was reminding himself of his mortality even in 1982 when he drove out to the airport to witness the shock and sorrow at bankrupt Braniff Airways.

The seeds of his own end were taking root. He had saved Chiapparone and Gaylord from jail. He'd made war on drug dealers in 1981 and reformed Texas schools in 1984. Perot knew that anything was possible for him. Now the world was catching on too. Back in the glory years, he told a reporter that the title to his life should be " 'It all starts with a telephone call.' I'm just sitting here doing business when someone calls and says 'Hey, we gotta do this.' "[6]

Those pleas are the one way Perot the east Texas horse-trader can be suckered. Perot, the billionaire defender of the underdog, is always in. Blue funk or not, he is certain to field a call one day that will cause him to saddle up once more and ride to the defense. If he is the last hope of the beleaguered group, and the odds are impossible, so much the better. Boswell, his eyes and ears at duPont in the early 1970s, watched him answer calls from Wall Street and Washington. "Dangling a challenge in front of Ross is like ringing the dinner bell," he says.[7]

Perhaps the Salomon Brothers bankers knew exactly what they were doing when, in 1984, they offered him an alliance with GM and a crack at the Japanese. Or perhaps they simply lucked into the one argument that would play to Perot's supreme confidence in his luck and his skills. It's an academic question now. Back in World War I, a Member of Parliament and contemporary of Sir Winston Churchill observed of the man: "It is no disparagement of Winston's qualities to say that his judgment doesn't quite equal his abilities, nor his abilities equal his ambition. The defect in him is that he sees everything magnified by his own self confidence."[8]

Such men don't dine on chicken feathers as often as we mortals. So Perot waits for the phone to ring, blames Roger Smith and Les Alberthal for his losses, and still misses the point. That's what makes Henry Ross Perot extraordinary. He won't accept that it, too, can all end with a telephone call.

REFERENCES

NOTES TO INTRODUCTION

1. William Wright, author's interview, April 10, 1989.
2. *The Wall Street Journal*, October 20, 1988.
3. *Dallas Morning News*, October 20, 1988.
4. Ibid.
5. Donald Ephlin, author's interview, May 11, 1989.
6. *Esquire*, December 1, 1980.
7. Gary J. Fernandes, author's interview, June 9, 1989.
8. *New York Post*, January 3, 1970.
9. *Look*, March 3, 1970.
10. Gary J. Fernandes, author's interview, June 9, 1989.
11. *Barron's*, February 23, 1987.
12. *Dallas Morning News*, February 19, 1986.
13. *Business Week*, October 6, 1986.
14. Perot speech, Dallas, October 20, 1987.

NOTES TO CHAPTER 1

1. Donald Rochelle, author's interview, April 27, 1989.
2. *Washington Post*, April 12, 1987.
3. The Perot family history is largely from the files of the Texarkana Historical Museum.

4. I drew on James M. Tennison's oral histories and other research for my account of Patty Hill School.
5. *Washington Post*, April 12, 1987.
6. Ed Overholser, author's interview, April 27, 1989.
7. Howard Waldrop, author's interview, February 13, 1989.
8. Bill Wright, author's interview, February 27, 1989.
9. Jim Morriss, author's interview, March 3, 1989.
10. Donald Rochelle, author's interview, April 27, 1989.
11. *Dallas Times Herald*, February 9, 1989.
12. D. W. Atchley, author's interview, March 12, 1989.
13. *Dallas Morning News*, February 1, 1986.
14. Perot speech, Dallas, February 8, 1989.
15. Dorothy Bakie, author's interview, March 13, 1989.
16. Jim Morriss, author's interview, March 3, 1989.
17. Hayes McClerkin, author's interview, February 28, 1989.
18. Jane Atchley, author's interview, March 12, 1989.

NOTES TO CHAPTER 2

1. Harold L. Schrewsbury, author's interview, February 19, 1989.
2. Arlis J. Simmons, author's interview, April 18, 1989.
3. Bob Inman, author's interview, March 23, 1989.
4. Mark Royston, author's interview, April 19, 1989.
5. Perot speech, Dallas, November 18, 1986.
6. Ibid.
7. Dean Campbell, author's interview, March 23, 1989.
8. Tom Spain, author's interview, March 7, 1989.
9. Ibid.
10. Gayle Tinsley, author's interview, March 2, 1989.
11. Dean Campbell, author's interview, March 23, 1989.
12. Henry Wendler, author's interview, February 24, 1989.
13. James Campbell, author's interview, March 6, 1989.

NOTES TO CHAPTER 3

1. *'D' Magazine*, January 1, 1984.
2. *Business Week*, October 6, 1986.
3. Jack Hight, author's interview, February 27, 1989.
4. James Campbell, author's interview, March 6, 1989.

5. Cecil Gunn, author's interview, April 20, 1989.
6. David W. Soelter, author's interview, April 25, 1989.
7. Cecil Gunn, author's interview, April 20, 1989.
8. Joe Wright, author's interview, April 5, 1989.
9. Cecil Gunn, author's interview, April 20, 1989.
10. Anne Ellis, author's interview, April 5, 1989.
11. Cecil Gunn, author's interview, April 20, 1989.
12. Ibid.
13. Charles Folsom, author's interview, April 8, 1989.
14. Ibid.
15. Ibid.
16. Jerry Dugger, author's interview, May 10, 1989.
17. Bill Seay, author's interview, March 2, 1989.

NOTES TO CHAPTER 4

1. Cecil Gunn, author's interview, April 20, 1989.
2. Malcolm Gudis, author's interview, July 21, 1989.
3. Perot speech, Austin, September 19, 1989.
4. *Dallas Morning News*, September 9, 1980.
5. Keane Taylor, author's interview, October 2, 1989.
6. Ibid.
7. Perot speech, Washington, May 24, 1981.
8. Keane Taylor, author's interview, October 2, 1989.
9. Perot press conference, Dallas, date unknown, 1983.
10. Perot speech, Washington, May 24, 1981.
11. Tom Beauchamps, author's interview, February 8, 1989.
12. Hearings before a subcommittee of the Committee on Government Operations, House of Representatives. September 28, 30; November 9; and December 1, 1971. U.S. Government Printing Office, 1972.
13. Ibid.
14. Ibid.
15. Ibid.
16. Richard Shlakman, author's interview, September 29, 1989.
17. Hearings before a subcommittee of the Committee on Government Operations, House of Representatives. September 28, 30; November 9; and December 1, 1971. U.S. Government Printing Office, 1972.
18. James Naughton, author's interview, April 12, 1989.

19. Hearings before a subcommittee of the Committee on Government Operations, House of Representatives. May 30, 31 and June 1, 1972. U.S. Government Printing Office, 1972.
20. Hearings before a subcommittee of the Committee on Government Operations, House of Representatives. September 28, 30; November 9; and December 1, 1971. U.S. Government Printing Office, 1972.
21. Tom Beauchamps, author's interview, February 8, 1989.
22. Hearings before a subcommittee of the Committee on Government Operations, House of Representatives. September 28, 30; November 9; and December 1, 1971. U.S. Government Printing Office, 1972.
23. Tom Beauchamps, author's interview, February 8, 1989.
24. Ibid.
25. *Dallas Morning News*, May 3, 1970.
26. *Dallas Morning News*, November 11, 1971.

NOTES TO CHAPTER 5

1. Jeffrey M. Heller, author's interview, May 25, 1989.
2. Ibid.
3. Cecil Gunn, author's interview, April 20, 1989.
4. Patrick F. McAleer, author's interview, May 26, 1989.
5. Gary Fernandes, author's interview, May 4, 1989.
6. Les Alberthal, author's interview, May 25, 1989.
7. Jim Meler, author's interview, May 21, 1989.
8. Gary Fernandes, author's interview, May 4, 1989.
9. Ibid.
10. Gary Griggs, author's interview, March 14, 1989.
11. Raymond Garfield, author's interview, March 21, 1989.
12. Gary Griggs, author's interview, March 14, 1989.
13. Patrick McAleer, author's interview, May 26, 1989.
14. Gary Griggs, author's interview, March 14, 1989.
15. Rob Brooks, author's interview, March 14, 1989.
16. Gary Griggs, author's interview, March 14, 1989.
17. Ibid.
18. Raymond Garfield, author's interview, March 21, 1989.
19. EDS brochure, "Success in Business," 1984.
20. Perot speech, Detroit, December 8, 1986.

NOTES TO CHAPTER 6

1. Rob Brooks, author's interview, March 14, 1989.
2. EDS brochure, "Success in Business," 1984.
3. Ibid.
4. Richard Shlakman, author's interview, September 29, 1989.
5. Robert Rhodes James, *A Study in Failure*, New York: World Publishing Co., 1970.
6. Perot speech, Dallas, February 8, 1989.
7. Richard Shlakman, author's interview, September 29, 1989.
8. Posner, *Leadership Challenge* (San Francisco: Jossey Bass, 1987).
9. Perot speech, Austin, September 19, 1989.
10. Perot speech, Dallas, September 23, 1986.
11. Perot speech, Austin, September 19, 1989.
12. Keane Taylor, author's interview, October 2, 1989.
13. Portia Isaacson, author's interview, March 21, 1989.
14. Perot speech, Dallas, September 23, 1986.
15. Richard Shlakman, author's interview, Dallas, September 29, 1989.
16. Pat McAleer, author's interview, May 26, 1989.
17. Jim Buchanan, author's interview, May 8, 1989.
18. Gary Griggs, author's interview, March 14, 1989.
19. *Dallas Times Herald*, March 14, 1974.
20. *Dallas Morning News*, July 6, 1989.
21. Bill Wright, author's interview, March 9, 1989.
22. Kotter, *Leadership Factor* (New York: Free Press, 1988).
23. Perot speech, Austin, September 19, 1989.
24. Richard Shlakman, author's interview, September 29, 1989.

NOTES TO CHAPTER 7

1. *Business Week*, March 27, 1971.
2. *Duns Review*, March 1, 1973.
3. *Fortune*, November 1, 1968.
4. John Brooks, *The Go-Go Years* (New York: Weybright & Talley, 1973).
5. G. Michael Boswell, author's interview, March 28, 1989.
6. Gary Griggs, author's interview, March 14, 1989.
7. *Duns Review*, March 1, 1973.
8. Gary Griggs, author's interview, March 14, 1989.

9. Alan Aldridge, author's interview, August 8, 1989.
10. James Lundquist, author's interview, August 9, 1989.
11. G. Michael Boswell, author's interview, March 28, 1989.
12. Carl Walston, author's interview, August 9, 1989.
13. Walter Auch, author's interview, October 30, 1989.
14. Ibid.
15. G. Michael Boswell, author's interview, March 28, 1989.
16. *Barrons*, January 28, 1974.
17. Walston, author's interview, August 9, 1989.
18. Richard Shlakman, author's interview, September 29, 1989.
19. *Barrons*, February 23, 1987.
20. Joe Glover, author's interview, May 31, 1989.
21. Portia Isaacson, author's interview, March 21, 1989.

NOTES TO CHAPTER 8

1. Perot speech, Washington, November 20, 1984.
2. Ibid.
3. Ibid.
4. Ibid.
5. *Dallas Morning News*, June 6, 1984.
6. Rick Salwen, author's interview, May 17, 1989.
7. Terral Smith, author's interview, March 3, 1989.
8. Ibid.
9. "Today Show," NBC, October 25, 1989.
10. Rick Salwen, author's interview, May 17, 1989.
11. Perot speech, Washington, November 20, 1984.
12. Charles Beard, author's interview, March 23, 1989.
13. Raymon Bynum, author's interview, March 23, 1989.
14. *Dallas Morning News*, June 6, 1984.
15. John Cole, author's interview, March 3, 1989.
16. Perot speech, Washington, November 20, 1984.
17. Raymon Bynum, author's interview, March 23, 1989.
18. John Cole, author's interview, March 3, 1989.
19. Ibid.
20. Charles Beard, author's interview, March 23, 1989.
21. Raymon Bynum, author's interview, March 23, 1989.
22. Gary Griggs, author's interview, March 14, 1989.
23. Raymond Garfield, author's interview, March 21, 1989.
24. Enso Bighinatti, author's interview, March 12, 1989.
25. Ralph Shannon, author's interview, March 9, 1989.

26. Lester Alberthal, author's interview, August 17, 1989.
27. Ibid.

NOTES TO CHAPTER 9

1. Gary J. Fernandes, author's interview, June 9, 1989.
2. Ibid.
3. Alex Mair, author's interview, June 15, 1989.
4. Jim Buchanan, author's interview, May 8, 1989.
5. Alex Mair, author's interview, June 15, 1989.
6. Jeff Heller, author's interview, May 25, 1989.
7. Gary J. Fernandes, author's interview, June 9, 1989.
8. Jim Buchanan, author's interview, May 8, 1989.
9. Paul Sims, author's interview, June 16, 1989.
10. Jeff Heller, author's interview, May 25, 1989.
11. Paul Sims, author's interview, June 16, 1989.
12. Evans deposition, May 18, 1987, *EDS* v. *Perot*; Circuit Court, Fairfax Co., Va.
13. Jeff Heller, author's interview, May 25, 1989.
14. Alex Mair, author's interview, June 15, 1989.
15. Jim Meler, author's interview, May 21, 1989.
16. Alex Mair, author's interview, June 15, 1989.
17. Jeff Heller, author's interview, May 25, 1989.
18. Smith deposition, March 3, 1989, *EDS* v. *Perot*; Circuit Court, Fairfax Co., Va.

NOTES TO CHAPTER 10

1. *Business Week*, October 6, 1986.
2. Donald Ephlin, author's interview, May 11, 1989.
3. Alex Mair, author's interview, June 15, 1989.
4. Perot speech, Austin, September 26, 1983.
5. Smith deposition, March 3, 1989, *EDS* v. *Perot*; Circuit Court, Fairfax Co., Va.
6. Ibid.
7. Johnson deposition, February 3, 1989, *EDS* v. *Perot*; Circuit Court, Fairfax Co., Va.
8. Smith deposition, March 3, 1989, *EDS* v. *Perot*; Circuit Court, Fairfax Co., Va.
9. Gary J. Fernandes, author's interview, June 9, 1989.

10. Smith deposition. March 3, 1989, *EDS* v. *Perot*; Circuit Court, Fairfax Co., Va.
11. Johnson deposition. February 3, 1989, *EDS* v. *Perot*; Circuit Court, Fairfax Co., Va.
12. Exhibit to Johnson Deposition.

NOTES TO CHAPTER 11

1. Les Alberthal, author's interview, August 17, 1989.
2. Wesley Hjornevik, author's interview, March 3, 1989.
3. Ibid.
4. *Texas Business*, March, 1981.
5. Richard Shlakman, author's interview, September 29, 1989.
6. Wesley Hjornevik, author's interview, March 3, 1989.
7. Robert W. Doubek, author's interview, April 12, 1989.
8. Ibid.
9. Ibid.
10. Ibid.
11. Jan Scruggs, *To Heal a Nation* (New York: Harper and Row).
12. *Retired Officer*, November, 1983.
13. Milton Copulos, author's interview, April 14, 1989.
14. F. Andrew Messing, author's interview, April 12, 1989.
15. Robert W. Doubek, author's interview, April 12, 1989.

NOTES TO CHAPTER 12

1. Smith deposition, March 3, 1989, *EDS* v. *Perot*; Circuit Court, Fairfax Co., Va.
2. Albert Lee, *Call Me Roger* (Chicago: Contemporary Books, 1988).
3. Ibid.
4. Smith deposition, March 3, 1989, *EDS* v. *Perot*; Circuit Court, Fairfax Co., Va.
5. Ibid.
6. Johnson deposition, February 3, 1989, *EDS* v. *Perot*; Circuit Court, Fairfax Co., Va.
7. Doron P. Levin, *Irreconcilable Differences* (Boston: Little, Brown, 1989).

NOTES TO CHAPTER 13

1. *Dallas Times Herald*, March 14, 1986.
2. Ibid.
3. Ibid.
4. Perot speech, Dallas, February 8, 1989.
5. Ibid.
6. *Dallas Morning News*, February 20, 1987.
7. *Texas Monthly*, December, 1987.
8. Bill Wright, author's interview, April 28, 1989.
9. *Newsweek*, February 18, 1974.
10. *Forbes*, June 15, 1972.
11. *Dallas Morning News*, November 24, 1970.
12. *Dallas Morning News*, June 2, 1980.
13. *Dallas Morning News*, June 28, 1981.
14. Nathan Adams, author's interview, August 2, 1989.
15. *Dallas Morning News*, May 18, 1986.
16. Keane Taylor, author's interview, October 2, 1989.
17. Troost memo, 1986.
18. *Business Week*, October 6, 1986.
19. Albert Lee, *Call Me Roger* (Chicago: Contemporary Books, 1988).
20. *Business Week*, October 6, 1986.
21. Gary J. Fernandes, author's interview, June 9, 1989.
22. Bill Wright, author's interview, April 28, 1989.
23. Les Alberthal, author's interview, August 17, 1989.
24. Smith deposition, March 3, 1989, *EDS* v. *Perot*; Circuit Court, Fairfax Co., Va.
25. Evans deposition, May 28, 1987, *EDS* v. *Perot*; Circuit Court, Fairfax Co., Va.
26. Ibid.
27. Ibid.

NOTES TO CHAPTER 14

1. Johnson deposition, February 3, 1989, *EDS* v. *Perot*; Circuit Court, Fairfax Co., Va.
2. Ibid.
3. Luce deposition, February 16, 1989, *EDS* v. *Perot*; Circuit Court, Fairfax Co., Va.

4. Perot testimony, October 19, 1989, *EDS* v. *Perot*, Circuit Court, Fairfax Co., Va.
5. Gary J. Fernandes, author's interview, June 9, 1989.
6. Alberthal deposition, February 6, 1989, *EDS* v. *Perot*; Circuit Court, Fairfax Co., Va.
7. Ibid.
8. Gudis deposition, February 22, 1989, *EDS* v. *Perot*; Circuit Court, Fairfax Co., Va.
9. Luce deposition, February 16, 1989, *EDS* v. *Perot*; Circuit Court, Fairfax Co., Va.
10. Johnson deposition, February 3, 1989, *EDS* v. *Perot*; Circuit Court, Fairfax Co., Va.
11. Ibid.
12. Luce deposition, February 16, 1989, *EDS* v. *Perot*; Circuit Court, Fairfax Co., Va.
13. Ibid.
14. Alberthal deposition, February 6, 1989, *EDS* v. *Perot*; Circuit Court, Fairfax Co., Va.
15. Ibid.
16. Perot deposition, February 9, 1989, *EDS* v. *Perot*; Circuit Court, Fairfax Co., Va.
17. Alberthal deposition, February 6, 1989, *EDS* v. *Perot*; Circuit Court, Fairfax Co., Va.
18. Gary J. Fernandes, author's interview, June 9, 1989.
19. Fernandes deposition, February 15, 1989, *EDS* v. *Perot*; Circuit Court, Fairfax Co., Va.
20. Luce deposition, February 16, 1989, *EDS* v. *Perot*; Circuit Court, Fairfax Co., Va.
21. Hamlin deposition, February 15, 1989, *EDS* v. *Perot*; Circuit Court, Fairfax Co., Va.
22. Johnson deposition, February 3, 1989, *EDS* v. *Perot*; Circuit Court, Fairfax Co., Va.
23. Ibid.
24. Perot press conference, December 1, 1986.
25. Ibid.
26. Johnson deposition, February 3, 1989, *EDS* v. *Perot*; Circuit Court, Fairfax Co., Va.
27. Millstein deposition, February 21, 1989, *EDS* v. *Perot*; Circuit Court, Fairfax Co., Va.
28. Les Alberthal author's interview, August 17, 1989.

29. Perot deposition, February 9, 1989, *EDS* v. *Perot*; Circuit Court, Fairfax Co., Va.

30. Johnson deposition, February 3, 1989, *EDS* v. *Perot*; Circuit Court, Fairfax Co., Va.

31. Perot deposition, February 9, 1989, *EDS* v. *Perot*; Circuit Court, Fairfax Co., Va.

NOTES TO CHAPTER 15

1. *The Wall Street Journal*, January 12, 1989.
2. Donald Ephlin, author's interview, May 11, 1989.
3. Perot speech, Detroit, December 8, 1986.
4. Perot speech, Dallas, February 2, 1989.
5. "How I Would Turn Around GM," *Fortune*, February 15, 1988.
6. David Cole, author's interview, May 8, 1989.
7. Donald Ephlin, author's interview, May 11, 1989.
8. "How I Would Turn Around GM," *Fortune*, February 15, 1988.
9. Alex Mair, author's interview, June 15, 1989.
10. "How I Would Turn Around GM," *Fortune*, February 15, 1988.
11. Ibid.
12. Ibid.
13. David Cole, author's interview, May 8, 1989.
14. "How I Would Turn Around GM," *Fortune*, February 15, 1988.
15. Les Alberthal, author's interview, August 17, 1989.
16. Jeff Heller, author's interview, May 25, 1989.
17. Jim Buchanan, author's interview, May 8, 1989.
18. Richard Shlakman, author's interview, September 29, 1989.

NOTES TO CHAPTER 16

1. *Parade*, November, 18, 1984.
2. *Dallas Morning News*, December 28, 1969.
3. Roger Shields, author's interview, April 4, 1989.
4. Ben Bradlee, Jr., *Guts and Glory* (New York: D. I. Fine, 1988).
5. "Nightline," ABC, December 1, 1986.
6. Perot speech, Washington, May 18, 1981.
7. Perot speech, Dallas, May 14, 1981.

8. Robinson Risner, *Passing of the Night* (New York: Random House, 1973).
9. Roger Shields, author's interview, April 4, 1989.
10. Perot speech, Dallas, April, 1980.
11. Ann Mills Griffiths, author's interview, April 11, 1989.
12. Hearings before the House Subcommittee on Asian Affairs, October 15, 1986.
13. Ibid.
14. Ibid.
15. Jack Anderson, United Features, February 25, 1987.
16. Hearings, Subcommittee on Asia Affairs, October 15, 1986.
17. *Time*, May 4, 1987.
18. *Newsweek*, January 9, 1989.
19. *Dallas Morning News*, February 25, 1988.
20. *Dallas Times Herald*, March 16, 1988.
21. Ibid.
22. Ibid.

NOTES TO CHAPTER 17

1. Frank deposition, March 9, 1989, *EDS* v. *Perot*, Circuit Court, Fairfax Co., Va.
2. Perot deposition, February 9, 1989, *EDS* v. *Perot*, Circuit Court, Fairfax Co., Va.
3. Richard Shlakman, author's interview, September 29, 1989.
4. Perot deposition, February 9, 1989, *EDS* v. *Perot*, Circuit Court, Fairfax Co., Va.
5. Luce deposition, February 16, 1989, *EDS* v. *Perot*, Circuit Court, Fairfax Co., Va.
6. Perot deposition, February 9, 1989, *EDS* v. *Perot*, Circuit Court, Fairfax Co., Va.
7. Alberthal deposition, February 6, 1989, *EDS* v. *Perot*, Circuit Court, Fairfax Co., Va.
8. Perot deposition, February 9, 1989, *EDS* v. *Perot*, Circuit Court, Fairfax Co., Va.
9. Les Alberthal, author's interview, August 17, 1989.
10. Bill Wright, author's interview, August 17, 1989.
11. Les Alberthal, author's interview, August 17, 1989.
12. Jeff Heller, author's interview, May 25, 1989.

13. Gary Fernandes, author's interview, June 9, 1989.
14. *New York Times*, June 3, 1988.
15. *Federal Computer Week*, June 27, 1988.
16. Frank deposition, March 9, 1989, *EDS* v. *Perot*, Circuit Court, Fairfax Co., Va.
17. Ibid.
18. Ibid.
19. Ibid.
20. *Dallas Times Herald*, July 8, 1989.
21. *Detroit News*, July 31, 1988.
22. *Gallagher Report*, July 25, 1987.
23. Perot testimony, October 19, 1988, *EDS* v. *Perot*, Circuit Court, Fairfax Co., Va.
24. *Dallas Morning News*, July 22, 1988.
25. Perot deposition, February 9, 1989, *EDS* v. *Perot*, Circuit Court, Fairfax Co., Va.
26. Frank deposition, March 9, 1989, *EDS* v. *Perot*, Circuit Court, Fairfax Co., Va.
27. Pat McAleer, author's interview, May 26, 1989.

NOTES TO CHAPTER 18

1. Johnson testimony, April 10, 1989, *EDS* v. *Perot*, Circuit Court, Fairfax Co., Va.
2. Johnson testimony, April 11, 1989, *EDS* v. *Perot*, Circuit Court, Fairfax Co., Va.
3. Richard Shlakman, author's interview, September 29, 1989.
4. Perot deposition, February 9, 1989, *EDS* v. *Perot*, Circuit Court, Fairfax Co., Va.
5. Ibid.
6. Gayden deposition, March 6, 1989, *EDS* v. *Perot*, Circuit Court, Fairfax Co., Va.
7. Perot deposition, February 9, 1989, *EDS* v. *Perot*, Circuit Court, Fairfax Co., Va.
8. *Detroit Free Press*, June 25, 1989.
9. Horner deposition, March 1, 1989, *EDS* v. *Perot*, Circuit Court, Fairfax Co., Va.
10. Reeves deposition, March 3, 1989, *EDS* v. *Perot*, Circuit Court, Fairfax Co., Va.
11. J. Livingston Kosberg, author's interview, August 7, 1989.

12. Smith deposition, March 3, 1989, *EDS* v. *Perot*, Circuit Court, Fairfax Co., Va.
13. John Castle, author's interview, August 17, 1989.
14. Perot testimony, October 19, 1989, *EDS* v. *Perot*, Circuit Court, Fairfax Co., Va.
15. Alberthal testimony, October 13, 1989, *EDS* v. *Perot*, Circuit Court, Fairfax Co., Va.
16. Johnson testimony, April 12, 1989, *EDS* v. *Perot*, Circuit Court, Fairfax Co., Va.
17. Johnson deposition, February 3, 1989, *EDS* v. *Perot*, Circuit Court, Fairfax Co., Va.
18. Tom Barr, closing arguments, April 13, 1989, *EDS* v. *Perot*, Circuit Court, Fairfax Co., Va.
19. Plummer decision, April 13, 1989; *EDS* v. *Perot*, Circuit Court, Fairfax Co., Va.

NOTES TO CHAPTER 19

1. *The Wall Street Journal*, October 6, 1989.
2. Perot speech, Dallas, September 23, 1986.
3. *D* Magazine, January 1984.
4. Perot speech, Austin, September 19, 1989.
5. "American Interests," PBS, The Blackwell Group, September 1989.
6. *Los Angeles Times*, May 11, 1986.
7. G. Michael Boswell, author's interview, March 28, 1989.
8. Robert Rhodes James, *A Study in Failure* (New York: World Publishing, 1970).

INDEX